D1075005

# WINNING WITH SYNERGY

# WINNING
# WITH
# SYNERGY

## How America Can Regain
## the Competitive Edge

Peter and Susan Corning

*1817*

Harper & Row, Publishers, San Francisco

Cambridge, Hagerstown, New York, Philadelphia, Washington
London, Mexico City, São Paulo, Singapore, Sydney

Material on page 27 is from *Introduction to Psychology*, Eighth Edition, by Rita L. Atkinson, Richard C. Atkinson, and Ernest R. Hilgard, copyright © 1983 by Harcourt Brace Jovanovich, Inc. Reprinted by permission of the publisher.

FIRST EDITION

---

**Library of Congress Cataloging-in-Publication Data**

Corning, Peter A.

  Winning with synergy

   1. United States—Economic policy—1981-    .
2. United States—Economic conditions—1981-    .
3. United States—Social conditions—1980-    .
I. Corning, Susan.  II. Title.  III. Title: Synergy.
HC106.8.C668  1986        338.973        85–45350
ISBN 0–06–250155–0

---

86  87  88  89  90   RRD   10  9  8  7  6  5  4  3  2  1

To our children—and their future

# Contents

Preface: On Taking the Long View     xi

Acknowledgments     xiii

1. Why Things Aren't Working     1

2. The Synergy Principle     12

3. The Synergy World View     23

4. Synergy and Dysergy     43

5. The Art of Synergistic Thinking I: Basics     63

6. The Art of Synergistic Thinking II: Values and Ideology     83

7. The Art of Synergistic Thinking III: Tools     111

8. Synergy (and Dysergy) in Families     135

9. Synergy in Communities     146

10. Synergy on the Bottom Line     168

11. The Synergistic Society     199

12. *E Pluribus Unum*     247

# Illustrations

*Figure 1.*  Cooperation and Competition          89
*Figure 2.*  Cooperation/Competition Matrix       94
*Figure 3.*  McKinsey's 7–S Framework            126
*Figure 4.*  The Synergy Model                   128
*Figure 5.*  Systematizer                        130
*Figure 6.*  Factor Analyzer                     132

*Table 1.*  Cost of Public Services             158
*Table 2.*  Residential Preferences             159
*Table 3.*  The Japanese Advantage              198

# Preface

## ON TAKING THE LONG VIEW

One of our traditional weaknesses as a society has been our short memory and limited foresight; we live in the present and take the future on faith. But this will no longer do. The future is not what is used to be, and the reasons are rooted in our past and present.

As this book goes to press, the short-term indications for our economy and society have turned positive: There is a buoyant stock market, a dramatic change in the dollar's exchange rate overseas, a decline in interest rates, plummeting oil prices, a federal deficit reduction act with real teeth, a historic tax reform bill, and, most important, a surge of public optimism about the future. Though these developments may seem to belie the deep concern expressed in this book about our collective future, from a longer term perspective we do not think so, and we have marshalled some of the evidence to support our view.

Taking the long view, we believe that this country continues to have deep-seated problems. Whether or not the reader agrees with our specific proposals is less important than winning support for our underlying thesis: That business as usual will not suffice to deal with our problems; they must be addressed in a more concerted and effective way. We speak of the need for a total mobilization of our energies and resources around a common purpose (that of regaining our competitive edge).

Yet a consensus on this issue is less important, we believe, than a recognition that synergy and its antithesis, dysergy, are vital determinants of our future; the lessons of synergy and dysergy contained in this book apply in equal measure to optimists and pessimists, conservatives and liberals.

This book is not, ultimately, about the causes of our trade deficit, or a 45-hour work week. It is about how to use synergy as a problem-solving and planning tool, as individuals, as organizations, and as a society.

# Acknowledgments

This book would have been stillborn without the gifted editorial midwifery of Clayton Carlson and his editorial team at Harper & Row San Francisco. Their vision of how to put all the pieces together was the catalyst that finally made it happen, proving once again that the relationship between a writer and an editor can be synergistic.

But the synergies at Harper & Row go even further. We were fortunate indeed that the production and marketing of our book—from the jacket design to publicity—was in the hands of such a talented and dedicated team, including Tom Dorsaneo, Steve Dietz, Brian Erwin, Mike Kehoe, Dorian Gossy, and Melanie Haage. They provided convincing evidence, if any was needed, that the successful publication of a book is a cooperative effort. We are very grateful.

Among our many other debts, we should acknowledge especially those we owe to Fred Hill, who understood what we were trying to do and never lost faith; also, to Mike Selmi, Tanya Blair, Susan Stocker, and Anne Corning, whose research assistance greatly enriched the final product; to Eric Seedman, whose graphics skills have so often managed to render our crude sketches intelligible, and to the staff of Corning & Associates, a tremendous source of strength.

Finally, an incalculable debt is owed to our clients, from whom we have learned so much. Though we have drawn upon our client experiences in the book, we have tried to avoid embarrassment and have not mentioned names. We trust our clients will understand.

# 1. Why Things Aren't Working

Our recent national euphoria bears an eerie resemblance to those classic Hollywood movies—happy illusions that for a time blot out unpleasant realities.

Despite appearances, this country is in deep trouble economically, and the long-range trend is ominous. Says the Nobel Prize-winning economist Paul Samuelson: "We are a people living in a happy daze.... Most people picture a rosy scenario that the statistical data do not support..."

In what was once called "the land of opportunity," millions of Americans are without work and without hope. Millions more who once enjoyed a middle-class standard of living have been reduced to poverty. And countless millions more, though gainfully employed, have been battered both financially and psychologically by the recent upheavals in our economy; last year alone, some 300,000 manufacturing jobs were lost to foreign competition as our trade deficit soared to an appalling $148 billion. As Samuelson puts it, we are on a spending spree—selling out the shop and the farm to foreigners rather than devoting our national income (and energies) to the defense of our economy.

In fact, America is under siege, and none of us can feel secure about the future of this country. In a recent *Business Week* cover story on the "hollowing" of American industry, the editors warn of an impending "national crisis."

## HOW IT WAS

Forty years ago, at the end of World War II, our nation was indisputably the richest and most powerful on earth. Among other things, we had:

- One-half of the world's total industrial production
- A dynamic, growing economy

- A highly favorable trade balance: the dollar was "almighty"
- Leadership in almost every field of science and technology
- By far the world's highest standard of living
- The world's best health-care and educational systems
- Competent (and generally respected) government
- Efficient public services
- Strong family and community life

Most of all, we had boundless optimism and rock-solid faith in a better future; a brash self-confidence was our most distinctive national trait. And justifiably so. We had earned our national pride the old-fashioned way.

## THEN AND NOW

How things have changed. Our once-vaunted industrial might has been devastated as one after another of our industries has lost out to foreign competition. Huge trade deficits are sapping our wealth, depressing the economy, and stunting our capacity for growth. The federal budget is still out of control, and escalating interest costs on the national debt are destined to become a heavy burden on future generations.

Meanwhile, persisting high unemployment and anemic industrial production (80 percent of capacity) testify to the fact that our economy never recovered completely from the last deep recession; in our once-mighty industrial heartland—now aptly referred to as the rust belt—unemployment in some areas stands at 25 percent, or worse. Perhaps most serious, many millions of youths (uncounted in the unemployment statistics) have been frustrated in their efforts to gain a toehold, and work experience, in the labor force.

Our agricultural sector is a disaster area, and farmers have become increasingly desperate. The petroleum industry has been hit hard by declining oil prices. The timber industry is wallowing in a long-term slump. Shoe manufacturers have closed 70 percent of their factories in the past few years, and machine tool makers have lost 60 percent of their markets in some key product lines. Our hospitals are in turmoil. The commercial insurance business is in disarray; skyrocketing rates have created a national crisis in the liability sector. Our banking industry is stretched to the limit; bank failures last year reached a post-Depression high. Even the computer industry has lost some of its luster.

As for the quality of life, many of our large cities are blighted by urban decay and declining public services; everywhere there is congestion, potholes, litter, graffiti—and poverty. And crime. In fact, our crime rates are a scandal. Though the dockets of our courts have become choked with pending cases and our aging prisons are filled to overflowing, we must still double-lock our doors and live in fear of one another. Harvard President (and former law professor) Derek Bok recently called our system of justice "the most expensive and inefficient in the world."

Many of our once-prized institutions show visible signs of deterioration. The agencies of our national government, a source of pride to a previous generation, are increasingly inefficient, ineffectual, or worse. The postal service, struggling to modernize, is bedeviled by red ink. The bedrock of social security has had a brush with bankruptcy. Our military establishment, which is bloated with expensive, high-tech weapons that perform poorly while maintenance, training, and munitions stockpiles get shortchanged, may no longer be capable of fighting a sustained war. And at the IRS, computer breakdowns, work backlogs, and other signs of slippage have created a mess in the tax system that has had ripple effects throughout the entire economy.

## SOME UNFAVORABLE COMPARISONS

As a nation we are not performing very well, either in comparison to other industrial nations or to our own past record, and the deficiencies are wide ranging. A few statistics reveal the breadth and depth of our difficulties:

- Per capita income in the U.S. now ranks twelfth among major nations; the Swiss enjoy an income level that is an astounding 50 percent higher than ours, overall.
- In the U.S., 15 percent of the population were living in poverty in 1984, the highest rate of any major industrial nation.
- Our competitors are currently spending far greater proportions of their GNP's on new plants and equipment than we

are (10 percent in Europe versus 3.4 percent in the U.S.), and worker productivity abroad is increasing more rapidly.

- North America has about 6 percent of the world's oil reserves, yet the U.S. alone accounts for 30 percent of world oil consumption; barring a radical change, we are doomed to be dependent on other nations.
- Domestic savings in the U.S., a key to future economic growth, was the lowest in the industrial world during the late 1970s and early 1980s; while Americans saved 18.9 percent of the GNP, the Japanese were saving 32.6 percent.
- In the past few years, the U.S. has dropped from second to seventh place among the industrialized nations in the skill level of its workers (according to education expert Melvin Bernstein).
- Our highways, which are arteries for much of our commerce, were estimated in 1983 to be deteriorating at twice the rate of repairs; in ten years, one-half of our highways may be unusable. At the same time about 40 percent of our 600,000 bridges are also in bad repair or obsolete.
- American companies are being sold to foreign investors at an unprecedented rate; the total is nearing $1 trillion.
- Of the 77,251 U.S. patents issued last year, 43.8 percent went to applicants from other countries—led by Japan.
- The personnel turnover rate for the electronics industry in the San Francisco Bay Area is about 25 percent a year, a serious burden for an industry under pressure.
- The U.S. has over 500,000 practicing lawyers, a reflection of the heavy cost to our society for litigation; Japan in 1982 had about 12,500 lawyers.
- Infant mortality in the U.S. (a sensitive indicator of a population's overall health) was about 13 per thousand in 1980; in Japan it was 7.9 per thousand.
- Each year some 50,000 children are kidnapped in this country; in Japan kidnapping is almost unheard of.
- Japan has about two robberies per 100,000 people every year; in the U.S., the figure is about 235.
- In New York City alone, almost 100,000 cars were stolen in 1983; in Tokyo, the number of car thefts is negligible.
- Credit-card fraud in this country far outstrips robberies; the

losses have been estimated to be nearly $1 billion a year, and this is in addition to the blizzard of bad checks.

- New York City has some 28,000 fires per year; Tokyo has about seven thousand.
- The divorce rate in Japan was about 1.2 per thousand in 1980; in the U.S. the rate was 5.2 per thousand; almost 40 percent of all U.S. marriages eventually end in divorce.
- Today some 20 percent of all American families are headed by a single parent, and the percentage continues to grow.
- In the 1984 election, roughly half of the U.S. electorate took the trouble to vote, the lowest turnout of any of the major democracies.

## A CASE IN POINT

Our educational system, a vital shaper of the nation's future, is a particularly important case in point. By the standards of most other industrialized countries, our secondary schools are turning out inferior goods. Roughly 20 percent of our population is functionally illiterate, and 85 percent are "technologically illiterate," according to a recent survey conducted at Northern Illinois University. Over nearly two decades, the combined Scholastic Aptitude Test scores of American high school students declined over 90 points. Teacher salaries remain abysmal, despite a growing shortage; truancy rates are epidemic in some areas (25 percent in California); and in New York City the school dropout rate is 45 percent. The system is so bad, according to the National Commission on Excellence in Education, that we are "putting the nation at risk." In a recent eight-nation test among sixth-graders, our test-takers ranked near the bottom in science, mathematics, and geography.

Higher education has suffered the consequences. Because only half our students take any mathematics after the tenth grade, our engineering schools are required to do two years of remedial work with entering students, on the average, which results in many poorly trained engineering graduates. In addition, inflation, declining enrollments, and cutbacks in aid to higher education have resulted in a marked decline in academic quality, along with an outflow of intellectual and scientific leadership from this country. Morale is so low among those who remain in college teaching that, in a recent poll by the Carnegie Foundation, almost 40 percent said they were seriously thinking of leaving the profession.

Meanwhile, we have a critical shortage of science and math teachers, our school and college laboratories are burdened with antiquated or worn-out equipment and, at the very time when our nation is being challenged as never before in science and technology, the federal government has been cutting back on aid to education. Yet even during the recent recession, 17,000 entry-level engineering jobs from coast to coast went unfilled. (To compensate for these deficiencies, American corporations these days find they must spend large sums on teaching the basics to many of their workers.)

The effects of these shortcomings are already visible. Our nuclear power plants have been jinxed; design flaws, construction problems, and huge cost-overruns have cast a pall over the entire industry, as well as increasing utility bills in many areas of the country. (In the state of Washington, the end result was an unprecedented default on utility bonds.) Our so-called Flxible buses, the only buses built in this country, performed so poorly at first that New York City took its entire fleet of 850 out of service and sued the manufacturer. Then there are those complex weapons systems, like the M-1 tank, that are enormously costly, perform below expectations, and are undependable to boot.

Today, Japanese companies are called upon to install control systems in our new steel plants because we don't know how to do it. Since domestic companies cannot design or build high-quality subway or railway cars, French and Japanese companies are winning the contracts. We turn to the Japanese, again, for help with high-speed rail systems and the latest in printing technology. Likewise, in consumer electronics these days it is the Japanese who are the innovators.

"We do not believe the educational system needs repairing," concludes a landmark Carnegie Corporation task force report published earlier this year. "We believe it must be rebuilt. . . . The cost of not doing so will be a steady erosion in the American standard of living."

## WE ALL SUFFER

It's like watching a beautiful old tapestry unravel before your eyes. Or like seeing a professional football team fall apart after a Superbowl championship. In one way or another we have all been affected by the gradual unraveling of our economy and society:

- All of us have been victimized by inefficient, error-prone, or overburdened systems, from New York's subways to Orange County's freeways.
- All of us are paying more than we need to for consumer products, health care, insurance, repair work, credit cards, and public services like telephones and electricity.
- All of us are subject to higher tax rates than would be necessary to pay for an efficient government and military establishment.
- Most of us have also felt personally the combined pinch of a higher cost of living and lower real incomes.
- For most of us, too, the kind of job we want has been harder to get, harder to hold on to, or nonexistent.
- All of us are less secure physically, economically, and militarily.
- And all of us have reason to feel that the future is in jeopardy.

## SOME OBVIOUS QUESTIONS

How did it happen? How did we manage to blow it? And why is it that we seem unable to reverse this dangerous trend? Why have so many of our economic and cultural gurus been so wide of the mark in understanding what has been happening to us? And why do their prescriptions so often seem to make the patient worse? Like the breakup of the telephone company, for instance—a nostrum that, so far, has resulted only in higher costs, lowered efficiency, complicated (and time-consuming) problems of coordinating various suppliers, more complex dialing procedures and, ironically, the opening up of new markets for foreign competitors.

There has been no lack of simplistic explanations:

- Some people blame the Japanese, or cheap foreign labor;
- Some blame high interest rates, and an overvalued dollar;
- Some think the unions are responsible;
- Some see failures in management;
- Some trace the problem to the welfare state;
- Some think government regulations are at fault;
- Some point to the corrupting influence of movies, TV, or various Supreme Court decisions;
- Some see the workings of inexorable forces: "Third Waves," "Megatrends," and the like.

## QUICK FIXES

Americans have always had a fondness for simple solutions and quick fixes, and this is no less true of our present predicament. For some people the solution is tariff protection, or import quotas. For others it is a cheaper dollar or a lower federal deficit. Still others think we need a national industrial policy, or a longer school day, or more aid to this or that beleaguered industry or interest group. For dyed-in-the-wool conservatives, the answer is more capitalism; let the free market cure our ills. For old-fashioned liberals, on the other hand, the answer lies in more government planning and government action.

Many people, though, have a sense that our problems are too numerous and too complex for simple solutions. "Death by a thousand cuts" is the way economist Lester Thurow has characterized what has been happening to our economy. Indeed, some see complexity itself as the villain and despair of finding a solution. In this view, the problems are simply too immense, or too inscrutable. We are helpless to do anything about them.

In some quarters, the result is a generalized sense of frustration, confusion, and powerlessness. A spiritual and psychological depression has set in, and there has been a distressing loss of hope. But equally disturbing is the high level of escapism. Pollyanna is alive and well, with millions of Americans simply refusing to face the problems while millions more have tuned out on the real world in favor of soap operas, the punk subculture, or baseball.

What is to be done? Is the situation beyond our control—our

problems insurmountable? Is there nothing that we can do, much less our leaders in education, industry, and government?


## THE ANSWER

The answer, of course, is no. Though the problems are indeed complex, there is a great deal that can and must be done if we are to turn the situation around. But how do we get a handle on it?

As we shall see, it is not any of the specific problems we face, or all of them put together, that lie at the heart of the matter. The underlying cause of the crisis is a deeply flawed way of understanding how the world works. Our troubles can be traced ultimately to how we have traditionally viewed the world—the way we have gone about solving our problems, managing our businesses, and running our government. The Germans have a word for it. The problem is our *weltanschauung*—our world view.

We are all guided, as individuals and as nations, by our images of how things (and people) work, or don't work, and how changes—personal, social, economic, political—come about. A *weltanschauung*, in other words, is a mental framework for organizing and understanding all the "variables" that we perceive to be important, our assumptions about cause and effect.

The first major step toward a long-term solution to our problems is a new, more sophisticated way of understanding how the world works. We need to break out of a mental straightjacket; we need a new way of thinking about and dealing with our problems, one which goes beyond such outworn nineteenth-century ideologies as capitalism and socialism—and beyond the linear thinking that has been characteristic of Western societies ever since the Enlightenment. Equally important, we need to improve on such future schlock as the "postindustrial society," the "Entropy Law," the "Third Wave" and other futuristic visions.

In short, we need to construct a new *weltanschauung* that is based on how things—and people—really do work. Unless we first go back to the basics, our responses will continue to be piecemeal, disorganized, wrongheaded, and, in the long run, insufficient.

## BACK TO BASICS

That is what this book is about: the basics. How the world in fact works. We are going to provide the elements of a new *weltanschauung* that is grounded in a new scientific synthesis, a general theory of how complex systems evolve, in nature and human societies alike.* More than that, we are going to offer a new way of thinking about both our national predicament and our own personal and work-related problems that will provide new insight and new understanding—in short a problem-solving tool with which to organize more effective responses to our problems, both big and small.

The key to this new *weltanschauung* is *synergy*. Every day, in a thousand different ways, our lives are shaped, and reshaped, by synergy—though most of us seem unaware of the fact. And so is our economy and society. For synergy is literally everywhere around us: It is one of the great governing principles of the natural world; it has determined the overall trajectory of life on earth; it played a decisive role in the evolution of humankind; it is vital to the workings of every modern society, capitalist and socialist alike; and it is no exaggeration to say that the fate of our civilization depends on it.

The synergy principle is not a new concept. It can be traced back to the ancient Greeks. Many of our most successful people use the synergy principle intuitively, as we shall see. And so do our most successful businesses. And so do successful nations, like Japan. Synergy has even become a buzzword in some quarters. Experts on corporate mergers, scientists who study drug interactions, and the followers of techno-visionary Buckminster Fuller, among others, have their own specialized uses for the term.

Most of us, though, seem to have little or no understanding of what the word "synergy" means, much less an appreciation of its pervasive influence—for better or worse—on all of our lives. Nor does synergy have a central role in our *weltanschauung*. Relatively few of us, in fact, use the synergy principle consciously as a problem-solving and planning tool.

---

*The theory was developed in detail in Peter Corning's *The Synergism Hypothesis: A Theory of Progressive Evolution*, New York: McGraw-Hill, 1983.

The challenge, then, is to do our homework—to develop a deep understanding of synergy and its vital role in all of our lives, and to learn how to use synergy in dealing with the problems we confront as individuals, as organizations, and as a nation. We need to learn how to think and act synergistically. We need to learn how to deploy the synergy principle to our own advantage, just as others have so often used it to our disadvantage. Because the stakes are so high, this is one educational investment that none of us can afford to defer.

## A "LESSON PLAN"

But before we begin our educational journey, it might be a good idea to take a brief look at a "lesson plan": In the next chapter we will introduce the synergy principle and give some examples designed to illustrate its universal importance. In chapter 3 we will anchor the synergy *weltanschauung* by examining briefly the central role of synergy in evolution and human history. Chapter 4 will introduce the negative side of the synergy principle—"dysergy"—along with the all-important distinction between "high synergy" and "low synergy."

A three-chapter section on the art of synergistic thinking begins in chapter 5, with some "basics" about the many different properties (and varieties) of synergy. Chapter 6 is concerned with why a synergy world view requires changes in our values and ideology, while chapter 7 introduces some specific "tools" for synergistic problem solving. Among these tools is an analytical framework that we developed for our business, which we call the *Synergy Model*.

Chapters 8 through 11 are devoted to applying the synergy world view to specific areas such as families, communities, the business world, sports, the arts, the professions, the military, government, and, indeed, society as a whole.

Finally, in chapter 12 we will address the problem of restoring America's competitive edge and arresting a progressive decline into national poverty and mediocrity. If our goal is to leave behind us when we're gone a country in which our children and grandchildren can flourish, we will have to fight for it.

# 2. The Synergy Principle

Let's begin at the beginning. What is synergy? And why do we make such extravagant claims for it? Can the synergy principle really provide a useful tool—a deeper understanding of the inner workings of things—or is it merely the latest in a long line of phony, pop culture cure-alls?

Synergy is one of those words that is at once easy to define and difficult to understand—truly understand. To put it simply, *synergy refers to combined effects—the effects produced by the cooperative actions of two or more parts, elements, or individuals.* The word synergy comes from the Greek word *synergos*, meaning to work together or, literally, to "co-operate." But we are concerned with the *effects* produced by "co-operation." Synergistic effects are not otherwise attainable. They arise only from cooperative interactions, and the results are often startlingly different from what any of the parts can do alone.

## A FEW EXAMPLES

The natural world is filled with commonplace examples. The light metal sodium and chloride gases are both poisonous to humans when ingested by themselves. But when ions of these two substances are combined to form sodium chloride—ordinary table salt—the resulting compound loses its poisonous properties and becomes positively beneficial to humans (in moderate amounts). The two elements "cooperate" to produce emergent new (synergistic) effects.

Likewise, when the two gases hydrogen and oxygen combine in a ratio of two parts to one, the miraculous result is a liquid with strikingly new physical properties. Water is in reality a product of synergy.

Synergy is also vital to the operation of living organisms. One example among the many that can be found in any major biology text involves muscle action. Say you want to lift this book from your lap up to your shoulder and back down again. In order to bend your hand and forearm first upward then downward, there must be a closely coordinated set of actions involving both your biceps (on the front side of your upper arm) and your triceps (on the back side). During the upward movement, the biceps will contract while the triceps relaxes. During the downward movement, the actions of the two muscles will be reversed. When you hold your arm steady in midair, both muscles will be contracted. The actions of these two "striated" or voluntary muscles are synergistic. They cooperate to produce a combined effect, the controlled movement of your hand and forearm.

Many different kinds of synergistic effects can be observed in the food we eat. For instance, there is a very good reason why tacos have been a staple in the diet of Central American Indians for many centuries. One cup of beans, eaten alone, provides the nutritional equivalent of two ounces of steak. Three cups of whole-grain flour consumed by itself provides the equivalent of about five ounces of steak. Because their constituent amino acids complement one another, when the beans and grain are consumed together they provide the nutritional equivalent of $9\frac{1}{3}$ ounces of steak, or 33 percent more usable protein. The whole taco is truly greater, nutritionally speaking, than the sum of its parts. This is a case where one and one almost literally equals three.

Synergy is also a routine aspect of the way we prepare our foods. The flavor of a lemon pie is the result of the combination of butter, eggs, lemon, sugar, flour, and salt. When some of these same ingredients are put together in a slightly different combination—say, butter, egg yolks, lemon juice, vinegar, salt, and pepper—and are prepared in a slightly different way, the result is hollandaise sauce. What our taste buds respond to are the different combinatorial (synergistic) effects.

Synergy is also commonplace in health care. One example is the effect produced by using atropine and Prednisone together to treat eye inflammations. The atropine serves to dilate the eyes, so that the Prednisone, an anti-inflammatory drug, can work more effectively.

## THE INVISIBLE HAND

Some of the most striking examples of synergy are embodied in human technology. Indeed, synergy is the "invisible hand" that guides the process of technological innovation and diffusion. Take chrome-nickel-steel, the man-made synthesis of natural elements which is stronger by at least 35 percent than all of its constituents added together. Or take the "glue-lam" composite wooden beams which are both stronger and less subject to warping than natural construction beams.

Or consider how Tandem Computers, one of the most successful of Silicon Valley's high-tech companies, utilizes the synergy principle in its computer system. Many organizations, such as banks and hospitals, need fail-safe computers for their high-priority jobs. The only way to achieve this is with redundancy—a backup system that can be brought on line if the main computer breaks down.

Before the Tandem system was developed, the necessary redundancy could only be obtained by purchasing two big "mainframe" computers, one of which might stand idle most of the time. But this solution was both expensive and inefficient. So Tandem's founders designed a new "nonstop" system that utilizes two or more small modules (and associated software) that can share the total workload. Then, if one module should fail, the other can temporarily pick up the high-priority work. In effect, the two modules back each other up. The result of this division of labor among two or more linked modules is a system that is lower in cost, more efficient, yet highly dependable.

Even something as ordinary as the humble clay brick, one of humankind's oldest inventions, provides a good example of synergy. When bricks are combined with one another and with mortar (itself a synergistic combination of cement or lime, sand, and water), they can be used to make an endless variety of useful structures: factories, houses, churches, prisons, garden walls, fireplaces, defensive fortifications, canals, roads, sidewalks, watchtowers—even kilns for making more bricks. The overall effect in each case depends on the bricks and the mortar, plus human purposes, designs, and skilled labor. And in every case, the "whole" has combined properties that the parts alone do not.

Human language provides yet another illustration of the synergy principle. The twenty-six letters in our alphabet make meaningful words only in precise combinations. (The words "I" and "a" are exceptions, of course.) We all had to learn in school that the word "their" has a very different meaning from the word "there." And it takes only a change in the order of the same five letters to convert "being" to "begin." Words are in reality small bundles of synergy.

By the same token, the ability of various word combinations to convey meaningful thoughts is dependent on how the individual words are strung together—how they cooperate. Consider the difference between "you will go" and "will you go?" A change in the word order can drastically alter the meaning. Thus, our language exhibits a two-level hierarchy of synergistic effects: a synergism of synergies. And the meaning that is triggered in your mind as you read the words on this page is a cooperative effect.

## SOCIAL SYNERGY

For reasons that will become clear later on, some of the most important forms of synergy for our purpose involve social cooperation. A striking example in animals involves the emperor penguin. When the Antarctic winter sets in and temperatures plunge to fifty degrees below zero, these hardy little creatures huddle together, often for months at a time, in dense masses that may number in the tens of thousands. In so doing, they provide insulation for one another and share precious body heat, with the result that each animal reduces its own energy expenditures by about 50 percent (by actual experiment). Without such "close" cooperation, it is unlikely that these heroic creatures could survive in such a bleak environment.

Or imagine this very human situation: It happens to involve the San Francisco 49ers versus the Detroit Lions in the 1983 National Football Conference playoff game, but it epitomizes thousands of similar situations in the history of football. With four minutes and fifty-four seconds remaining in the game, the Lions scored a touchdown and pulled ahead of the 49ers, 23–17. The Lions' kickoff put the 49ers on their own 30-yard line. It was the moment of truth.

"I can't be too happy with what we did overall today," said center Fred Quillan afterward. "But I will remember that last series for the rest of my life. Together, we had to do it. And we did—together."

"There is no way to describe what we had in that huddle," added tight end Russ Francis. "Energy. It came down to us from the stands, and from each of us standing side by side. There are a lot of things about football that you can argue about, but that feeling is something that is so amazing—that striving for a common goal and knowing, somehow, you'll make it." The final score: 24–23.

Less dramatic but just as relevant to our purpose is the synergy produced by trade associations like the California Avocado Commission. Twenty years ago, only 5 percent of U.S. households bought avocados, and many people thought they were fattening. But thanks to the commission's member-supported advertising campaign, today the percentage of households buying avocados has risen to 50 percent and the domestic industry's sales volume has increased more than fourfold.

Or consider Stanford University's new Center for Integrated Systems. CIS is, as one writer put it, a quantum leap forward. Stanford has long enjoyed various consulting and research relationships with both private industry and government agencies. But now a consortium of twenty electronics firms has put up $15 million to help construct a major electronics research facility on campus, while the Department of Defense has kicked in another $10 million plus $25 million (so far) in grants for research activities at the new center. The motivations behind this partnership are varied: The electronics industry wants to stay ahead of the Japanese; the Pentagon wants to stay ahead of the Russians; and Stanford wants to stay ahead of rival universities. To compete more effectively, they have decided to cooperate more closely. The result is a program that none of the partners could have undertaken alone.

## THE COMPETITIVE EDGE

It is synergy that, very often, spells the difference between failure and success—between the also-rans and those who get written up in the history books. And it is synergy that, more frequently than most of us realize, gives one competitor the critical edge over all the others. "Synergy has become more than a buzzword in today's corporation," notes consultant Philip Harris in a recent issue of the *Journal of Business Strategy*. "In many cases it's the key to survival and prosperity." Look at a few testimonials:

- "Synergy is one of our greatest strengths," says the 1984 annual report for 3M Company. "The ability to share resources and expertise throughout the organization makes us a strong competitor in the many markets we serve."
- "The merger is completed; the synergy is just beginning," proclaims a full-page *Wall Street Journal* ad announcing the linkup between SmithKline Corporation, a world leader in the manufacture of drugs and other health care products, and Beckman Instruments, one of the biggest names in laboratory equipment and related technologies.
- "The synergies in the companies were never really utilized when we acquired them," explains the chief executive of Gulf & Western Industries, Martin Davis, in the *Wall Street Journal*. "Now we hope to have better controls and to put all the creative forces in the organization at work together."
- "Synergy at last," exults Vice President Charles Frank in *Fortune* magazine over the first joint deal ever between his investment bank, Salomon Brothers, and the commodity trading firm Philbro. The two firms had been uneasy merger partners for five years without any visible evidence of cooperation between them.
- "Synergy is our business" claims a Japanese electronics manufacturer in a *Business Week* ad, which includes a picture of a pair of scissors and a caption that reads: "It takes more than one blade to make a cutting edge in the modern world."

## SYNERGY AND INNOVATION

The people (and organizations) that are out there on the cutting edge, whether they are aware of it or not, are, almost without exception, exploiting the synergy principle. For it is synergy that lies at the heart of true innovation—the putting together for the first time of different things, or ideas, or people that were previously separate. For example:

- Cogeneration—the ingenious idea of coupling steam- and electricity-generating systems in such a way that waste heat (usually a high percentage of the total) is minimized; energy cost-savings are so dramatic that cogeneration systems typically pay for themselves in three to five years.
- The phenomenal success of Club Med, which is able to provide its "members" with high-quality, low-cost vacation packages, including travel, accommodations, meals, recreation, and more at nearly 100 luxurious "vacation villages" around the world.
- The dynamite merger between Nabisco and Standard Brands (now part of R. J. Reynolds), two diversified food companies that complement each other in their product lines, their organizational strengths, and their marketing capabilities.
- Buckminster Fuller's remarkable geodesic domes, which now number in the hundreds of thousands, a felicitous architectural innovation that combines a spherical design (the strongest and most space efficient form for its weight and size) with an exceedingly strong yet economical framing geometry (namely, geodesic, or "great circle" tetrahedrons). This results in structures that are extremely strong, yet light in weight, easily constructed, and low in cost.
- "Live Aid," the superbowl of rock concerts and an organizational nightmare that nevertheless succeeded in bringing together 52 rock stars for 16 hours of live entertainment beamed via 14 satellites and 107 broadcast stations to an audience estimated at an astounding 1.5 billion people in 140 countries, and which netted some $60 million for African famine relief.

# THE UBIQUITY OF SYNERGY

As should already be evident, synergy is not some exotic phenomenon that can only be observed by trained scientists using high-powered instruments. Nor is it some rarified experience that only the rich, the specially gifted, or the anointed few can appreciate. Synergistic effects are ubiquitous. They are of central importance to such fundamental sciences as physics, chemistry, and biology. They are deeply embedded in the subject matter of economics, sociology, and psychology. They are the absorbing preoccupation of engineers, architects, clothing designers, business entrepreneurs, housewives, and artists.

The synergy principle is embedded in such familiar institutions as airlines, banks, hospitals, hotels, insurance companies, libraries, newspapers, postal systems, railroads, supermarkets, telephone systems, and much more. It is utilized in our poetry, music, theater, movies, painting, and photography. It is widely employed in politics and government: in legislatures, political parties, reform movements, revolutionary conspiracies, and social security programs. It affects how we design our homes, how we plan and cultivate our gardens, how we decorate the interiors of our homes, how we dress ourselves, and how we "do" our hair. It is even a major facet of our sports, our military, and our family relationships—as we shall see.

Look at just a few of the English words that have the prefix "syn"—meaning "with," "together," or "at the same time." These "syn" words are indicative of synergy's many dimensions: syndicate, synagogue, synthesis, syndicalism, synchronize, synthetic, syntax, synod, syngamy, synoecism. There are also a number of English words formed from the equivalent prefix "sym": symmetry, symphony, symbiosis, sympathy, symposium, symptoms, and others.

Indeed, the natural world is a great pyramid of synergistic effects, stacked layer upon layer, from the basic substances that make up our material environment to the inner workings of the human mind (and all of its products). And at every stage in the evolution of this cosmic pyramid, over some 3.5 billion years, synergistic effects were responsible for the underlying trend toward more complex forms of organization. Not only are synergistic effects a common denominator but, more important, they have been one of the primary causal agencies in evolution, and in human history. (See chapter 3.)

## TUNING IN TO SYNERGY

How can it be that most of us have had so little appreciation for something which is so elemental, so indispensable as synergy? There are many reasons, we think, and it is important to take note of some of these before we go on to explore how to make use of the synergy principle in a more conscious and deliberate way.

For one thing, we may be too close to the synergy principle; in a sense we have been unable to see the trees for the forest. Precisely because synergy is so commonplace, our familiarity with it may have bred, if not contempt, at least a kind of comfortable complacency. We are so accustomed to it that we simply take it for granted. Or else we limit our understanding of the term to some narrow aspect of our lives or work (corporate mergers, drug interactions, "win-win" therapy groups, and the like).

By contrast, our nineteenth-century forebears were enraptured by the wonders of technology and marveled at its effects. To them, a civilization that could produce steam engines, power looms, railroads, cameras, electric lights, telephones, automobiles, and motion pictures could do anything. The synergistic effects achieved by technology underpinned their faith in human progress.

What a contrast between their exuberant optimism and our relatively blasé attitude even toward something as infinitely complex and heroic as the space program. Often as not these days we treat high technology as a menace, as a dehumanizing or destructive influence. Some of us yearn for a decentralized technology controlled by "the people," or technology on a "human scale," or an "appropriate technology," or even the abandonment of technology and a return to rustic simplicity. There are even some modern-day Luddites among us who, like the workers who smashed the knitting machines in nineteenth-century English cotton mills to protest against industrialization, would like to prevent the introduction of new technology.

A second reason for our indifference to the synergy principle may have to do with the way our minds seem to work. For most of us, it appears, synergy is not something that we can easily envision. We are not very good at thinking about complexity, or at holding many interacting factors in our minds at once. We tend to economize mentally, to reduce the "blooming, buzzing confusion" of the world around us to neat categories and simple "prime movers." When we think about complex systems, we tend to focus either on the "whole" (the house, the car, the human being, the Russians) or some "part" (the door, the spark plug, the heart, Mikhail Gorbachev).

We are especially prone to thinking about the parts in isolation from one another when something goes wrong with one of them. We are not very good at thinking about both the whole and the parts together—how the parts interact, how the whole constrains and shapes the actions of the parts, and vice versa. We notice the effects either of the parts or of the wholes but not the effects of parts *in* wholes. Whether this way of thinking is merely a habit of mind or a quirk of the mind, it has been an obstacle to a deeper understanding of how the world works.

Our intellectuals, with their Babel of "paradigms," "models," and "theories," have not helped matters either. Until very recently, the central tendency in the academic world was to move away from unifying, holistic views of man and society and toward specialized, one-dimensional perspectives. This has been the case especially among social scientists, who were often rewarded for creating theories based on simplistic assumptions about human nature and social life.

Thus, elaborate theoretical structures were erected to advance the postulate of an economic man, a sociological man, a power-seeking political man, a behaviorist psychological man, a humanistic "self-actualizing" man, or what have you. Often it did not seem to matter how naive a particular theory was so long as it was "rigorous," meaning that it could be expressed in terms of a mathematical model. But mathematics is only a tool, a kind of language for expressing relationships between things. It was as if someone were to claim that anything he says is true, so long as it can be translated into French.

## BLIND MEN

Perhaps the single most important reason for our failure to appreciate the importance of the synergy principle is that, for most of us, the pieces have not been brought together before. We are like the proverbial group of blind men who, being able to touch only the different parts of the elephant, variously describe it as being like a wall, a tree, a rope, a snake, and a fan. Because we have not seen the elephant as a whole, we have failed to exploit fully its prodigious ability to serve our needs. Synergy is a mighty pack animal that can carry much of the burden of ensuring our survival and well-being in a complex world; if we have the wisdom to use it to full advantage, the synergy principle can help us blaze our path into the future.

# 3. The Synergy World View

The foundation for the synergy world view lies in the natural world, and in the evolutionary history of our species.* Indeed, the origins of synergy can be traced back to the very beginnings of the universe itself.

In the course of cosmic evolution following the so-called Big Bang, all of the more complex elements apparently arose through "nucleosynthesis"—the thermonuclear fusion first of hydrogen nuclei to produce helium, then each of the more massive elements. Remember what we learned in school? Such "wholes" as oxygen, carbon, and lead are actually different combinations of the same subatomic building blocks. In other words, our physical environment consists of progressively more complex cooperative effects.

The same holds true for various chemical compounds. New properties arise when two hydrogen atoms combine with one of oxygen to produce water, when three hydrogen atoms combine with one of nitrogen to produce ammonia, or when chromium is combined with iron in the steelmaking process to produce stainless steel—a synthesis of the corrosion resistance of chromium and the strength of steel.

## CATALYSTS

Catalytic reactions of various kinds also involve synergy. A catalyst facilitates a chemical reaction by decreasing the activation energy required. For instance, if hydrogen and oxygen gases are simply mixed together, nothing will happen. But add a little platinum to the mixture and the explosive result will be water. Yet in the process the platinum will remain unchanged.

---

*We can only provide a brief overview here. For a more exhaustive discussion of the role of synergy in evolution, see *The Synergism Hypothesis* (New York: McGraw-Hill, 1983).

Synergistic effects are also found in crystals. A crystal is a precise geometrical arrangement of atoms or molecules in one of a number of different lattice structures, and the properties exhibited by a particular crystal (appearance, hardness, optical properties, conductivity, etc.) are a result of both the chemical properties of the underlying substance and the type of structure it assumes. Thus when we put diamonds in drill bits, or silicon "wafers" in semiconductors, we are using one form of synergy to help create another.

As humans have come to understand better the nature of the physical universe, we have also learned how to manipulate some of its forces to produce new forms of synergy. Space flight and nuclear power are obvious examples. So are the many useful effects produced by lasers—narrow beams of "coherent" light waves that have been focused, organized and synchronized so as to produce powerful cooperative effects that would otherwise be impossible, from communications at the speed of light to microsurgery. The same applies to superconductivity, the reduction or elimination of electrical resistance in a conductor when it has been cooled to minus 452° Fahrenheit, which causes the electrons that serve as electrical conduits to become aligned with one another.

## SYNERGY IN LIVING SYSTEMS

If all matter is synergistic, this is doubly the case for the organic compounds that serve as the raw materials for living systems. Indeed, as we begin to move up the "great chain of being," in the ancient phrase, we can observe the emergence of a vast hierarchy of synergistic effects.

"Life" begins with (primarily) carbon, oxygen, hydrogen, nitrogen, and energy. The major biological molecules—proteins, carbohydrates, lipids, and nucleic acids—are each composed of three or more of these elements. The carbohydrates, for example, consist of carbon, hydrogen, and oxygen in the approximate ratio of 1:2:1, and the type of carbohydrate that is produced depends on the number and physical arrangement of these atoms. Some are very familiar, like the "fuel" substances glucose and fructose. Others, like erythrose (an intermediate in photosynthesis), are not so well known.

By far the most complex and diverse of the basic biological building blocks, both structurally and functionally, are the proteins. Some proteins serve as the structural materials from which living cells are constructed. Others serve as the enzymes (catalysts) that drive cellular activities. Still others provide mobility for cells and cell parts.

Yet, in spite of their diverse functions, all proteins have a similar structure, consisting of one or more long chains of subunits called amino acids. Only twenty different amino acids are used initially by cells to make different proteins, and the properties of each protein are determined by its size and amino acid sequence. Since the total number of amino acid subunits can range from a minimum of about fifty in the smallest proteins to giant molecules containing more than fifty thousand, an almost endless variety of proteins is possible.

What is especially significant about these so-called macromolecules is that, even before we arrive at the self-sustaining, self-renewing processes that epitomize "life," we can observe the basis for an organic division of labor. Thanks to the synergies that occur at the biochemical level, it was possible to develop the "parts" that were required to construct the more complex synergistic wholes that constitute living systems.

How life itself began, and when, remains uncertain and mired in controversy. One thing seems increasingly certain, however. The first one-celled "prokaryotes," the microscopic ancestors of modern bacteria and blue-green algae, were organizations of co-operating parts and processes that included, at the minimum, an outer envelope of some sort, molecules that could store the "coded" instructions needed for directing the construction and ongoing activities of the cell, molecules that could translate the coded information into biological structures, and (not least) metabolism—the ability to capture, use, and perhaps also store energy. Each of these interdependent functions in turn required a precisely integrated set of cooperative activities.

## SURVIVAL OF THE FITTEST

Assuming that a process of natural selection was going on even during these earliest stages of biological evolution (a period which may have lasted one billion years or more), the fact is that the most successful competitors—the forms that ultimately came to predominate—also happened to be the most effective co-operators; the "fittest" among the earliest one-celled creatures were the ones that (1) were able to perform all of the functions that are necessary to sustain life, (2) developed the most efficient combinations of cooperating parts, and (3) were the most compatible with the conditions that existed in the environment of three billion years ago, or more. The formula for success that we can see in operation at this still early stage of biological evolution (and we will meet it again) can thus be stated simply as: *competition via cooperation*. Competition has been a selecting agency (an editor), but cooperation has produced selective advantages that have shaped the overall trajectory of the evolutionary process toward increasing organizational complexity.

## MULTILEVEL SYNERGY

How did multicellular organisms like flatworms, or humans, arise? Competition among individuals cannot explain it. And neither can a simple process of growth in size or numbers; even the simplest of multicellular creatures displays some specialization of parts.

Though the evidence is not conclusive, it appears likely that the three major branches among the so-called metazoans—fungi, plants, and, animals—arose independently by a process of amalgamation and symbiosis among colonies of one-celled creatures. It was the synergies associated with a division of labor and cooperation that led, step by step, from one-celled creatures to humans. For any large organism is first and foremost a vast cooperative enterprise involving many billions of specialized cells that are bound to one another in a tight web of interdependency. For instance, without the structural support provided by a rigid skeleton, the emergence of large animals would have been impossible. Indeed, a complex organism is the product of at least six hierarchical levels of synergistic effects; each one of us is a multileveled synergism of synergies.

## SYNERGY AND THE MIND

Consider just one part of the human anatomy, the agglomeration of perhaps 100 billion specialized nerve cells that constitutes the brain. Though we think of this extraordinary organ as being a single, unified entity, in fact the "mind" is an intricate network of many interconnected "subsystems" whose "outputs" (our thoughts, words, and actions) are synergistic effects—products of an internal collaboration. (Millions of electrochemical impulses, traveling at speeds of up to three hundred miles per hour, keep the different areas of the brain in touch with each other at all times.) Even the most routine human actions are the combined result of an exceedingly complex division (and integration) of mental labor that is still only partly understood. Psychologists Rita and Richard Atkinson and Ernest Hilgard in their *Introduction to Psychology* offer as an example the act of stopping your car at a red light:

First of all, you must see the light; this means that the light must attract the attention of one of your sense organs, your eye. Neural impulses from your eye are relayed to your brain, where various features of the stimulus are analyzed and compared with information about past events stored in your memory. (You recognize that a red light in a certain context means "stop.") [The result of this analysis is a "decision," which you may not even be conscious of, to stop your car.] The process of pressing the brake begins when the motor area of the brain signals the muscles of your leg and foot to respond. In order to do so, the brain must know where your foot is as well as where you want it to go. The brain must have some sort of register of the position of the body parts relative to one another, which is used to plan directed movements. You do not stop the car with one sudden movement of your leg, however. A specialized part of your brain receives continual feedback from leg and foot muscles so that you are aware of how much pressure is being exerted and can alter your movements accordingly. At the same time, your eyes and some of your body senses tell you how effectively the car is stopping. If the light turned red as you were speeding toward the intersection, some of your endocrine glands would also be activated, leading to increased heart rate, more rapid respiration, and other metabolic changes associated with fear; these processes would speed your reactions in an emergency. Your stopping at a red light may seem quick and automatic, but it involves numerous complex messages, and adjustments.

Every human act, every thought we think, and every word we utter is a synergistic effect. Each of us is a huge bundle of co-operative effects, and the many ways in which we can become "disabled" (or worse) testifies to how dependent the whole is on the smooth functioning of all these parts.

Moreover, the synergy that we produce as we go about our daily lives is not only an effect of human evolution; it is also the underlying cause of our emergence as the dominant species on earth. To appreciate why this is so requires a word of explanation about the causes of progressive evolution.

## EVOLUTIONARY CAUSATION

In biological evolution, causation runs counter to our intuition. Our everyday experience teaches us to think in linear terms about causes leading to effects. In evolution, though, the process runs in reverse, for it is the functional effects, or consequences, produced by a given set of causes in a given environment that determine whether the agency of those causes will persist and be passed on to the next generation, or fall by the wayside. In other words, it is performance that matters, and the ultimate test of "fitness" in a contingent world is whatever contributes to survival and reproduction.

In essence, then, Darwin's theory of natural selection is a theory about effects as causes. Natural selection is not an active selecting agency, or a "mechanism." It is a way of identifying and characterizing those effects produced within organisms, and between organisms and their environments, that are responsible for causing differential survival and reproduction. Contrary to the many misinterpretations of Darwinism, the theory of evolution is not primarily a theory about competition; it is a theory that emphasizes the role of functional effects in directing the course of evolution.

Now, the point is that the same kind of causal dynamic applies to synergistic effects as well. Any synergistic effect (behavioral or otherwise) that provides an advantage in terms of survival and reproduction will be "favored" by natural selection. So in answer to the question, what has been responsible for the evolutionary trend toward larger, more complex synergistic systems, in a nutshell it was the very same synergistic effects that are the hallmark of these systems. When the synergy produced by a complex system provides a selective advantage, it is likely to persist and be favorably selected; insofar as cooperative effects contribute to ensuring survival, whether in competition with others or not, it is the cooperators who are the "fittest."

Over the course of evolutionary history, moreover, synergy begat more synergy until, looking backward from our present vantage point, we can see what looks like a directed, deterministic trend. No wonder so many theorists of the past were persuaded that our fate was being guided by some higher intelligence, or perhaps some "law" of progress. What theorists like Aristotle, Comte, Marx, and Spencer were in fact observing was the evolutionary progress of the synergy principle.

## SOCIAL EVOLUTION

It is not known exactly when the first cooperative "social" relationships arose between multicellular organisms, but the many modern-day examples include some species with an ancient ancestry. One of the best known is lichen, a symbiotic partnership between an alga and a fungus in which one partner provides the capability for photosynthesis and the other provides a secure attachment means and water retention capabilities. Though the two species can exist independently, together they are able to occupy many otherwise uninhabitable areas. Often they are the first migrants into a barren location.

There are also the bacteria that live in the digestive tracts of cattle and other ruminant animals, where they provide an indispensable service by breaking down the cellulose in the grasses consumed by their hosts. Or take the blue-green algae that attach themselves to the roots of legumes and rice plants and fix nitrogen for their hosts in return for being provided with an anoxic (low oxygen) environment, and other amenities. Ants and aphids also form symbiotic relationships on occasion, with the ants specializing in defending and nurturing the aphids while the aphids milk and process the sap of various plants, both for their own consumption and for the benefit of their protectors.

Symbiosis in fish is also fairly common. For example, there are some fifty-odd species of "cleaner fish" that earn their livings by removing parasites and other debris from larger fish (who oblige by not eating their smaller relatives and, often, by serving as protectors). In sea anemone–crab partnerships, on the other hand, the former provide camouflage and defensive weapons against predators while the latter provide a set of legs and mobility.

Synergy also explains the evolution of social cooperation among members of the same species. One of the most storied examples (in fact an inspiration for social theorists and poets ever since ancient Athens) is honeybees. These creatures have an elaborate social system that features a division of labor among biologically specialized "castes." Reproduction is performed exclusively by a "queen," with the assistance of many servants, while various workers engage in construction and maintenance of the hive, joint defense of the hive, activities designed to heat or cool the hive (by generating extra body heat or by fanning the hive with their wings), and an elaborately organized pattern of cooperative foraging activities that are dependent in part on a primitive communication system, the famous "waggle dance."

Is synergy really the explanation for this model economy? Yes, because the system developed by the honeybees enables them to occupy a great variety of habitats and to predominate over solitary competitors. In fact, the advantages provided by their survival strategy explains why they were able to adapt so readily when our ancestors brought them to this country. The key to their competitive success has been close cooperation.

## COOPERATIVE STRATEGIES

Though the cooperative behavior of honeybees is one of the more dramatic examples, the strategy of competition via social cooperation has been observed (and analyzed) on every rung of the ladder of life. For instance, aggregates of microscopic myxobacteria, which move about and feed en masse, secrete digestive enzymes that enable them collectively to consume much larger prey than any one of them could unaided. Similarly, the evasive maneuvers employed by "schools" of dwarf herring against predatory barracudas dramatically reduce their joint risk of being eaten.

Among the highly social African wild dogs, cooperative hunting strategies result in kill probabilities that are vastly superior to those of less social carnivores. And the great tits that coordinate their foraging activities locate food much faster than do solitary birds living in the same environment.

Collective action may also aid in self-defense. Primatologist Hans Kummer studied the awesome defensive maneuvers used by groups of Hamadryas baboons and found that they significantly reduce the risk to each animal. And baboons are only one of many social mammals, and birds, that engage in collective defense.

Cooperative action can also help in coping with various environmental stresses. The emperor penguins were mentioned earlier. Another striking example is the Mexican desert spiders, which cluster together in the thousands during the dry season in order to minimize the loss of body moisture and avoid dehydration.

In each of these cases, and many others, social organization and cooperative behaviors provide significant "economies" for the participants that would not otherwise be possible. The cooperators are the fittest. However, it remained for an obscure offshoot of the primate line known as the hominids to demonstrate just what social cooperation could accomplish. For we are quite obviously in a class by ourselves; we are the paramount synergy producing animal.

## THE EVOLUTION OF HUMANKIND

What accounts for the emergence of our transcendent species? How can our unprecedented accomplishments be explained? This "ultimate question" has tantalized scientists and thoughtful laymen alike at least since Aristotle's time, and, over the years, countless theories have been advanced. With few exceptions, though, these theories have tended to focus on a single prime mover: climate changes, tool making, our erect posture, the development of our outsized brain, aggression and war, language, the nuclear family, technology, social organization, and so forth.

As it turns out, all of these factors may have been important, but none was sufficient. In actuality, there was no prime mover. The evolution of humankind involved a concatenation of factors that interacted with one another; it was a cooperative effect. The accumulating evidence (both direct and indirect) makes it increasingly clear that the answer to the riddle of human evolution is, in a word, *synergy*.

Human evolution was shaped by a fortuitous combination of mutually reinforcing traits, including: (1) "pre-adaptations" (traits developed in one context that can be used in some new context) that we owe to our primate heritage, (2) the development of bipedal walking, (3) the evolution of versatile hands with opposable thumbs (another form of synergy), (4) our increased intelligence (and inventiveness), (5) the invention of language, (6) the prolonging of childhood dependency (and learning), (7) the tools and technologies that have been an integral part of our survival strategy for millions of years, and, not least (8) a general trend toward more intensive, more elaborate forms of organized cooperation. It turns out that group living traces far back in our evolutionary history and played an important causal role in our biological evolution.

Some 3 million years ago, long before the emergence of large-brained, language-using humans, a diminutive, small-brained ancestor called *Australopithecus afarensis* walked erect, lived in groups, enjoyed a diversified diet, and, probably, had some division of labor, as evidenced by recent fossil finds. Like modern chimpanzees, these creatures also probably knew how to make and use primitive tools.

A somewhat later human ancestor, the so-called *Homo habilis* of 1.5 to 2 million years ago, left behind fossil remains that reveal the extensive use of stone tools made by specialists at "factory sites," the construction of crude shelters, and, most important, organized social scavenging and (probably) hunting of large animals. Yet these remarkably accomplished creatures had neither large brains nor language.

The final transition from *Homo habilis* to *Homo sapiens* paralleled closely further improvements in technology and social organization. Fire, for instance, added another important form of synergy to the advantages our ancestors already enjoyed. Fire permitted the occupation of colder regions; it became a tool that facilitated the capture of prey; it was probably used for defensive purposes; and it enabled our ancestors to add to their diets foods that are toxic if eaten raw. The result was further improvement in our ability to compete with other species.

On the other hand, the use of fire required fire tenders and firewood gatherers, not to mention readily available sources of wood for fuel. Similarly, the development of highly specialized stone tools required the skills of specialized toolmakers and sources of suitable raw materials such as flint or obsidian, just as the large-scale hunting of big game animals required careful planning, organization, and leadership. Such technological innovations almost always imposed requirements for new forms of cooperation and a greater elaboration of the division of labor.

In other words, the ancestors of modern *Homo sapiens* defined the trajectory of their own subsequent evolution by virtue of the strategies they developed for coping with changing environmental conditions. These responses included inventions, both in technology and in organization, whose synergies enabled a relatively disadvantaged primate (anatomically) to gain an edge over various competitors. These behavioral changes in turn triggered new selection pressures that favored the development of a more humanlike anatomy. The formula for success, once again, was competition via cooperation.

Much of the cooperative competition among our ancestors was indirect and economic in nature. But some was not. There can be little doubt that the synergies produced by organized, cooperative violence have also played a part in spurring the development of human societies. By the same token, synergy has also contributed, regrettably, to various forms of economic exploitation, ranging from sweatshop working conditions to outright slavery. Though we may deplore such practices, we must also recognize that, as long as the potential benefits (synergies) to exploiters outweigh the costs, the temptation will always be there.

In any case, synergy in various forms has been the key to our ultimate success as a species. Without it we would most likely have remained an undistinguished primate waiting, perhaps, to be studied by some other species that had managed to put all the pieces together. For better or worse, we are the ones who learned how to realize the full potentialities of the synergy principle—and we are not done yet.

## SYNERGY AND HISTORY

"History smiles at all attempts to force its flow into theoretical patterns or logical grooves," write historians Will and Ariel Durant in the summation of their multivolume opus, *The Story of Civilization* (1968). "It plays havoc with our generalizations, breaks all our rules; history is baroque."

The Durants' fire is directed especially at the many theorists, past and present, who have viewed human history as a kind of organic process like biological development, or the life cycle of an organism. Aristotle, for instance, used the metaphor of an acorn growing into an oak tree. Likewise, during the Enlightenment Bernard de Fontenelle treated the development of a single man as an "allegory" for the progress of civilization, although he assured us in his "Discourse Concerning the Ancients and Moderns" that: "To abandon the allegory, men will never degenerate and there will be no end to the growth and development of human wisdom."

In the nineteenth century, Herbert Spencer went even further and formulated a universal "law" of progressive evolution in which the development of "superorganisms" (organized societies) was only the latest stage. "Progress," Spencer declared in his famous monograph "Progress: Its Law and Cause," "is not an accident, not a thing within human control, but a beneficent necessity."

In *Social Change and History*, a thought-provoking critique of such organismic theories of history, sociologist Robert Nisbet asserts that this entire tradition is based on a misplaced metaphor:

No one has ever seen a civilization die. . . . Nor has anyone ever seen a civilization in a literal process of decay and degeneration. . . . Nor, finally, has anyone ever seen—actually, empirically seen, as we see these things in the world of plants and animals—growth and development in civilizations and societies and cultures. . . . All we see are the mingled facts of persistence and change.

What, then, is the alternative? Is history merely a cascade of disconnected events without any discernible patterning or direction? Is the idea of "progress" fatuous and illusory? Is it possible that so many astute observers of the human condition, spanning so many centuries, were misled by a metaphor?

The truth, as usual, lies in the middle. History may be baroque, but it it not chaotic or unintelligible. Neither random chance, nor a predestined "fate," nor the "free will" of human actors can account for its inexorable flow. Theories of history that are based on some prime mover—whether it be the actions of "great men" or the relentless march of some sort of technological determinism (as techno-philosopher Jacques Ellul would have it) or even Karl Marx's dialectical conflicts—are all insufficient to account for the often perverse twists and turns of the human narrative.

In fact, the historical process combines and synthesizes chance factors, deterministic elements, and the ideas and actions of human actors. These influences "cooperate" to produce the stream of historical events. And if there are no iron laws of history, it is perfectly obvious that there have been some profoundly important trends, however contingent they may be.

## AN ILLUSTRATION

The process can be seen in microcosm in the California Gold Rush. Contrary to the mythology that has grown up around this renowned historical episode, most of the mining activity was not done by individual prospectors wading in mountain streams with tin pans. In fact, over a five-year period from 1848–1853 the ontogeny of gold-mining technology in effect recapitulated our entire technological history up to that time.

Within the first year, individual panning was largely supplanted by three-man teams using shovels and "rocker boxes," an innovation that increased the quantity of material that could be processed in a day from ten or fifteen buckets to more than one hundred buckets, or at least twice as much per man.

Shortly thereafter the wooden sluice made its appearance. Though it required six- to eight-man teams, a sluice could handle four hundred to five hundred buckets of material per day, or about twice as much per man as a rocker box.

Finally, when hydraulic mining was introduced in 1853, teams of twenty-five or more men were required to process the materials and manage the water pumps, hoses, etc., that were used to blast away the faces of entire hillsides. Yet the amount of material processed daily also jumped to one hundred tons or more. Thus each advance in technology created a new imperative for social cooperation, even as it produced more powerful synergies.

## THE TIDES OF HISTORY

There is a saying that "you can never do just one thing," meaning that every human act is embedded in a complex matrix and has ramifying effects. If you go out to a movie, you may also use personal income, burn gas, wear your tires, depreciate your car, pollute the environment, use time that might have been spent some other way, add to traffic congestion, support your local theater, help the movie industry turn a profit, contribute to the GNP, add to state sales tax revenues, and so on.

The converse of this important but often unappreciated axiom is that human history is never shaped by just one cause. The tides of history have been driven by the ebb and flow of synergy; the great lesson of history is that its major sea changes are almost always the result of a confluence of many interacting, cooperative effects. Consider just one example.

## THE AUTOMOBILE "REVOLUTION"

Automobiles are so much a part of our lives today that we take them for granted, except when they break down. In fact, cars are almost as plentiful as people in this country; as of 1984, registered motor vehicles numbered some 168.6 million. (The worldwide total was over 456 million.) What's more, as a nation we are heavily dependent on motor vehicles.

Yet the first practical gasoline-powered car in the U.S. dates only to 1896, and at the turn of the century the total population of U.S. automobiles (steam, electric, and gas-powered) numbered about 8,000 (versus some 25 million horses). Up to that time, automobiles were produced mainly for experimental purposes and as playthings for the rich—and venturesome. One reason was that these machines were hand tooled and retailed for $3,000 or more (in 1900 dollars), compared to a range of $600 to $1,500 for a horse and carriage. Another reason was that, at this stage in their development, cars could not clearly outperform horses in meeting basic transportation needs. They were still relatively slow (top speeds seldom reached even 20 miles per hour); their engines and brakes were unreliable; having to start the car with a hand crank resulted in many broken arms; steering with a tiller was awkward and sometimes dangerous; and the solid rubber tires and stagecoach suspension systems used in the early cars gave passengers a teeth-rattling ride. To top it off, the engines had to be drained and the cars stored during the winter months.

At first the U.S. seemed an unlikely candidate for the leading role it was to play in the automobile revolution. Progress in developing automobile technology had been centered mainly in Europe during the latter part of the nineteenth century, and American roads were notoriously bad. In 1904, the U.S. had only 153,000 miles of "improved" roads (gravel or paved) out of 2.1 million miles altogether. As one early car maker put it, "The American who buys an automobile must pick between bad roads and worse." On the other hand, our railroad and trolley systems were among the best in the world.

Despite our slow start in developing automotive transportation, during the first decade of this century the U.S. was able to seize the leadership. While the European auto industry poked along in making improvements and expanding production, the Americans moved aggressively to realize the full potential of automotive transportation. Competition was keen, and by 1908 some 515 companies had formally entered the business, of which more than half had already failed. (There were also many backyard tinkerers who never actually produced vehicles for sale.)

In this climate, improvements came rapidly, and within a few years the industry crossed the critical takeoff threshold. By 1906, the number of registered vehicles hit 108,000. By 1912, the total had surpassed 1 million (thanks in part to Henry Ford), and by 1925 there were 17.5 million cars on the road. Only the Great

Depression of the 1930s and World War II temporarily slowed further growth to the point where, in the 1970s, Detroit was manufacturing as many as 9 million cars per year.

The reason why the automobile revolution occurred when it did, and where it did, involves a unique combination of factors—a synergistic nexus including the following:

1. *The Internal Combustion Engine*: Though obviously important, its superiority was not at first clear-cut and there was much more to it than that. In fact, as late as 1900 the number of steam and electric vehicles in the U.S. outnumbered gasoline-powered cars by 3:1.
2. *Technological Refinements*: Ultimate success also depended on a series of inventions, which converted the automobile into a fast, reliable, all-weather means of transportation. These inventions included, among other things, more powerful and efficient engines, lightweight (but strong) vanadium steel for making enclosed car bodies, inexpensive, fast-drying paints for protecting car bodies from rust, better brakes, the electric self-starter, headlights, steering wheels, and, not least, antifreeze.
3. *Balloon Tires*: This was a major factor. Originally developed for bicycles, the use of balloon tires in cars eliminated a serious constraint on performance by permitting much higher speeds and a much smoother ride. In fact, some of the earliest car-manufacturing companies were spinoffs from the bicycle-making business.
4. *Petroleum*: The availability of an abundant, efficient, and easily transported fuel supply was another major factor, along with improvements in gasoline-cracking methods during the critical years, which more than doubled the yields per barrel and dropped the price dramatically.
5. *Mass Production*: The development of assembly-line production methods was also an important factor, because it drove prices steadily downward to as low as $290 for one of Henry Ford's Model T's (about 10 percent of the average 1900 price). Our pioneering in mass production was a reflection of the distinctively American development strategy, which emphasized low-cost transportation for the masses rather than status symbols for the rich. However,

this strategy was in turn dependent on the fact that the U.S. already led the world in manufacturing standardization, and in the use of interchangeable parts.

6. *Raw Materials*: There was also the fortuitous fact that the U.S. alone among the industrialized nations of that time was blessed with huge quantities (at cheap prices) of such key raw materials as iron ore, coal (for steel making), wood, and especially petroleum.

7. *Geography*: Equally fortuitous was the fact that Detroit was close to all of the necessary raw materials (which were then concentrated in the Midwest) and was already a manufacturing center for all of the component technologies: carriage making, bicycle making, and the production of gasoline engines for various industrial uses, as well as such ancillary trades as leather-working, upholstering, carpentry, and machine-tool making.

8. *Government Assistance*: Road improvements and other measures undertaken by the government also played a major role. For example, the budget for the Federal Office of Public Roads jumped from a meager $87,000 in 1908 to $500 million by 1925. (Contrary to the mythology of capitalism, government and industry were partners in developing automotive transportation.)

9. *The Marketplace*: As it happened, there was an astonishing increase both in population and in national wealth during the very period when automobile technology was reaching the breakthrough stage. Not only did the population of the U.S. grow by some 30 million people between 1900 and 1920 (40 percent), but national income rose from about $14.5 billion per year at the turn of the century to $79.1 billion in 1920. While the European nations were squandering their wealth in the carnage of World War I, America was getting rich—in part by serving as a supplier to the warring nations. (Even allowing for some inflation, per capita income rose by one-third during this twenty-year period.) Furthermore, the distribution of income was much more equitable and the general standard of living in America was higher than in Europe. The result was that many more people in this country had surplus income

available to invest in a new mode of personal transportation. To put it in economics terminology, a vast potential "demand" for mass-produced automobiles was there waiting to be tapped.

10. *Promotion, and Cultural Factors*: Finally, automotive transportation was heavily promoted in the U.S. and attracted many investors and entrepreneurs. Even before the full benefits of mass production were realized, cars were perceived to be cheaper to operate than horses and carriages. They took up much less space on congested city streets and, believe it or not, were less prone to collisions. They were also viewed as requiring less upkeep and as being cleaner. (Horses produced some twenty-two pounds of manure per day, which posed monumental refuse and health problems for any large metropolis.) Then there were the psychological factors: the sense of adventure, freedom, and independence that automobiles increasingly provided for their owners.

When all of these factors and more were combined, the result was a mode of transportation that was much cheaper, faster, more efficient, and even more comfortable than the horse and buggy. A doctor with a car could make five house calls when before he could make only one. A local department store could reduce by more than half the cost of making deliveries. A farmer could reduce the cost of shipping his produce to market from about 30 cents per ton to 14 cents per ton, and ship it over a much longer distance to boot (when the roads were good).

Clearly, there was no "prime mover"; the causes of the automobile revolution were manifold. It was a synergistic phenomenon. Moreover, it was the combined effects—the "payoffs"—that, in the final analysis, were responsible for directing the course of this historic change.

## THE LESSONS OF HISTORY

What can we learn from a synergy view of history? One response is that we must begin to think about historical processes the way ecologists think about nature. To embellish the old saying, we must learn to avoid focussing either on the forest or the trees. Instead, the forest must be viewed as a complex "ecosystem" which, like Darwin's famous "entangled bank," contains many different forms of plants, animals, insects, birds, and trees. All of these living things, Darwin stressed, are intensely interdependent, sometimes in very oblique ways.

So it is also with the complex ecosystems that constitute human societies. The process of historical change is complex beyond our capacity to comprehend. Many different factors combine to shape the contours of the human narrative. Pick any factor you like to explain the automobile revolution, or the current computer revolution for that matter, and it can be shown that it would not have been sufficient. Conversely, if any major factor were to be removed from the equation, the end result would not have been the same.

## THE SYNERGY WORLD VIEW

The very essence of the synergy *weltanschauung* is the notion that history is not a linear progression but a contingent, configural process involving, most often, a great many codetermining, context-dependent causes. Not only are all these codetermining causes necessary, but a small change in any one of them can produce drastic changes in the pattern as a whole, and in the outcomes.

Thus, the synergy world view involves a richer view of reality. Indeed, the synergy world view mocks simplistic, deterministic visions of the future, even as it puts much of the burden for shaping that future in our own hands. Many years ago, the prominent British archeologist V. Gordon Childe wrote a classic treatise on the so-called agricultural revolution entitled *Man Makes Himself*. In a very real sense, this sums it up. Not only has our species shaped its own evolution, and its own recent history, but to an increasing extent we are shaping the continuing evolution of the earth and all of its inhabitants, whether we know it or not.

The synergy world view also suggests that there is a symmetry, logic, and wholeness in the architecture of the natural world. To see this unity clearly, in all of its many ramifications, is truly to see the world from a new perspective. At least to us, this unity—this intelligibility—is both comforting and inspiring.

Finally, the synergy world view transcends such outworn nineteenth-century ideologies as capitalism and socialism. The capitalist and socialist models of society have been earnestly debated by generations of scholars and revolutionaries alike as if they more or less define our choices. In light of the synergy principle, however, it can be seen that neither of these one-sided caricatures provides more than a partial understanding of how a modern economy operates (see chapter 6). For better or worse, we live in a world that is at once highly competitive and highly cooperative, self-interested and interdependent. Because our interdependence is inescapable, we must learn how to live with this duality and use it to our advantage.

## THE POWER OF SYNERGY

It should be abundantly clear by now: There is something at once mysterious and immensely powerful in the workings of the synergy principle. It is at the center of all creativity; it has been the engine of our evolution as a species; it has shaped the trajectory of human history; and, as we have seen, its products have ranged from the unexpected to the almost magical. Like the remarkable division of labor and combined effects produced by the roughly seven octillion cells in each of our bodies. Or the graphite and epoxy resin compounds that collaborate to produce a tough new material with similar strength and greater heat resistance than steel. Or the exalted fabric of sound produced by the precise blending of hundreds of voices and instruments in Beethoven's magnificent Ninth Symphony. Or the microscopic precision and exquisite complexity of a microcomputer. Or the monumental complexity of a modern supercarrier.

Make no mistake: Those who understand how to use the full creative potential of the synergy principle hold in their hands a tool that rivals—no, transcends—the gift of fire.

# 4. Synergy and Dysergy

Before we go on to show how the synergy principle can be used as a tool to help us cope with our problems, big and small, there is some additional groundwork to be done. The many forms of "positive" synergy that we have already described are, it turns out, only half the story. Unfortunately, there is also a dark side to the synergy world view.

The antimatter, so to speak, of the synergy principle is "negative" synergy, or dysergy—cooperative effects that are undesired or destructive in nature. Like its more felicitous counterpart, dysergy comes in many forms. Among them are:

- The drug interactions that can cause side effects ranging from mildly irritating to fatal;
- The combination of electrical appliances that succeeds in blowing the fuse;
- The corporate mergers that go sour, producing wholes that are *less* than the sum of their parts;
- The computer errors that result in thousands, or tens of thousands of erroneous "notices," billings, even disbursements;
- The corrosive effect of automobile exhaust gases on the facades of historic buildings;
- The street gangs and prison gangs that are incubators of collective violence;
- The one small glitch that prevents the computer software from running;
- The overcrowded beaches that dilute the fun of getting away from it all;
- The salt (instead of sugar) that turns the cake batter into a culinary disaster;
- The single dialing error that results in getting a wrong telephone number;
- The groaning crop surpluses that depress farm prices and

turn the successes of many individual farmers into a collective failure;
- The overloaded transit systems that work fine, except during the rush hour.

## A CLOSER LOOK

Let's look at dysergy in a little more detail. One of the most common forms of dysergy occurs when there is too much (or too many) of a good thing. Up to a certain point, it may be beneficial to have more transit riders, more telephone users, more cars on a toll road, more airline flights, or more "development" of vacation resorts. Beyond that, any *more* of the same may produce dysergy—sardine-can commutes, "please hold" messages, traffic jams, snarled air traffic systems, or an exodus of disappointed vacationers. Indeed, many of the current problems in our society—from congested national parks to environmental pollution, inflated land prices, water-rights controversies, and a host of other things—can be traced at least partly to the relentless increase in our population.

Likewise, in the business world, when there are too many restaurants or gas stations in one small town, or when the makers of, say, smoke detectors or video games become too numerous, what began as a bonanza for some can turn into a bloodbath for all.

## SOME VARIATIONS

There are many variations on this theme. Take the airlines' practice of "overbooking" flights in the expectation that there will be a certain number of cancelations. When everyone shows up for the flight, the result can be costly to the airline. A number of compensatory payments might have to be made to the passengers who get "bumped."

Another example involves the signs in public places (in some states) warning that occupancy by more than so many persons is "dangerous and unlawful." Occupancy laws are a product of hard (even tragic) lessons in what can happen when too many people are crowded into a given space.

Our food-consumption behavior provides still another example. Even an irresistible treat like an ice-cream sundae, beyond a certain amount, can give us indigestion, or worse. We know a local creamery that used to sell something called the "Awful Awful." The proprietors used to advertise these humongous confections with the low-risk offer (to them) that anyone who could eat two Awful Awfuls would get a third one free.

Or consider the Los Angeles smog. When the exhaust fumes from millions of automobiles combine with an atmospheric "inversion" and the topography of the Los Angeles Basin, the effects can range from unpleasant to life threatening. And this is paltry compared to what many scientists believe may be happening to the overall climate of the earth as a combined result of our burning of fossil fuels. The so-called greenhouse effect is also, unfortunately, an example of negative synergy.

## WHEN A PART FAILS

The failure of a major part in a synergistic system can also produce dysergy. When a commuter train carrying, say, four hundred passengers is a half-hour late because of the avoidable failure of a small part, the combined effect may be the loss of 200 man-hours of productive labor. Likewise, the failure of a single component in an electrical power system can, under some circumstances, black out an entire city. Or a single pothole in a heavily used highway may produce thousands of misaligned front ends.

Or worse yet, an insurance industry nightmare came true recently when an elderly lady, confused and disoriented in a heavy fog, stopped her car in the middle of a causeway on Interstate 80, setting off a chain collision involving ultimately more than 70 cars and, luckily, only 15 injuries. Though we don't usually think of it in such terms, the motorists who make use of a highway are, for the duration, parts of a system.

Or consider this lead in the *Wall Street Journal*: "It was the smallest of mistakes. A detail in a joint, incorrectly designed, weakened a walkway suspended over a lobby of the Hyatt Regency Hotel in Kansas City. The walkway collapsed during a crowded dance party last July, killing 113 people and injuring 186 more."

Individual actions in a social situation can also be the cause of negative synergy. When two people are talking at once a listener may not be able to understand either of them. One loud and boisterous group in a crowded restaurant can force all the other diners to speak up, with the result being a din in which no one can be clearly heard and everyone gets a bit hoarse. One disruptive child in a schoolroom can completely frustrate the teacher's efforts to get the job done. And the actions (or inactions) of a key employee in a business firm can have a drastic impact on morale, productivity, and ultimately the viability of the organization as a whole. The paradigm case was Captain Queeg in *The Caine Mutiny*.

## VICTIMS OF DYSERGY

Though we seldom (if ever) stop to reflect on it, our lives are frequently disrupted by the loss of synergy due to the failure of some component part in a complex system. Thus the economy of a city (or a part of it) can be crippled when there is a power outage or a water main break. When the air traffic controllers go out on strike, the airline industry can be crippled. When there is a transit strike, commuters may despair of getting to work. And when there is a trucking strike, the grocery shelves may quickly be emptied by hoarders.

The Iranian hostage rescue mission in 1980 failed because of the "coincidence" of three small but critical failures in three of the eight RH-53 helicopters that were involved in the mission. A clogged cooling vent that had inadvertently been covered led to the failure of two key navigation instruments on one of the choppers. A cracked nut led to a hydraulic leak and consequent failure of the hydraulic pump on the second craft. And a dangerous hairline crack in one of the rotor blades apparently downed the third. (Remember the children's story about how the war was lost for want of a horseshoe nail?)

By contrast, when the Israelis succeeded in rescuing 103 hostages at Uganda's Entebbe airport back in 1976, everything (and everybody) worked perfectly.

At a more personal level, we may be late for work because a transformer malfunctioned on one of our antiquated subway cars; we may lose the softball game because of an error by the center fielder, or we may storm out of the movie theater in frustration and demand our money back because a transistor failed in the sound system. (Just try watching the in-flight movie without earphones.)

For better or worse, we live in a world where perfectionism must be the rule if we hope to meet our needs and accomplish our goals. It is not good enough for GM's X-cars to work 99 percent perfectly, except for the brakes. Or for everything to work perfectly at the Three Mile Island nuclear power plant, except for some "human errors." Or for everything to work fine on the space shuttle Challenger, except for... (NASA's moon exploration program was successful in part because "zero defects" was both official policy and a religion within the organization.) And when we speak of having had "bad luck," often as not it involves an unpredictable small failure in, and consequent breakdown of, a synergistic system.

## WRONG COMBINATIONS

Another common form of negative synergy occurs when people put things together in the wrong way, or without a proper sense of the relationship between the parts and the whole. When someone builds a garish modern house in a neighborhood dominated by charming old Victorians, the one "eyesore" can spoil the aesthetics of the entire neighborhood.

Likewise, a person's appearance is the combined result of many factors: health and physical conditioning, complexion, hair styling and care, clothing and accessories, even one's outlook and mental state. And all it takes to spoil the effect is to have disheveled and dirty hair, or the wrong tie or scarf, or even a sleepless night.

By the same token, how many of us have had the experience of being impressed with someone else's home, except for the ugly wallpaper, or the neglected garden, or a disorderly mess that detracted from the overall effect?

Indeed, there are innumerable opportunities for negative synergy in our daily lives. Our personal health, as advocates of the so-called holistic health movement stress, is an obvious case in point. The likelihood of having a heart attack or getting cancer depends on a number of "risk factors" that may be working in combination, including family history (genetic predisposition), diet, exercise, work-stress, life-style, etc.

Or consider such "vicious circles" as the experience of an acquaintance who developed a drinking problem when work pressures and marital quarreling (and probably also a genetic factor) combined to create severe personal stress. His drinking problem in turn led to the loss of his job, which contributed to a separation from his wife, which led, finally, to a breakdown and hospitalization.

More mundane (but commonplace) was the dysergy experienced recently by another acquaintance, who had to break a window to get into his own home. He had inadvertently locked himself out, and a neighbor of his who had been given a spare key for just such occasions had gone away for the weekend. (Taking a leaf from Tandem Computers, our absent-minded acquaintance has now distributed two extra emergency keys.)


BUSINESS DYSERGY

Many more examples of dysergy can be observed in the business world. Corporate mergers consummated primarily to realize quick profits for some takeover artist and his lawyers or to avoid taxes, rather than for functional reasons, can often lead to unfavorable consequences on the bottom line. What do oil companies know about the computer industry, and vice versa? And what does a communications company know about rental cars? This is one reason why "divestitures" have become so popular these days.

Likewise, many an office has been wracked by a "personality conflict" between two key people. And many a business failure has been due, to restate an old saying, to the combination of straws which together broke the camel's back.

For instance, when Lionel Corporation, the one-time maker of toy trains, filed for bankruptcy during the 1982 recession, the management blamed the state of the economy in general and poor Christmas sales in particular. Yet Lionel's major competitors were able to survive the very same economic downturn. Looking beneath the surface, it was clear that much more was involved in Lionel's demise: the abandonment and sale of its faltering toy train business and a shift into toy retailing; the purchase of existing retail toy stores that were often of marginal quality and poorly located; concentration on acquiring more stores, rather than strengthening the performance of earlier acquisitions; lack of sufficient capital to keep its stores adequately stocked with merchandise year-round, or to engage in the kind of aggressive marketing that competitors like Toys 'R' Us could do; and, finally, some ill-timed acquisitions that put an added burden on the company's cash flow just as the recession hit. What was responsible for Lionel's failure? All of the above.

## A SYMBOL: NEW YORK'S SUBWAYS

If ever there was a symbol of the dysergy that besets our nation, it is the New York City subway system. When it was built in the early part of the century, it was a model of technological sophistication. It was also lovingly constructed by skilled craftsmen, who did many of the stations in varying patterns of hand-laid tiles. With 6,150 subway cars and 832 miles of track (230 route miles), New York's subways carry three-quarters of the nation's total rapid transit passengers (more than 1 billion a year). Each day hundreds of thousands of New Yorkers either get to work on time, or late, or not at all depending on the performance of the subways.

Despite its vital role in the economy and social life of one of our key cities, the system is a mess—no, a Faustian nightmare. For more than a decade the system has been in radical decline, and now the situation is desperate. "The subway system is having a nervous breakdown," the new transit authority chairman Robert Kiley told a reporter for the *New York Times*.

Its stations are filthy, dark, and dangerous. The rolling stock are subject to frequent breakdowns, fires, and malfunctions; subway cars go only one-quarter of the distance between breakdowns that they did twenty years ago. The system's antiquated, poorly maintained tracks are the cause of innumerable delays, derailments, and fires. Losses of power, failures of tunnel signals, and water seepage into the tunnels have become routine occurrences. Three out of every ten trains fail to finish their runs within five minutes of the scheduled time, and the number of trains forced to bypass stations is three times what it was a decade ago.

## FEAR OF THE SUBWAYS

Fear of using the subways is pervasive, and with good reason. Despite the presence of some 3,600 transit police, there are on the average 38 felonies reported on the system every day and many more go unreported. (The so-called subway vigilante, Bernhard Goetz, became a folk hero when he fought back and shot his attackers.) Cheating the system by jumping over or ducking under the turnstiles to avoid paying fares (a misdemeanor) is rampant. In one eight-hour crackdown, 300 police officers made 117 arrests and issued 530 summonses, the vast majority of which were for fare-dodging.

The subway system has an annual budget of over $2 billion, but with ridership currently at roughly half what it was in 1947 (due to changing demographics, fare increases, and the alienation of many riders who have found alternatives) the system is running a deficit of $500 million a year.

Still, that very substantial budget is not being wisely spent. Virtually all of the subway cars in the system are completely covered, inside and out, with spray-painted graffiti. The effect is intimidating to those who aren't used to it—a whiff of anarchy. Vandalism is also endemic, especially the smashing of car windows. Yet, incredibly, none of the system's fifteen yards was fenced until very recently.

## POOR ADMINISTRATION

In 1982, when a major study of subway operations was undertaken by the city, the administration of the system had not been significantly improved since the 1940s. In the age of computers, simple information about where a particular car is located proved difficult to obtain, and inventory procedures were hopelessly out of date.

Purchasing for the system was found to be chaotic, and repairs were frequently delayed for lack of parts. A computer system intended to alleviate the problem is often overtaxed and breaks down.

Some 250 employees in various parts of the system were assigned to data collection and processing, a rather large number. Yet no department was responsible for coordinating and integrating these data-processing activities.

Over $100 million was being spent annually to staff the system's 753 token booths, a cost that, the study concluded, could be cut more than 25 percent if bulk purchases of tokens was permitted. Another way of saving money might be to use vending machines to dispense tokens, as some other systems do, but in New York the likelihood is that any savings would be offset by vandalism.

Major financial decisions by management over the years have also contributed to the system's decline. The sophisticated new cars that were purchased some years ago to replace some of the oldest equipment were not adequately field-tested beforehand and proved to be unreliable. Despite declining ridership and budget deficits, a decision was made in the 1960s to construct new routes. Ten years and $1 billion later, none of the new routes are yet in service and they may never be.

## MAINTENANCE PROBLEMS

Meanwhile, maintenance needs have been sorely neglected, especially during the city's fiscal crisis in the mid-1970s. To make matters worse, a generous new pension plan introduced in 1968 (half pay after twenty years) led to massive retirements among the most experienced of the system's 40,000 workers. The subway's infrastructure was decimated within three years, and replacements for what had once been a high-quality work force have been far less qualified, inadequately trained, and fewer in number.

Nevertheless, the performance of the system could be markedly better than it is were it not for a labor force that is, to put it mildly, out of control. Work practices are incredibly lax and sloppy, with such commonplace abuses as sleeping on the job, leaving early but claiming overtime, and fulfilling one's pre-scribed work quota within a few hours then quitting for the day. Training and supervision are completely inadequate, and many workers are only marginally competent. Some recent adminis-trators seemed grateful that the workers did anything at all; oth-ers took the General Patton approach and so antagonized the workers that they responded with sullen noncooperation.

To remedy this situation, a massive rebuilding program is un-derway that could ultimately cost more than $10 billion, and an aggressive new management team has been brought in to try and turn the situation around. So far, things seem only to have gotten worse, and the new team seems to have repeated the mistakes of their predecessors with regard to labor relations. It remains to be seen if the system can be turned around.

## DYSERGY AND HISTORY

Negative synergy, like its better-known twin, has also left its imprint in the history books. Let's examine briefly one of the classic cases—the mutually reinforcing pattern of factors that combined to produce what might have been anything but a "Great Depression."

Almost every schoolboy learns that the stock market crash of October 1929 signaled the onset of the worst economic disaster in modern history. This is the legend, but it's not true. The Depression had actually been gathering momentum for some time before a wild, out-of-control stock market, usually a good bellwether of business conditions, caught up with economic real-ity and made an already bad matter worse. In fact, the specu-lative fever that gripped the stock market during the latter part of the 1920s was itself, ironically, one of the avoidable causes of the underlying depression.

The roots of the Depression can be traced to a fundamental imbalance in the U.S. economy that grew worse as the decade neared its end. In a nutshell, "supply" had begun to run away from "demand."

In part this was due to a transformation that was occurring in the agricultural sector. Mechanization of the farm, with tractors and trucks beginning to replace horses, meant increased productivity and yields, especially in the Midwest grain belt and the so-called bonanza farms of the Far West. At the same time, a sharp decline in the population of horses greatly reduced the demand for fodder (some 20 percent of our total grain production in 1900). In addition, there was a big decline in overseas demand for our farm products as European agriculture began to recover from World War I. Between 1919 and 1927, wholesale farm prices dropped more than 50 percent. With more than 30 percent of our population still living on farms (and in farming communities) in those days, the economic impact was widespread.

As the agricultural sector slid into a dysergy-induced depression, a similar imbalance between supply and demand began to appear in the industrial sector as well. And, again, several factors contributed. One was an increasing gap between the incomes of the rich and the poor. Between 1920 and 1929, the income share of the wealthiest 5 percent of the population went up 14 percent, while the average wages of blue-collar workers were stagnant. Indeed, industrial productivity increased 43 percent during the 1920s, but much of this improvement was retained as profits rather than being passed on either to the workers in the form of higher wages or to consumers in the form of lower prices.

This had the dual effect of fueling financial speculation and, more important, excess capital spending on factories, office buildings, equipment, and the production of goods while, at the same time, throttling down consumer purchasing power. Despite the boom in automobile production, for instance, by the end of the decade only one American in six owned a car. Likewise, only one in five had a bathtub and one in ten had a telephone.

High protective tariffs and a general economic weakness overseas (as a result of the war) further dampened demand for American industrial products, as did a collapse in the price of silver, which had the effect of cutting sharply the volume of silver-based purchases from the Orient. Even the speculative fever gripping Wall Street, perversely enough, began to have an adverse effect on consumer purchasing power. As the great bull market of the latter 1920s roared ahead, stock speculation became a national mania. Get-rich-quick schemes multiplied, and money that might have been spent on consumer goods went into playing the market.

For those who were sensible enough to pay heed, the signs of a downturn in the industrial sector began to appear many months before the stock market crash. Some economists and many more private citizens duly noted these signs at the time, but mostly they chose to interpret them as being a temporary slump. They believed that the booming stock market would override and in time reverse the downtrend, and that continued economic growth was assured.

## A HOUSE OF CARDS

Unfortunately, the optimists were placing their confidence in a financial house of cards. Credit, especially for speculation, had become grossly inflated in an era when government restrictions were few and enforcement was lax. For instance, broker loans for speculation in stocks, which were already vastly overpriced, increased 25 percent in 1927 alone. Banks had also become heavily dependent on the stock market. Not only were many of their assets tied up in stocks but many of their loans were secured by stocks.

Then there was the pernicious practice of "pyramiding"—the creation of investment trusts that held stocks in holding companies, which owned the stocks of banks, which in turn had affiliates that owned holding companies, etc. When the panic struck, this intricate edifice came crashing down, carrying with it a large number of banks and other financial institutions.

The effect of the stock market crash, then, was to augment the negative forces that were already at work in the economy. The dysergy it produced turned what might have been a mild depression into a rout—a self-propelled downward spiral that was unstoppable until 25 percent of the work force was unemployed and industrial production hit bottom at 50 percent of capacity. Indeed, despite the New Deal of the 1930s the economy didn't fully recover until World War II.

If one could go back and rewrite the script for that human tragedy, a change in only one or two of the major factors might have produced a very different outcome. Such "what ifs" and "might have beens" are, of course, the favorite parlor game of historians. No one can say for certain what the outcome might have been under different circumstances. One thing we can be certain of, though, is that the Great Depression was the result of negative synergy—a concatenation of forces that fed on one another while the people who had the power to contain these forces did nothing, or else did too little and too late, or else did the wrong thing altogether.

## SYNERGY VS. DYSERGY

Though it may seem contradictory, especially in light of everything that has been said so far, the fact is that synergy is neither inherently "good" nor "bad." It just is. The distinction between "positive" and "negative" synergy depends entirely upon our values, and interests.

It so happens that many of our values are shared so widely that most if not all of us can agree on how to label the synergies that impact on those values. Hardly anyone was happy about the Great Depression, aside from some communist ideologues. And is there anyone who would view a nuclear holocaust as a good thing? If someone like Superman's nemesis, Lex Luthor, really wanted to create mayhem, then he or she might take pleasure in traffic jams, blackouts, even nuclear disasters. But, luckily, there seem to be very few real-world people who hold such values.

Aside from the many synergies that impact on our widely shared values, however, there are a great many instances in which the distinction between "positive" and "negative" synergy depends on who you talk to. Even when the stock market is going down, the professional "traders" may still make money by selling short. Rapid price movement of any kind may be good for their business, and the only form of dysergy for them is a stable market. Likewise, stock brokers make commissions on either side of a stock transaction. So they can be relatively sanguine about a sell-off in the market.

In a closely fought football game, an inspired offensive drive represents positive synergy for the team that has the ball. But their opponents will doubtless view the matter more negatively. For someone who likes hot chili, more chili powder in the recipe may be good. But for someone who does not like it hot, more is less.

By the same token, the snowstorm that delights the skiers may, at the same time, snarl the transportation systems of nearby urban areas and, in the longer run, cause spring flooding. And the farm surpluses that conspire to keep farm prices low may be a boon to consumers at the cost of driving the farmers deeper into debt.

When thirteen of the oil-producing nations banded together to form a price cartel (OPEC) and were able by joint action to jack up the prices sharply, the results were clearly beneficial for the producers but certainly not for the consumers. With OPEC now in disarray, the consuming nations are plainly delighted, while the producing nations are obviously frustrated.

## ACCEPTING THE INEVITABLE

If positive synergy is an inescapable part of our daily lives, so is dysergy. Most of us would agree that overburdened urban transit systems, littered public parks, street gangs, recessions, water pollution, and the like are synergies we can do without. Likewise, there can be lethal dysergy when a person mixes alcohol and barbiturates; or merely aggravated discomfort when two or more allergy-producing agents are present simultaneously; or increased stress when a family tries to squeeze six kids into a house designed for two or three. And, when a symphony orchestra is warming up, the resulting cacaphony (dysergy) may be just irritating enough to heighten the almost magical effect that ensues when, after a brief round of applause for the conductor and a moment of silence, the orchestra pours forth in perfect synchrony (positive synergy) the powerful opening measures of Brahms's great First Symphony.

Indeed, this familiar concertgoing ritual can serve as a metaphor for just how fragile, complex, and context-dependent may be the relationship between synergy and dysergy. If the pieces of any whole come together in the wrong way, the results may range from displeasing to catastrophic. And what may be a beneficial combination in one context can be destructive in another. Thus what may be the right spare part for one auto engine can severely damage another. Likewise, what starts out as a mass of well-disciplined protest marchers may degenerate into an uncontrolled mob, turning what could have been a powerful political statement into a bloody, backlash-producing riot. Even an orderly protest march at the wrong place and the wrong time may be counterproductive. And if an effective demonstration lifts the spirits of the protest leaders, it may at the same time depress and discourage members of the old guard.

Synergy and dysergy, therefore, are not absolutes. They constitute a vast congeries of open-ended, dynamic processes that ebb and flow with the tides of history and the vicissitudes of our economic, political, and personal lives. In either case, though, their effects are inescapable.

## HIGH AND LOW SYNERGY

If positive and negative synergy are ubiquitous, so are high and low synergy. Many years ago, the anthropologist Ruth Benedict drew a useful distinction between organizations or societies in which the potential for synergy is more or less effectively realized. Her point was that much can depend on how well the pieces are put together; some systems hum with efficiency while others are, as the systems theorists would say, "suboptimal." For better or worse, our society has an abundance of both kinds of systems. The examples are almost endless:

- The recipe that didn't turn out the way Julia Child did it on TV;
- The high school orchestra—bless its heart for attempting the first movement of Dvorak's *New World Symphony*;
- The Broadway shows that close before they open;
- American automakers in the 1970s, when their cars were poorly engineered, shoddily built, and overpriced;
- The disorganized, demoralized football teams that are destined to end the season in the cellar;
- The "greasy spoon" restaurants that exist in every town and city.

Sometimes it is objective factors—the very design of the system—that make the difference between high and low synergy.

## AN EXAMPLE

Consider the two new restaurants that opened in a nearby town at about the same time some five years ago. One was a small French restaurant that seated about 45 people and charged $11 to $13 for the entree alone. The other was something very different, an upscale natural foods restaurant that seated 250 people and charged $5 to $7.95 for the entree, including rolls and soup or salad. Five years later the first restaurant was limping along on a low-profit margin (and had changed ownership), while the second was well on its way to becoming a national chain.

Economies of scale had something to do with the differences in performance, but that was hardly sufficient. Lots of large restaurants go out of business. And so do restaurants whose principal virtue is low prices. Conversely, very small restaurants sometimes do exceedingly well. The explanation for the differing fortunes of these two business ventures, it turns out, is both more complex and more interesting.

The natural foods restaurant started with the advantage of a strikingly new and different menu, which includes a profusion of innovative (and tasty) dishes, drinks, and desserts. The food and the service are also of very high quality which, together with low prices, makes it extremely competitive. While the French restaurant's food is of similar quality, it is not notably better, or lower priced, than three other French restaurants in the area.

The natural foods restaurant also has a better location; it is on the main street in the center of town, as well as being adjacent to two city parking lots. The French restaurant, on the other hand, is located on a side street with very limited parking.

But most important, the natural foods restaurant has a formula for achieving a very high volume, which is the key to how it can be so profitable with such low prices. First, it remains open continuously from 7 A.M. to 11 P.M., seven days a week, serving everything from breakfasts to late-night snacks. And second, it has a highly efficient kitchen that makes extensive use of microwave ovens and woks for heating the many dishes prepared in advance. Thus customers can usually be served within a few minutes of being seated, which results in a much faster turnover. Indeed, right from the beginning there has almost always been a short waiting line (no reservations are allowed), and few seats ever remain empty for long.

In contrast, the French restaurant is open only six days a week during specific lunch and dinner hours, mainly by reservations which, if canceled at the last minute, might result in a loss of perhaps 5 percent in revenue for a given meal.

In short, the natural foods restaurant has a winning combination: a distinctive menu, high quality, and the ability to achieve a very high volume with relatively low prices. It is a high synergy operation, while its neighbor has low synergy.

## MANAGEMENT STYLES

If synergy by design is responsible for many standout performances, in many other cases the difference between a high and low synergy operation can be traced to the qualities of leadership and management. Two strikingly similar hospitals provide a clear-cut illustration. (We will name no names, since they are former clients.)

Hospital A and Hospital B were so much alike that they came about as close as one could get in the real world to having a controlled experiment. Both were privately owned, nonprofit institutions operated by religious orders; they were in the same state and were therefore subject to the same regulatory environment; both were located in urban, residential, low-income minority areas; they were of comparable size; and they had about the same socioeconomic mix of patients in terms of the reimbursement received for services.

Nevertheless, Hospital A was producing a consistent 6 to 8 percent net income, while Hospital B had averaged less than 1 percent over the previous five years and had lost money in one year.

As far as could be determined, the differences in financial performance did not lie in any of the externals. If anything, Hospital A had a disadvantage in that regard. It had an older physical plant, fifty fewer beds, a slightly higher load of charity and low-reimbursement patients, and a high volume of maternity patients (a traditional loss leader in the hospital business), while Hospital B had no maternity patients at all. Hospital A even had double-occupancy rooms while Hospital B had single-occupancy rooms. At least in theory, double-occupancy rooms are harder to keep filled, because of the problem of matching the sex, smoking habits, and other characteristics of the patients.

The most significant difference between the two hospitals, it turned out, was in the quality of the management. Hospital A provided a model of how to run an institution; Hospital B provided a model of how to blow it.

The chief executive officer (CEO) of Hospital A was open, supportive, and sensitive to his staff and the needs of the institution. He was also decisive, well organized, and committed to the development of his hospital. Hospital A had a formal planning and control system that ran throughout the organization. Planning was thus an integrated, systemwide process in which each unit participated in developing overall hospital goals, as well as annual plans. The management also tried to promote a sense of everyone participating in a common effort. And because everyone was brought aboard, the staff tended to line up behind organizational objectives; nobody was sabotaging the plans.

In addition, Hospital A had made extensive efforts to build a good image in its community. The board of trustees was drawn primarily from the community, rather than from the religious order. And members of the community were serving on every one of the hospital's boards and committees.

As a result, Hospital A ran a lean, highly efficient operation with tight cost controls. Patient volume was an incredibly high 95 percent of the maximum attainable rate. One could even sense the difference in the hospital environment: Staff morale was high; the staff was friendly and cooperative but businesslike; people were busy; no one was killing time.

In contrast, the CEO of Hospital B was authoritarian and closed. He handed down orders rather than consulting with his staff. Because he was ambitious and wanted to move up in the corporate hierarchy of the religious order, he calculated his actions accordingly. The hospital had no formal planning process at all. When planning was done, it was ad hoc and often at cross-purposes with what other parts of the organization were doing. Furthermore, every one of the hospital's trustees were members of the religious order, and from out of town.

As a result, Hospital B ran a very lax operation; staff productivity was low; there was a chitchat organizational culture and many operating inefficiencies. Patient volume was only 75 to 80 percent of the maximum, despite the hospital's supposed advantages. Overall operating expenses were about 10 percent higher than for Hospital A.

The conclusion seems well founded. Given similar resources and capabilities, good management can make the difference between a high- and low-synergy performance.

## "GREATNESS" REDEFINED

The distinction between high and low synergy gives us a handle on how to define the elusive concept of "greatness." The characteristic that all "great" human achievements have in common is high synergy—an excellent whole composed of many excellent parts:

- A great athlete combines exceptional native ability with tremendous drive, self-discipline, training, and even intelligence.
- A great restaurant has it all—setting, decor, service, management, wines, and, of course, a great menu prepared by a great team of chefs and kitchen personnel using the very best ingredients.
- A great automobile is not only a joy to drive—a product of exceptional engineering—but is handsome to look at, painstakingly constructed, and of the highest quality in every detail.
- A great Broadway musical, the stuff of legend, is one that brings together a classic story, memorable music, clever lyrics, imaginative choreography, lavish staging and sets, outstanding performers, brilliant direction, and much more.
- A great nation strives for, and achieves, excellence in every area—family life, education, science, the arts, government,

agriculture, business, the military, sports, recreation, even religious institutions. Greatness is an accolade that many nations seek, few attain, and fewer still sustain for very long.

For many of us—as individuals, organizations, or nations—the aspiration for greatness may become an end in itself—a challenge just because it's there to be had and because it provides, as a reward, a sense of achievement and pride. Of course, a high synergy performance also wins the admiration of others.

But the most important attribute of high synergy is that it bestows on its possessor a competitive edge. If competition via cooperation has been a winning strategy in evolution generally and in human history specifically, high synergy is the high road to competitive success.

The challenge, then, is to perfect the art of synergistic thinking—and action. This is what the wisest individuals, organizations, and nations already do, whether knowingly or intuitively. We must all learn how to use the synergy principle as a conscious tool to achieve (or maintain or regain, as the case may be) the high synergy that, over the long run, our competitive success requires.

# 5. The Art of Synergistic Thinking I: Basics

More than anything else, the synergy principle provides a mind-stretching tool, a way of confronting systematically the enormous complexity and interdependence of things. The art of synergistic thinking begins, therefore, with an anatomy lesson. Let's look a little more deeply into the nature of synergy.

## 1 + 1 = 3

When the term "synergy" is introduced into a conversation, it is often associated with the catch-phrase: "The whole is greater than the sum of its parts" $(1 + 1 = 3)$. Such formulations are certainly suggestive. The whole automobile demonstrates cooperative effects that cannot be achieved by any of its 5,000 or more parts acting alone, or even by all of its parts if they were arranged in a different way. As the great economist Joseph Schumpeter put it in his classic text *The Theory of Economic Development*: "Add successively as many mail coaches as you please, you will never get a railway thereby."

The same thing applies to airplanes, boats, houses, and computers. Add as many wings, sails, doors, and disk drives as you please, but you will not get a functioning system. For complex systems of all kinds, whether they are organizations of human actors (say a football team or a symphony orchestra) or technological hardware (say a camera or a bicycle), depend for their operation on the precise arrangement and integrated functioning of various specialized parts, or "roles."

One way of determining whether or not a given effect is the product of a synergistic system is to remove a major component and observe the result. Take away the center from a football team, or the violin section from an orchestra, or the camera's lens, or the bicycle's handlebars. It's not difficult to imagine the consequences. Indeed, the repairmen who fix our cars, refrigerators, computers, telephones, and TVs depend for their livings on the fact that these technological wholes involve effects that are produced by a set of precisely designed parts acting in concert. Our repairmen practice what might be called applied synergy; in essence, they are concerned with the maintenance (or restoration) of various synergistic effects. For that matter, so are the repairmen who minister to the various parts of our bodies— perhaps the most complex system in the natural world.

However, the slogan "the whole is greater than the sum of its parts" is actually a very narrow characterization of the synergy principle and may even be misleading. It would be more accurate to say that the whole produces combined or cooperative effects that are not otherwise attainable. These effects are not necessarily "more than" whatever the parts can do alone. Just different. (Sometimes, in fact, the parts can't do anything at all by themselves.) Nor is synergy confined to organized "wholes."

## THE DIVISION OF LABOR

To be sure, some of the most important forms of synergy involve the coordinated action of different parts. Plato was perhaps the first social theorist to appreciate that synergy lies at the very base of human societies—that the "division of labor" produces mutually beneficial results because different people have different aptitudes and because specialization increases a person's skill and efficiency. In *The Republic*, Plato wrote: "Things are produced more plentifully and easily and of a better quality when one man does one thing which is natural to him and does it in the right way, and leaves other things."

## SYNERGY IN ADAM SMITH

Even Adam Smith, who is generally acknowledged to be the founding father of capitalism, recognized the cooperative basis of a complex society and, in *The Wealth of Nations* (1776), penned what ranks as one of the classic appreciations:

Observe the accommodation of the most common artificer or day-la-
bourer in a civilized and thriving country, and you will perceive that
the number of people whose industry a part, though but a small part,
has been employed in procuring him this accommodation, exceeds all
computation. The woolen coat, for example, which covers the day-la-
bourer, as course and rough as it may appear, is the product of the joint
labour of a great multitude of workmen. The shepherd, the sorter of
the wool, the wool-comber or carder, the dyer, the scribbler, the spinner,
the weaver, the fuller, the dresser, with many others, must all join their
different arts in order to complete even this homely production. How
many merchants and carriers, besides, must have been employed in
transporting the materials from some of those workmen to others who
often live in a very distant part of the country! How much commerce
and navigation in particular, how many ship-builders, sailors, sail-mak-
ers, rope-makers, must have been employed in order to bring together
the different [dyes] made use of by the dyer, which often come from
the remotest corners of the world! What a variety of labour too is necessary in order to produce the tools of the meanest of these workmen!
To say nothing of such complicated machines as the ship of the sailor,
the mill of the fuller, or even the loom of the weaver. . . . If we examine,
I say, all of these things, and consider what a variety of labour is employed about each of them, we shall be sensible that without the assistance and cooperation of many thousands, the very meanest person in
a civilized country could not be . . . accommodated.

Adam Smith also provided us with one of the textbook examples of the division of labor. At a pin factory that he had
personally observed, ten workers performing ten different tasks
were able to manufacture about 48,000 pins per day, Smith reck-
oned. But if each of the laborers were to work alone, attempting
to perform all of the tasks associated with making pins rather
than working cooperatively, Smith doubted that on any given
day they would be able to produce even a single pin per man.

Adam Smith's pin factory is often used by modern-day economists (especially the writers of introductory college texts) as an
example of the division of labor, but this characterization ob-
scures the deeper principle of synergy. Another way of looking
at the pin factory is in terms of how the various specialized skills
and production operations were *combined* into an organized "system." The system included not only the roles played by each of
the ten workers (which had to be precisely coordinated) but
also the appropriate machinery, energy to run the machinery,

sources of raw materials, a supporting transportation system, and (not least) markets where the pins could be sold to recover production costs.

Not only that, but the pin factory required "management"— people who were responsible for hiring and training the workers, for planning, for production decisions, for marketing, for bookkeeping, and so forth. Thus the economic benefits (the synergies) realized by Adam Smith's pin factory were the result of the total system. In fact, the pin factory entailed several different kinds of cooperative relationships: There was cooperation among the workers, cooperation between the workers and the managers, cooperation between the workers and their machines, and cooperation between the factory as a whole and various parts of its social, economic, and political environment.

## MODERN COUNTERPARTS

Today's corporate behemoths—a GE, IBM, or Ford—dwarf Adam Smith's paradigmatic pin factory. Indeed, that microcosm of the industrial revolution could be housed in one small corner of a modern production line. Yet the same underlying principle applies.

Our telephone system, for instance, is much more than simply a division of labor. In fact, it is complex beyond our ability even to comprehend. Before its recent breakup, AT&T alone comprised a statistical cornucopia: $114 billion in assets, more than a million employees in 6,500 different job descriptions, 750 million shares of stock divided among 3 million shareholders, 24,000 buildings, ranging from tiny microwave towers on remote hilltops to Western Electric's vast manufacturing facilities, plus 18,000 local offices, 177,000 motor vehicles, 17 airplanes and a miscellany of helicopters, cable-laying ships, private railroads, horses and bicycles, not to mention 30 million telephone poles, 138 million phones, 120 million directories, and enough wire to reach the sun and back three times.

Each year, some 45,000 different suppliers provided the system with 200 million paper clips, 3 million ball-point pens, 500 million paper towels, 20,000 motor vehicles, 400,000 tons of paper, and 250,000 telephone poles, among many other items. All this and more just so that you could call almost any one of the other telephones in the country, if you chose to do so.

Of course, there are also many modern-day systems that are as small as or even smaller than Adam Smith's pin factory. A baseball team consists of only nine different "roles," and there are only two in families where the two "partners" divide up various responsibilities and chores.

There are also a great many mom-and-pop businesses. We know of a husband and wife team that manages a large number of rental properties. She handles the personal contacts with the property owners and renters and keeps the books, which she does extremely well, while he does all the maintenance and handyman work, his trade for twenty years. Neither of them could run the business alone; together they have a very successful operation.

## SYMBIOSIS

As we suggested above, the division of labor is not confined to cooperation among human actors. Symbiosis between humans and their tools represents another class of synergistic effects; in a very real sense, a skilled craftsman produces effects that depend on close cooperation with his or her tools. In fact, there is a little-known but rapidly growing science called "ergonomics" that specializes in improving and harmonizing human-machine cooperation, from office work stations to airplane cockpits.

Symbiosis between humans and animals represents yet another variation on the division of labor. Since the dawn of history, humans have utilized the remarkable physical, sensory, and (not least) social capabilities of dogs to help achieve a variety of objectives, including tracking and hunting game (or other humans), herding sheep and cattle, guarding the home, towing sleds, controlling crowds, providing eyes for the blind, and, lately, even sniffing for hidden caches of drugs. In fact, we have often systematically "improved" various breeds by artificial selection. At various times and places we have also formed symbiotic relationships with, among others, cats, horses, donkeys, elephants, oxen, llamas, and even numerous species of birds.

An interesting recent example involves the use of pigeons by the Coast Guard for air-sea rescue work. It takes good eyesight and good concentration to spot a life raft from a helicopter during a search operation that may last several hours. So pigeons have been trained (on an experimental basis) to provide an extra set of eyes. After being "conditioned" with suitable rewards to peck a key every time they spot a life raft or similar object in the water, the pigeons have been put aboard search and rescue helicopters at specially designed observation posts to augment the regular crews. Not only do the pigeons have better eyesight for such tasks than humans do, but as their trainer, Bob Gisiner, put it, "they don't get bored and they're cheap." Preliminary results show that the use of pigeons can, under some circumstances, double the chances of spotting a survivor in the water.

## AGRICULTURE

Though less appreciated by most of us, symbiosis also plays an important role in our agricultural system. For instance, the honeybees that were brought to America by our Pilgrim Fathers to produce honey for colonial dining tables today also oblige us by pollinating about one-third of our food crops, a service that benefits the bees, the plants, and humans alike.

Similarly, legume crops such as beans, peas, and soybeans depend for their productivity on symbiotic relationships between their root systems and various nitrogen-producing microorganisms that live in the soil such as the bacterium *Rhizobium*. Thus an indirect cooperative relationship between human food producers, their crops, and other living creatures produces mutually beneficial results that are vital to our very survival.

In the future we can also expect to see a vast increase in the number of symbiotic relationships between machines alone, with little or no human involvement. A model is the Fujitsu Fanuc factory at Kobe, Japan, that manufactures robots. A cooperative relationship between computers, robots, and production machinery makes it possible for the factory to run twenty-four hours a day with minimal human intervention (especially at night, when there are no human workers present).

## FORTUITOUS COMBINATIONS

However, it is also important to recognize that the synergies arising from the division of labor comprise only one slice of the pie. Much of the synergy that we encounter in our daily lives involves fortuitous combinations of factors, or of human actions, that do not in any sense entail a specialization of roles. It takes two to make a seesaw work, but both participants play the same role. The goose down inside my sleeping bag "cooperates" in producing an extremely light but highly efficient layer of insulation for those nights when we are backpacking in the high country. (All of the many kinds of insulation that humans employ involve synergistic effects.) Likewise, the maple leaves that produce the summer shade over our neighborhood park bench did not grow for the purpose of producing that effect, yet it is a cooperative effect, and one that gradually dissipates come the fall.

## COST AND USE SHARING

Far more important for our purpose, though, are the many forms of synergy that result from cost and/or use sharing. Though most of us never think of it in such terms, whenever we rent a car, ride a bus, go out to a restaurant, or take in a movie, we are tacitly cooperating with others. We share not only the use of the facility, or product, but also the associated costs. It is a matter of efficiency. If we have only a limited need for particular goods or services, we can "economize" by sharing them with others and paying only a proportionate part of the costs.

Come to think of it, most of the services and facilities that make our civilized life possible, if not enjoyable, involve such shared-use synergies: airlines, banks, barbershops, cable TV, cleaning services, consultants, copy shops, dentists, doctors, Disneyland, equipment leasing, highways, hospitals, hotels, lawyers, libraries, museums, parks, railroads, repair services, rock concerts, sidewalks, sporting events, the telephone system, live theater, time-share vacation condos, tuxedo rentals, vending machines—the list is almost endless. Indeed, some of the most innovative and promising new businesses these days involve new applications of the same synergy-producing strategy, from computer rentals to luggage rentals to the rental of feature films on video tapes.

Insurance is a particularly important example of synergy via tacit cooperation. As Winston Churchill once put it, insurance brings "the magic of averages to the rescue of millions." It is also one of the most ancient forms of risk and cost sharing, dating back to the funeral societies of ancient Greece. Since it is obviously not possible to predict exactly when a person will die, the people of Athens conceived the idea of banding together and making small annual contributions to cover the funeral expenses of whoever happened to die during the succeeding year, rather than requiring everyone to be "self-insured" for the full amount. Today, using the same basic strategy, we tacitly cooperate in insuring ourselves against almost every conceivable risk, from earthquakes to dental caries.

Mutual funds involve a slight variation on this theme. By pooling your money with that of other investors, you jointly subsidize the services of investment experts and, more important, spread your risk by having the appreciation in your "shares" pegged to the aggregate performance of the entire "portfolio." To modify an old metaphor, it amounts to being able to divide up one egg among many baskets.

## ECONOMIES OF SCALE

The synergies associated with cost and use sharing also underlie the "economies of scale" that form a bedrock of economic theory. Economies of scale can take various forms. Sometimes it may involve spreading "fixed costs" or "overhead costs" over a larger number of users, or customers. Sometimes it involves taking advantage of a division of labor, or technology, to reduce the "unit cost" of production. Sometimes it entails being able to purchase raw materials or component parts in larger quantities, and at lower cost. In any case, the benefits enjoyed by any one user or customer are dependent on similar actions by others. Thus if the demand for pins in eighteenth-century England amounted only to a few hundred a day, there would not have been any pin factories for Adam Smith to write about.

Likewise, when microcomputer sales were running at less than ten thousand a year just a few years ago, software packages usually cost $500 or more. With sales now at more than 8 million a year (according to InfoCorp, a market research company), some software programs are selling for a fraction of that amount, not because they cost any less to produce and sell but, to quote from an advertisement for a program called Wordvision: "The large number of personal computers that IBM is selling lets us spread our costs over lots more copies than earlier programs."

## THE "LAWS" OF ECONOMICS

Synergistic effects are also involved, as we have seen, in such "macro-economic" phenomena as stock prices, inflation, recessions, and that sacred cow of the economics profession, the "laws" of supply and demand. These are all phenomena in which individual decisions and actions combine to produce what may often be unintended and unforeseen collective effects, effects that may alter prices and/or the volume of business activity.

For instance, one of the laws of economics states that, in a "perfect" market (meaning one that is free of any real-world constraints), the equilibrium price for a given type of good or service will be determined by the intersection between the curves on a graph that describe the varying levels of "supply" and "demand" that different price levels can be expected to stimulate. That is, the combined effect of the interactions between all of the prospective sellers and all of the prospective buyers will determine (or, more realistically, influence) the resulting price levels, just as price levels can influence supply and demand. Adam Smith characterized the workings of the marketplace as an "invisible hand," and economists ever since have been prone to get dewy-eyed and mystical about what is, in fact, just another kind of synergistic effects.

## THE VARIETIES OF SYNERGY

Synergy, as we have also seen, comes in every conceivable size, shape, and form. Some synergistic effects are so commonplace as to be prosaic. The vast array of colors with which we enrich our lives are nothing more than mixtures in varying proportions of the three primary colors. Tunafish salad (or any other cold salad combination) is a cooperative effect that is very different in flavor and texture from either of its primary constituents. Then there are the countless household implements that use synergy, from tweezers to kitchen tongs, nail files, handsaws, whisks, strainers, brushes, graters, even eating utensils.

Likewise, the properties of a window screen—the ability to allow light and air to enter a room while keeping bugs out— arise from the crisscrossing of hundreds or thousands of thin strands of wire. (Similar applications of the synergy principle can be found in nets, sieves, strainers, and various kinds of filters.) And the remarkable closure strength achieved by a Velcro fastener is the combined result of the interactions among the many tiny plastic hooks and loops on its two facing parts. (The curved closure strength of one of the standard varieties is about 22 pounds per square inch, according to the manufacturer.)

Indeed, a simple "thought experiment" can be used to demonstrate the importance of synergy in our homes. Imagine the consequences when a scissors has only one blade, when the fork is missing from a carving set, when a strainer or window screen has a large hole in it, or when a styrofoam cup has even a small hole.


## MULTIPLE SYNERGIES

While many of the synergies we encounter in our everyday lives are plain to see, others are surprisingly complex.

Take your local restaurant, for example. In reality, this familiar institution embodies multiple, interacting forms of synergy; it is a synergism of synergies. For starters, it utilizes the classic division of labor among the chefs, dishwashers, waiters, busboys, bartenders, cashiers, cleaners, maitre d', bookkeepers, and managers.

In addition, its supporting infrastructure involves a vast division of labor that includes architects, interior designers, construction firms, the manufacturers of stoves, refrigerators, kitchen and dining room equipment and supplies, plus farmers, ranchers, fishermen, distillers, vintners, canners, bottlers, transportation and distribution systems, commercial laundries, the advertising media, public utilities such as the mail service, the power company, the telephone company, and, not least, water, sewage, and garbage disposal services.

Restaurants also enjoy economies of scale in their ability to purchase and prepare food in large quantities. Then there is the tacit cooperation that occurs among the patrons, who may be required to make reservations, wait in line to be seated, conduct themselves "properly," and then contribute a proportionate share of the overall cost of supporting the restaurant.

There is also nutritional synergy in the food combinations that, in a *table d'hote* meal, provide complementary sets of nutrients. Furthermore, when a restaurant is located in a shopping center or is part of a well-known restaurant chain, there may be synergies in being linked to these external organizations.

Restaurants also depend on the synergistic properties of our written and verbal language. Though we take it for granted, language plays an indispensable role in the many social transactions that occur in a restaurant—among the employees, between the employees and the patrons, and between the restaurant and its external environment.

## INTENDED VS. UNINTENDED SYNERGY

While some forms of synergy are intended and the result of deliberate design, others are unintended. The four-color patterns of tiny dots that produce the synergistic effects in a magazine or a book that we call "pictures" are the result of a highly specialized technology. But the frustrations associated with rush-hour traffic tie-ups are the fortuitous (and undesired) cooperative result of many individual decisions and actions.

Whether intended or not, some forms of synergy are highly predictable while others are not. The recipe for a chocolate cake if followed closely will produce the expected synergistic effect (except at high altitudes). In contrast, the slot machines at Las Vegas are deliberately designed so that the sequence of winning combinations cannot be predicted by the players, though the relative frequency with which the tumblers will produce three cherries or three bells is well known to the manufacturers and casino operators. Many card games, likewise, are based on the consequences of unpredictable combinations. Poker is an obvious example.

## "NATURAL" VS. MAN-MADE SYNERGY

A contrast can also be drawn between forms of synergy that are embodied in the natural environment and those that are the product of human invention. A river, for instance, is in reality a cooperative effect that is produced by the confluence and loose adhesion inside a naturally formed channel of many billions of water droplets that have been aggregated, usually, from a large water "catchment" area. Though humans had no hand in creating rivers, it is hard to imagine how human civilizations could have arisen without this important form of synergy. For we are dependent on rivers in various ways: for drinking water, irrigation water, energy, commerce, seafood, sewage disposal, and even (historically) for defense.

Similarly, the snowpack that our skiers revel in during the winter months is a synergistic effect. Each cubic foot of snow contains about 18 million frozen water droplets that have condensed into crystals, no two of which are exactly alike. Moreover, each crystal contains many trillions (yes, trillions) of water molecules. And if the air temperatures should vary by only a few degrees, the result may instead be an icy rain, a layer of slush, and/or a hard crust.

On the other hand, human engineering is responsible for "Maltron," a new way of arranging the keys on a typewriter keyboard that is superior to the conventional "QWERTY" layout (so called because of the sequence of letters at the beginning of the top row). Another product of the science of ergonomics, the Maltron keyboard (a name derived from one of its two British inventors) significantly improves human performance levels because there is high synergy; the new layout meshes better with the properties of our written language and with our manual abilities.

Not surprisingly, many forms of synergy involve both natural and man-made elements. The skier depends both on a good snowpack and a properly designed set of skis (not to mention learned skills). And human exploitation of rivers have been increasingly augmented by technology, from dugout canoes to oceangoing vessels, and from waterwheels to massive dams with huge hydroelectric power plants.

Our economists tend to emphasize the role of technology in the "economies" that are achieved by a complex society, but in reality nature also frequently plays a part, so that in a sense it is also possible to speak of cooperation between humans and their environments.

## AN ILLUSTRATION

A classic illustration can be found, again, in Adam Smith's *The Wealth of Nations*. Smith did a comparison between the transport of goods overland from London to Edinburgh in "broad-wheeled wagons" and by sailing ships from London to Leith, the seaport that serves Edinburgh. In six weeks, two men and eight horses could haul about four tons of goods to Edinburgh and back, Smith found. However, in the same amount of time, a ship with a crew of six or eight men could carry 200 tons to Leith, a load that, if transported overland, would require 50 wagons, 100 men, and 400 horses.

Now, the synergy produced by these merchant ships, which gave the English a powerful economic advantage, was only partly a result of the division of labor, the technological hardware, and such other necessities as capital, markets, and a navy (to protect the merchantmen). It also happened to include an ecological factor—the opportunity for waterborne commerce between two large human settlements located, not coincidentally, near navigable waterways with suitable channels, tidal currents, and prevailing winds. Without these additional (often unacknowledged) contributions from nature, economies such as Smith observed could not have been realized.

Adam Smith's example illustrates yet another aspect of the synergy principle. While some forms of synergy involve radically new effects that could not have been produced in any other way, others may involve only an improvement on an existing means.

Thus the steel axes that have replaced those made of stone in every corner of the world are not fundamentally different but are roughly five times as efficient at felling trees (by actual experiment), while chain saws may provide a 20: or 30:1 advantage. Likewise, the increasingly powerful desktop microcomputers of today and tomorrow, costing only a few thousand dollars, are beginning to replace (and even outperform) the big, multimillion-dollar mainframe computers that filled entire computer centers only a few years ago.

## COMPLEMENTARITIES

It is also important to distinguish between those forms of synergy that arise from a union of parts (or people) with similar characteristics and those that depend on "complementarities"— the "yins" and "yangs" which, in the traditional Chinese cosmology, work together to make a complete system. Thus on the one hand there are the synergistic effects produced by the row of identical teeth on a comb or the bristles on a hairbrush (or by the opposed rows of teeth in our mouths and the hair on our heads, for that matter). By the same token, in the economic marketplace there are the many individual purchases that combine to produce the synergistic effects we call a "best seller" or a "blockbuster" movie.

On the other hand, microcomputers and their software programs serve complementary functions and are dependent on each other to make the system as a whole work. Similarly, a great many business partnerships and "joint ventures" depend on the melding of complementary skills or resources. In the joint venture between GM and Toyota, GM had an unused $130 million plant and the need for an economical small car in its line, while Toyota had the car and the need for a manufacturing plant in this country. Likewise, in the husband and wife management company mentioned above, he had the maintenance skills and she had the administrative skills. And in a successful small marketing consortium that we're familiar with, one partner is an expert in market surveys, a second is a superb planner and strategist, and the third is skilled at pubic relations and advertising.

Together, they can offer their clients an integrated, "soup-to-nuts" package of marketing services.

## ADDITIVE VS. MULTIPLICATIVE EFFECTS

While some forms of synergy involve "additive" effects, others may be "multiplicative" in nature. Add one more player to either side in a tug-of-war and the war may soon be over. Add one more passerby to those who are helping to push a stalled car out of a snowbank and the combined effect may quickly shift from failure to success. Or, add one more passenger to an airline flight and it may mean the difference between operating at a loss and turning a profit.

In contrast, the miracle of compound interest is achieved by multiplying the combined total of the principal and previously accumulated interest at the end of each successive payout period, and the shorter the time between each compounding the more rapidly might a poor but prudent saver become rich.

Such multiplier effects can also have negative consequences. The reason why the Reverend Thomas Malthus and some of his successors among the current generation of demographers are prone to be alarmist about population growth is that it tends to be "exponential." As Malthus put it in his famous monograph, *An Essay on the Principle of Population* (1798): "Population, when unchecked . . . increases in a geometrical ratio . . . [while] the means of subsistence, under circumstances the most favourable to human industry, could not possibly increase faster than in an arithmetic ratio." Accordingly, Malthus envisioned relentless population pressures that could only be checked by "the ruthless agencies of hunger and poverty, vice and crime, pestilence and famine, revolution and war."

An elegant example of the power of a multiplier effect is the riddle used with French schoolchildren. Suppose you have a pond on which a water lily is growing, and the plant doubles in size each day. If allowed to grow unchecked, the lily pond will be completely covered in thirty days, choking off all other forms of life in the water. If you decide to cut the lily back when it covers one-half of the pond, on what day will that be? The answer, of course, is the twenty-ninth day. You will have only one day left to save the pond.

## THRESHOLD EFFECTS

Malthus's dour vision also illustrates another important aspect of the synergy principle. Whether additive or multiplicative, many forms of synergy involve what are called "threshold effects." We have already encountered them. Add more passengers to the bus and, up to a point, the consequences may be beneficial. Increased ridership means that fares (or public subsidies) can be kept low. Beyond that point, though, the bus may become uncomfortably crowded and its schedule may be disrupted by the problems associated with loading and unloading passengers. True, the bus line may make more money, but its rolling stock may wear out more quickly. Also, if more buses were to be added to the route to accommodate the increase in passengers, the overall number of riders per bus could actually drop. In other words, there may be a rapid shift from positive to negative synergy.

Similar threshold effects are associated with some of the dysergies we noted in chapter 4: rush-hour highway traffic tie-ups, the overloading of telephone circuits on holidays, food that has been too heavily spiced, indigestion from eating too much Thanksgiving turkey, and a host of other everyday experiences. (Besides being involved in threshold effects, the synergy principle often travels incognito under the headings of "critical mass," "linkage effects," and "optimum number.")

Another example of a threshold effect in the economic sphere is protective tariffs. When a tariff is deliberately added to the price of an import for the purpose of making it slightly more expensive than the homegrown product, the result may be to shut out the import.

The inexorable growth of human populations can also produce threshold effects—overcutting of forests, overexploitation of fish and game species, pollution of rivers, and so forth. This was illustrated by biologist Garrett Hardin a few years ago in his classic (and much-reprinted) *Science* article, "The Tragedy of the Commons."

In the Middle Ages in England, many villages provided a "common" pasture where the local farmers could graze their excess cattle, much like public parks today provide a common recreational area for humans. The problem was that no limits were set on how much the commons could be used and there were no charges levied. Therefore, everyone had an incentive to use the commons as much as possible. Though no single farmer was responsible for the inevitable result, the combined effect was the frequent overgrazing and deterioration of the ground cover when the "carrying capacity" of the land had been exceeded. To quote Hardin: "Freedom in a commons brings ruin to all."

The solution, of course, was to "enclose" the commons by collective political action designed to regulate its use, a synergistic solution that we are now applying for similar reasons to such overcrowded national parks as Yosemite, Glacier, and the Grand Tetons.

## SOCIAL/PSYCHOLOGICAL SYNERGY

In addition to the many cooperative effects that we can observe in the material world, there are also many social and psychological synergies. Some of them are enshrined in such familiar expressions as "team spirit," "mob rule," and "the business climate." Others are reflected in homilies like "there's strength (or safety) in numbers," "two heads are better than one," "success breeds success," and "many hands make light work."

Then there is the saying "you scratch my back and I'll scratch yours." To most people the saying connotes reciprocity, but a deeper analysis reveals that it involves synergy. When you stop to think about it, somebody else can probably scratch, or rub, your back better than you can yourself. Thus two mutual backscratchers are likely to be better off than two soloists. Maybe this hidden synergy explains why the expression is so popular.

By the same token, additive dysergy is reflected in sayings like "too many cooks spoil the broth," "misery loves company," "two's company, three's a crowd," and, of course, "the straw that broke the camel's back." (A variation on this old saw can be found in the children's story by Pamela Allen, *Who Sank the Boat?* It was not the mouse that caused the rowboat to sink, needless to say, it was all the animals together.) On the other hand, a breakdown of synergy is implied in aphorisms like "divide and conquer" and "the squeaky wheel gets the grease."

Psychologists have documented some of our synergetic traits. For one thing, our sensory equipment was designed with synergy in mind (so to speak), and there is a branch of psychology called "Gestalt theory" which specializes in the natural ability of the human mind to perceive "wholes." Contrary to the old saying, we generally see the forest first and only later pick out individual trees. When we listen to an orchestra we are naturally inclined to hear the "blend" and must make a special effort to hear a particular instrument (unless the composer or conductor intended us to hear it). When we are house hunting, we tend to respond first to the overall "gestalt"; a house which "shows well," as any experienced realtor will tell you, is one where the various elements (architecture, interior design, paint colors, carpeting, furnishings, garden, etc.) create a pleasing combined effect. We also possess the remarkable ability to "read" the time on an old-fashioned clock with a mere glance at the combined position of the two hands.

Gestalt theorists point out that the human mind even has the ability to perceive the whole when some of the parts may be missing or garbled—an ability that cartoonists and poor spellers (among others) depend on. For instance, anyone who can read this book should be able to recognize the term "m__ddle-class" and knows that the missing letter is different from the one in "m__ddle-headed," even though the remaining five letters are the same in each case. But this is trivial compared to what a skilled crossword puzzle player can do.

Consider this incident: on the way to the office in our car, we spotted on the highway up ahead a large sign with a flashing yellow arrow directing us to change lanes, and we responded accordingly. But, as we pulled abreast of the sign, we realized that the arrow was really composed of twelve separate lights and, moreover, that two of the lights were out. Nevertheless, we got the message. (One of the major shortcomings of present-day computers is that they do not have our ability to fill in the gaps; they are extremely literal and perfectionist. However, computer scientists are currently working to endow the next generation of computers with humanlike interpretive skills.)

## SOCIAL SYNERGY

There are also many synergistic effects that arise from our social interactions. For instance, a study by psychologist David Gumpert, reported in the *Harvard Business Review*, has shown that "teams" are more likely than individuals to be successful as entrepreneurs. And a consulting firm called Human Synergetics routinely demonstrates in its training sessions with client groups that the decisions made by groups in various contrived "survival situations" are generally better (more likely to succeed) than the decisions that each individual might make alone.

Similarly, psychologist J. A. F. Stoner, in a series of experiments reviewed in *Advances in Experimental Psychology*, found that individuals are more likely to take risks and make risky decisions when they are members of a group, a finding that is confirmed by various studies of street gangs. Stoner calls this phenomenon the "risky shift."

More subtle is the influence of what psychologist Robert Zajonc called "social facilitation." It has been observed in humans and many other animals that the mere presence of another member of the species can positively affect the behavior of the individual: Food consumption, speed of learning, and work output, among other things, may be measurably increased. And generations of actors have averred that there is a special "chemistry" associated with performing before a live audience.

There is also the research on "mob psychology," going back to Gustav Le Bon's classic work *The Crowd* (1896). What Le Bon called the "collective mind" is in part the mutually facilitative effect of participating in a large-scale social event, whether it be a rock concert, a political rally, or a brawl. People in crowds often behave in ways they never would if they were not "caught up" in what others are doing, a susceptibility that has been exploited by generations of demagogues, political agitators, and *agents provocateurs*.

Perhaps the most disquieting form of social synergy, though, is what Stanley Milgram calls the "aggressive triad." In a famous series of experiments, reported in *Human Relations*, Milgram showed that a division (and sharing) of responsibility for aggressive behaviors serves as a facilitator. When one person can make the decision and give the orders without having to carry them out, while a second person merely carries out the orders but bears no responsibility for making the decision, the synergistic result is heightened aggression.

## FEELING SYNERGISTIC

Finally, there is good evidence in the research literature of social psychology that we not only work better (most of us) when we are part of a "team" but we also *feel* better; we derive intrinsic satisfaction from working with others in pursuit of what the experts somewhat pretentiously refer to as "superordinate goals." So powerful are these psychological synergies, in fact, that we may even make sacrifices to obtain them, as the leaders of various cults well know.

The point was driven home to us personally a few years ago, when one of the authors participated in the development of a new public policy course at Stanford University. In a departure from the usual practice, a major element of the course was a requirement that the students work together in small teams on a "casebook" policy problem and present their findings and recommendations jointly to the rest of the class. Not only did the course generate great excitement but a clear majority of the students rated the course as being among the most rewarding they had ever taken. The reason given in their course evaluations was the unique opportunity (in academia, at least) of being able to work with others.

We are, indeed, "social animals." Together we produce synergy, and in a myriad of ways we also benefit from the results. To humanists, such rewards have long been viewed as ends in themselves. In fact, good human relations is also good business. Only recently has the business community begun to appreciate that our potent social/psychological motivations, if properly harnessed, can have a powerful, positive effect on the bottom line.

# 6. The Art of Synergistic Thinking II: Values and Ideology

As we have seen, synergy is not a one-dimensional or easily grasped phenomenon. It doesn't lend itself to simple formulas or easy answers, and it can't be distilled into some neat acronym. It doesn't promise to give you shortcuts. Nor does it make Olympian predictions about the future. Indeed, the synergy principle teaches that the future is destined to hold surprises. We don't pretend to be gurus, seers, or visionaries. On the contrary:

- We've seen too many five-year plans that were outdated before the ink was dry.
- We've seen too many megatrends that dissolved as soon as the latest best seller dropped off the charts.
- We've seen too many *wunderkinder* and cutting-edge ventures that have gone belly up because of blind spots or Achilles' heels.
- We've also seen the insidious workings of complacency, the deadly enemy of those who have already achieved success.
- Worse yet, we've even seen some high-synergy systems fail because of unexpected or uncontrollable external forces.

What the synergy principle involves, in fact, is something more fundamental than a formula, or a dubious prediction. It involves, most importantly, a new way of understanding how the world works—a new *weltanschauung*—that may require changes in our values, our ideology, our understanding of cause and effect, our approach to analyzing problems, our strategies for dealing with these problems, and our view of the future. Let's get down to specifics.

The "American Creed," a tradition that can be traced back to our frontier days, stresses freedom, rugged individualism, and private enterprise in an atmosphere of "free competition"; in our self-image, we are the quintessential capitalist society. We see ourselves as being endowed with "inalienable rights," and we display relatively little concern as a nation about "duties" or reciprocal obligations. In an earlier era, we also esteemed industry, hard work, and efficiency, but in the hedonistic climate of the post–World War II era these aspects of our value system have eroded. Compared with some other industrialized nations, our work habits today are second-rate.

## THE REALITY

The reality, though, is that we live in a vast sea of synergies, both positive and negative. Every day we are the beneficiaries of the efforts, ideas, enterprise, skills, hard work, and even the altruism of others. More important, we are deeply dependent on others—the farmers, teachers, grocery clerks, policemen, mechanics, truckers, barbers, plumbers, and so forth—who are all instrumental to meeting our personal needs.

At the same time, we are also assaulted daily by low synergy, or negative synergy—inefficiencies, errors, antisocial actions, the "laid-back" work ethic, and even deliberate attempts to deceive or defraud. (For example, it costs the taxpayers of the Los Angeles area $9 million a year just to pick up the litter that fellow citizens throw on the highways. Likewise, we all pay higher interest rates to cover the 5 to 6 percent of all loans that end up in default.)

Overall, our frontier values have served us well. But so have some other values—values that are more conducive to high synergy. These synergetic values have often been undervalued and underutilized, but the time has come to put them in the forefront. They include:

- *Excellence*—a striving to achieve the highest quality in every area, every detail, and every part;
- *Perfectionism*—an essential ingredient of sustained success, not just a neurotic compulsion;
- *Discipline*—a quality that is essential to personal, corporate, and national excellence;

- *Duty*—a necessary counterbalance to our preoccupation with "rights";
- *Teamwork*—cultivation of a national ethic that emphasizes working together on our common problems, large and small;
- *Cooperation*—the antidote for an overdose of free market rhetoric, which has given competition too much of the credit for our success;
- *Equity*—a concept that implies a "fair share" for anyone who contributes to the collective effort.

## COMPETITION AND COOPERATION

Let's look a little more closely at the relationship between competition and cooperation.

Shortly after denouncing the Soviet Union as an "evil empire" and "the focus of evil in the world," President Reagan approved a new five-year grain export agreement with the Russians and enunciated a new policy toward this supposedly perfidious regime of "credible deterrence, peaceful competition, and constructive cooperation." In a later speech he added: "We would welcome negotiations. . . . We who are leaders in government have an obligation to strive for cooperation. . . ."

Hypocrisy, you say? Election-year rhetoric? Of course. And yet, behind these contradictions lies an equally contradictory reality. For we live in a world that is a mixture of intense competition and extensive, often unappreciated cooperation. Competition and cooperation are not at the opposite poles of an "either-or" world but are parts of an inextricable duality—like the north and south poles of a single magnetic field. Sometimes we may be located closer to one pole than the other, but we are still embedded in a field.

Though we are stuck with this duality—it is inherent in human existence—many of us seem to be uncomfortable about it. Idealists, on the one hand, aspire to enhance cooperation and reduce, if not eliminate, the competitive forces in our society. These well-meaning people tend to blame our culture, our economic system, or perhaps some fatal flaw in human nature for the supposed "evils" of competition.

Self-styled "realists," on the other hand, tend to view competition as if it were a law of nature, if not a positive good, and see cooperation as a necessary evil, or worse. To some of these tough-minded thinkers, cooperation may even be a bit suspect— a ploy, perhaps, that the disadvantaged use as a means for extracting concessions from the more favored among us. In this view, cooperation can obstruct the workings of nature; it can weaken the otherwise beneficent effects of "free" competition.

"Free competition without government interference has been the key to our economic success," asserted candidate Ronald Reagan. Federal Trade Commissioner Michael Pertschuk was quoted by the *San Francisco Chronicle* as claiming that "competition is the strongest weapon we have in the war against inflation." And private citizen Robert Herrmann, in a letter to the editors of *Time* regarding its cover story on capitalism today, argued: "There is no other conclusion. Capitalism appeals to those with a winner's instinct and socialism to the losers."

## THE REALITY

The reality is that both competition and cooperation play an important role in our society, and either one may be beneficial or destructive depending on the situation. Indeed, the interplay between competition and cooperation is such that one may condition the expression of the other. Thus the violent, high-stakes competition among professional football teams is constrained by both compulsory and voluntary forms of cooperation, including most visibly the "rules" that are enforced each week by the referees and the annual player-selection process called the "draft."

Conversely, many of our churches, despite their dedication to such uplifting human values as love and charity, must nowadays compete for parishioners in an effort to combat declining attendance and fickle loyalties. The competition is usually very discreet, of course. Many of the traditional forms of cooperation among local churches—"ecumenical" relief projects, combined services during the summer vacation months, and so forth—continue to be observed. Moreover, 32 different Protestant and Orthodox churches routinely collaborate in supporting the National Council of Churches. Nevertheless, hard economic realities have heightened competitive pressures.

Our nonprofit hospitals, many of them run by religious orders, face a similar dilemma. Competition among them for "market shares" has greatly intensified in recent years and promises to get worse. The "marketing" of hospitals has become a growth industry, and there are fears that many of these institutions will go under before the end of this decade.

Yet, paradoxically, competing hospitals may also collaborate in a variety of ways, including the joint purchasing of supplies, shared ownership and use of expensive capital equipment like CAT scanners, or even cosponsorship of an outpatient center. Two or more hospitals might also agree to divvy up certain specialized services (say obstetrics or sports medicine) in order to avoid duplication and unnecessary competition. And all of the hospitals in a given area may jointly support the activities of an overhead association that provides mutually beneficial services ranging from data collection and dissemination to lobbying and educational programs.

It is the same, of course, with business firms and nation-states. Several competing oil companies may nevertheless "joint venture" a high-risk oil exploration project and share both the risks and potential rewards. Two or more Hollywood studios, once fiercely independent, may collaborate in producing a film in order to minimize the increasing risks and costs associated with moviemaking. And, despite President Reagan's rhetoric, the U.S. and the USSR cooperate in a myriad of unobtrusive ways.

Both nations respect the international rules of the road on the high seas and the rights associated with each other's territorial waters. Furthermore, under the terms of a 1972 accord, the Russian and American navies have pledged not to interfere with each other's operations or to act in ways that could be construed as threatening. And when an American merchant ship foundered at sea recently, a nearby Russian ship kept faith with an ancient tradition among mariners and sped to the rescue.

Both nations adhere to the mail-handling procedures that have been established by the International Postal Union, as well as to the procedures for using international airways (including, among other things, the use of the English language in all communications).

In their diplomatic dealings, both nations honor long-established norms and privileges, from the sanctity of diplomatic missions (except for eavesdropping devices) to the rights associated with diplomatic immunity. They even cooperate in maintaining a telephone "hotline" that is designed to minimize the risk of an accidental nuclear confrontation.

## EXPLAINING THE PARADOX

One way to make sense of this pervasive paradox is to appreciate the synergies that social cooperation can produce. Cooperation, as we have seen, may result in otherwise unattainable effects, and many of these may be advantageous to all the participants. Communications and transportation systems are prime examples.

In other words, cooperation need not be based on altruism. Most cooperation, in fact, is based on enlightened self-interest. Individuals, or organizations, or nations, are most likely to cooperate when it is in their self-interest to do so, and egoistic forms of cooperation far outweigh those that involve self-sacrifice. We may dignify it by calling it "enlightened," but it is still self-interest.

Often, as we noted, people may engage in both competition and cooperation at the same time, depending on whether there are potential rewards for doing so. A way of illustrating this interplay is with one of the Venn diagrams that mathematicians use. (See figure 1.) Each circle represents an entire "bundle" of interests for two actors, A and B, and the area of shaded overlap between them represents that portion of A and B's interests which can be served by cooperating. The rest of each actor's bundle consists of nonoverlapping and possibly competing interests.

Sometimes the area of overlap is very small. At other times it may be very large. But seldom is there no overlap at all, or a complete overlap. Furthermore, the area of overlap may vary as conditions change. During World War II, America and Russia were allies against a common enemy, and we donated vast quantities of arms, ammunition, food, and medicines to that beleaguered country. Now things are very different, of course. More recently, America and Communist China were bitter enemies

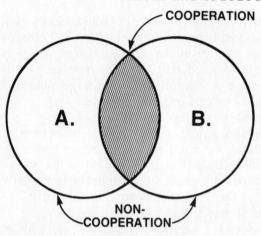

*Figure 1*

and fought one another in Korea, but this relationship too has changed dramatically.

This is not to say that people always cooperate, or compete, when it is in their interest to do so. For one reason or another we may settle for less than what would best suit our interests. Sometimes we may unwittingly cooperate with an unrecognized competitor, and sometimes we are so driven by competitive pressures that we miss opportunities to cooperate. Fear and distrust often stand in the way of constructive cooperation (look at Israel and the Arabs), just as a lack of confidence may discourage us from competing when an opportunity presents itself. However, many of us do learn to strike a balance, to walk a tightrope that enables us to cooperate or compete as the occasion warrants.

## RECIPROCAL INFLUENCES

Not only do competition and cooperation often go hand in hand but they frequently influence one another. It has been an axiom of political life ever since Machiavelli's day that the presence of an external enemy can enhance internal cooperation. In colonial America, the thirteen fractious colonies maintained an uneasy peace and might have ended up at war with one another had it not been for a common enemy, the British. (Later on, of course, the North and South did fight a bloody civil war.) Remember Benjamin Franklin's admonition in 1776: "We must all hang together, or assuredly we will all hang separately." Indeed, it is generally agreed that the formation of "a more perfect union" under the Constitution was in large measure due to the continuing threat of European intervention.

When an alliance is formed between two or more countries, a nonparticipating neighbor is likely to perceive it as threatening. The result may be heightened competition and, quite possibly, a counter-alliance. NATO and the Warsaw Pact are thus part of a long historical procession that stretches from the Peloponnesian Wars to the Iroquois "nation" to the Atlantic Alliance of World War II days.

Or consider what happened when the "Iron Chancellor," Otto von Bismarck, succeeded in unifying the previously quarrelsome German states. Eventually, Bismarck's success precipitated a close alliance between two other European nations that had been making war on each other for centuries—England and France.

By the same token, when the European Common Market was established after World War II, several previously warring nations (including France and Germany) joined forces in an explicit effort to offset the size advantages enjoyed by the two "superpowers." Today, the European nations are cooperating in a variety of economic ventures, from the Airbus commercial airliners to space rocketry and the cross-Channel tunnel. And, despite the recent troubles among the Common Market members, the dream of a United States of Europe still lives.

## THE BUSINESS WORLD

The interplay between competition and cooperation is also apparent in the business world. Recall how the otherwise fiercely competitive computer makers have joined forces to counteract competition from the Japanese. Or recall how GM and Toyota teamed up to produce small cars in the U.S.

Consider also the recently announced plan of five of the largest California banks to introduce a system that will enable their customers to use their automatic teller cards with merchants in lieu of cash or a credit card. As one spokesman explained, previous efforts to set up such a system have failed because "you need a critical mass of card-holders and merchants with a high volume of activity to make the system work."

Or ponder the advertising slogan mounted outside of a nearby shopping arcade: "Inside—sixteen restaurants competing for your appetite." Not only have these sixteen eateries co-located within the same building but they share the cost of joint promotional activities.

In the same way, there are innumerable examples of small companies that have combined to offset the size advantage of their competitors. That's how General Motors got its start against the then-dominant Ford Motor Company, and that's how many big firms with amalgamated names, such as Dean Witter Reynolds or the Chase Manhattan Bank, got to be so big.

Another form of competition via cooperation are the ubiquitous "coalitions"—loose associations of organizations sharing a limited common goal. Coalitions of otherwise competitive business firms may join forces to fight union-backed legislation; coalitions of unions may unite to boycott the products of nonunion producers; coalitions of environmentalists and local businessmen may concert their efforts to stop the latest offshore oil-drilling scheme; and so on.

Sometimes, though, various competitors may decide to cooperate simply to minimize destructive competition among themselves. A case in point is the Antarctic Treaty of 1959, which constrains the activities of the fifteen signatories, including Russia and the U.S.

In the world of business, both gentlemen's agreements and government actions have been used at various times to create an "orderly" market, to allocate market shares, or to fix prices and confine competition to such nonfinancial areas as the quality of service. The agreement in the 1920s that led to government allocation of radio frequencies, and later TV channels, is a notable example. So are the federal regulations that, until recently, strictly limited competition in the trucking, airlines, and banking industries. And so was the major oil companies' systematic practice over many years of sharing price and marketing data among themselves.

Similarly, in the world of charity, some two thousand of this country's charitable organizations now do their fund raising under the umbrella of United Way. It has been found that it is much more effective to make one concerted appeal on behalf of many charities than to bombard the public with innumerable individual appeals. Accordingly, many of these often competitive agencies have concluded that they are better off splitting a large purse than trying to go it alone.

## COMPETITION AND SYNERGY

Though we have stressed the ways in which social cooperation can produce synergistic effects, it is important to appreciate that competition may also produce positive synergy.

In sports, for instance, it is no less important for being a truism that competition can stimulate all the participants to do better, thus improving everyone's performance. Competition can also be depended upon to draw a crowd, which is what pays for the sometimes stratospheric salaries of professional athletes, not to mention the organizations that support them. Few people will bother to go see a boxer who is working out with a sparring partner or a football team that is scrimmaging, even when admission is free. Yet millions of "fans" may be willing to pay for the opportunity to see a real contest between well-matched contenders, and both the winners and losers may benefit by getting a share of the "gate."

Competition can also play a positive, if not indispensable, role in politics. Recognizing the dangers inherent in absolute power, our Founding Fathers in their wisdom designed a "checks and balances" system that divides and limits power and requires open competition for various offices. Despite such close calls as Watergate, the rivalry between our two major parties does help to police the system, keep politicians responsive to the electorate, and, most important, provide the citizenry with a choice. As the political philosopher Edmund Burke observed after witnessing the carnage of the French Revolution: "A state without the means of some change is without the means of its conservation."

As free market advocates keep reminding us, competition can also play a mutually beneficial (synergistic) role in the business world. Competition may put pressure on all of the "players" to reduce production costs and prices, to introduce improvements more rapidly, to enhance the quality of the product or service, to promote it more aggressively, and to be more responsive to customer needs. The positive effects may include better products at lower prices and more rapid growth of the industry as a whole. Consumers will be more willing, and able, to buy the product. Banks and venture capitalists may be more willing to loan money to start up companies that are in that line of business and talented professional people may be more interested in working in that field. The result may be a larger pie for all to share.

Of course, if there are too many competitors in any field, or if the rules of the game are not carefully defined and enforced, competition can also produce negative synergy. If a market becomes too crowded with suppliers, or if it becomes "saturated," an industry can begin to look like an overloaded life raft; as the craft slowly begins to sink, there may be cutthroat competition for a handhold. Thus ruthless cost cutting may lead to a general decline in quality. Look at some of the airlines.

Likewise, the presence of numerous "splinter" parties in a political system may so divide the electorate that nobody can put together a majority coalition capable of running the country. Italy and France have been plagued by this kind of competitive dysergy over the years, and there have been occasions in this country when third-party movements have temporarily fractured the electorate and produced a political stalemate.

In a nutshell, then, competition or cooperation (or some combination of the two) may produce either synergy or dysergy, depending on the particular situation. This is illustrated in figure 2. In case 1, competition among two or more actors produces beneficial effects (better performance, lower costs, higher quality, etc.). In case 2, competition produces mutually destructive effects (for example, the competition among European powers that culminated in World War I or the nuclear weapons stockpiles that are the fruit of the current arms race). In case 3, cooperation produces positive effects, while in case 4 the effects are negative (as in the many examples cited earlier where a growth process exceeds some optimum level).

There is no simple formula that can be applied to predict in every case when competition or cooperation will produce syn-

| RELATIONSHIP | SYNERGY | DYSERGY |
|---|---|---|
| COMPETITION | 1 | 2 |
| COOPERATION | 3 | 4 |

*Figure 2*

ergy or dysergy. But in general, both as individuals and as institutions, we seem to function best when there is a mixture of the two—some balance between necessary (or even desirable) competition and mutually rewarding cooperation. Competition may create challenges, spur innovation, produce a striving for excellence, reward skill and efficiency, and provide a testing ground for alternatives—whether it be laundry detergents or presidential candidates.

Cooperation, by contrast, encourages order, efficiency, stability, constraint, and living by the rules. It is the vehicle for coordinating efforts to the extent that it is mutually beneficial (and/or more economical) to do so. Professional football without rules and referees (and penalties) would most likely result in unrestrained and frequently lethal violence, an outcome that none of the players (and few of the fans) want.

Of course cooperation is by no means always voluntary. Though some people insist on equating cooperation with voluntary compliance, in reality a large proportion of the cooperation that occurs in human societies is enforced. At one extreme are the slave systems that benefit mainly the slaveholders. At the other extreme are the taxes that pay for such "public goods" as fire and police protection, national defense, and the like.

And, in the business world, gentlemen's agreements without antitrust laws and the like can lead to exploitative price fixing, manipulation of stock prices, monopolies, and an assortment of other business practices that are ultimately destructive to consumers. Ironically, in order to make our capitalist system work "efficiently" it has been necessary to set many limits on the ways in which our businessmen are allowed to cooperate, in addition to the many limits on competitive practices.

A good rule of thumb for understanding the interplay between competition and cooperation is that the relative value of each in a given situation depends on whether or not you are dealing with parts or wholes. Among the parts of any larger system, cooperation must take precedence. Though there may be some competition among the parts (say for promotions within a business organization), it tends to be constrained by the needs of the whole. Internally, the dominant theme is usually cooperation.

On the other hand, *between* wholes competition tends to be the dominant theme. Not always of course, but more often than not. We've already noted that there has been a historic trend toward larger, more encompassing systems. In the longer run, emergence of an embracing common interest among competitors has been one of the most important means by which cooperation has superseded (or at least reduced) competition.

## CHANGES IN IDEOLOGY

In theory, capitalism has been an "engine for the creation of affluence," to use the metaphor of the neoconservative writer Irving Kristol in *Two Cheers For Capitalism*. But, as we have shown, only part of the credit belongs to capitalism per se.

Capitalism has a number of proven virtues. It produces an economic environment in which creativity, personal ambition, and hard work are encouraged; it is achievement oriented. It also prizes efficiency and is more likely to punish the inefficient and incompetent. It provides an atmosphere conducive to innovation and technological progress. Indeed, it is especially well suited to a rapidly changing economic environment.

Capitalism is also more democratic and pragmatic. It is oriented to what the consumers themselves determine that they need—to the free play of supply and demand—not to what some utopian, or some bureaucrat, decrees that we *should* need. Thus, it tends to diffuse economic and political power; it is more compatible with personal freedom and pluralistic government.

## CAPITALISM'S WEAKNESSES

However, as various critics have noted, capitalism (even in theory) has some serious weaknesses. First, because it does not acknowledge any superordinate goals—any public interest or general welfare—it provides no justification for, and may even oppose, the claims of patriotism and positive government. Calls for sacrifices to ensure the well-being of the whole may violate the sanctity of the self-interest motive, or else stretch the meaning of "enlightened self-interest" far beyond its normal connotation.

Our adherence to morality may also run counter to the capitalist creed. We certainly have ample evidence that the rules of the game are not self-enforcing; the history of capitalism is replete with examples of price fixing, monopolistic practices, predation against competitors, attempts to mislead gullible consumers, and even outright fraud. The thick web of laws, regulations, and ethical precepts that in fact limit the free play of self-interest in our economy have evolved in spite of the tenets of capitalism (strictly construed), not because of them.

Capitalism is also widely accused of creating a spiritual vacuum; with its materialistic focus on "getting and spending," it aspires to nothing more uplifting than an increase in the quantity of goods and services.

Finally, "pure" capitalism tends to be callous toward losers. It is indifferent to bad luck; it is blind to human needs that are not backed by disposable income; and it gives no quarter to those who may have been handicapped from the start. It does not recognize "equity" but only "freedom," property rights, and the sanctity of contracts.

Unfortunately, over the years many capitalists and capitalist writers have taken the assumption of unrestrained egoism to heart. In the nineteenth century the doctrine of laissez faire decreed that government should take a hands-off attitude toward the economy; let free competition in an unrestricted marketplace determine the course of the economy. According to the Social

Darwinists, nature itself provided justification. "While the law of competition may be sometimes hard for the individual," intoned steel magnate Andrew Carnegie in his "Gospel of Wealth," "it is best for the race because it ensures the survival of the fittest."

Many capitalists have lived by Carnegie's gospel. Carl Hovey's biography of financier J. P. Morgan notes that during the great financial debacle of 1907, in which he played a significant part, Morgan shrugged: "I owe nothing to the public." When asked by a TV interviewer some years ago what he does for his country, multimillionaire H. L. Hunt replied: "I provide jobs." More recently, in *Time* magazine, computer pioneer Jack Tramiel paraded his tough-minded personal philosophy without apologies: "Business is war."

## MODERN CAPITALISM

On the whole, the views of contemporary theoreticians are more moderate, though they are also less faithful to the capitalist creed. The model for this stance, ironically, is Adam Smith himself, whose companion volume on *The Theory of Moral Sentiments* (1817) stressed that the marketplace must operate within the framework of a moral and spiritual order; a free market is justified, ultimately, by its superior ability to increase the wealth of the whole—the wealth of *nations*.

Listen to the views, in a 1982 speech, of former treasury secretary and now presidential chief of staff Donald Regan, the very model of a modern capitalist: "The only way capitalism can work," Regan says, "is when it is tied to morality, when equity, fairness, and compassion are the hallmarks of its people, and when the limited government that oversees the system is ready and able to help those who cannot help themselves."

Listen also to conservative economist Milton Friedman, commenting in *San Francisco Focus* on the federal government's rescue of the beleaguered Continental Illinois Bank:

The Depression led to the establishment of the Federal Deposit Insurance Corporation and to the recognition that you should not allow a major bank to fail. [That is, it would be against the "public interest."]

In other words, modern capitalists try to have their cake and eat it too. On the one hand, they defend the free market and the free play of self-interest. On the other hand, they recognize the superior claims of the community, of human needs, and of "equity"—the buzzwords of socialism. They also tacitly acknowledge the transcendent authority of the political order, especially when it is democratic and (presumably) embodies the will of the "people." And they justify the rights (and profits) of individual capitalists in terms of the benefits to others—to society as a whole. "The market is only one section of society," writes Wilhelm Roepke in *The Economics of the Free Society* (1963). "It is a very important section, it is true, but still one whose existence is justifiable and possible only because it is part of a larger whole which concerns not economics but philosophy, history, and theology." (And, he might have added, biology. And politics.)

Accordingly, the welfare states that have been superimposed on capitalist systems during this century are contradictions of the underlying logic of capitalist ideology. Growing out of the socialist tradition, the welfare state is a pragmatic, compromise solution that was designed to save capitalism from itself, or, more precisely, from the undesirable consequences of taking its assumptions too literally.

## A LOOK AT THE RECORD

In fact, all great civilizations have owed their success in substantial measure to a "partnership" between government and the private sector (though conflicts between the two have also been frequent), in general, thriving economies have been associated with a cooperative and mutually supportive relationship between the public and private sectors. (Indeed, in many cases the public and private sectors have been closely intertwined.) As columnist George Will observes in *Statecraft as Soulcraft*: "Government produces the infrastructure of society . . . a precondition for the production of wealth."

Witness the case of the United States, supposedly the most capitalistic nation of all. Going back to colonial times, government at various levels has always been involved in our economic life. Our "manifest destiny" as a nation was greatly facilitated by federal government purchases, or conquests, of huge tracts of land that were then given away or sold at low prices to encourage settlers. Our military provided much-needed protection for the hardy souls who ventured into these new territories. Government land grants were used to foster such specific ends as higher education and railroad construction. And many a nineteenth-century entrepreneur in the timber, mining, coal, and oil industries benefited from the government's willingness to give away, or sell cheaply, the right to exploit (and profit from) these assets.

Over the years the federal government, as a matter of national policy, has also assisted—either directly or indirectly—in the development of our merchant marine, our railroads, agricultural technology, the automobile industry, aviation, space technology, nuclear power, electronics, biotechnology, and much more. Indeed, the federal government has been a silent partner in most of this country's leading edge technological ventures.

The federal government also has a long history of aiding the private sector with respect to foreign trade—ranging from import quotas to export subsidies and tariffs. Thus, in the 1820s, tariffs were imposed to protect infant industries such as steel making and textiles from the vicissitudes of "free" competition with the British. A hundred years later, when these same industries were again threatened by foreign competitors, tariff measures were again invoked.

## GOVERNMENT SERVICES

Then there are all those government services that are often treated as natural rights: At the national level there is the postal system, the national parks, the Public Health Service, the Coast Guard, the Patent Office, the Library of Congress, the federal judiciary, the federal treasury, and much more. And at the state and municipal levels there are the public roads, sewers, transit systems, health services, schools, police and fire protection, etc., all of which are vitally important to the private sector.

Public education, upon which modern industry is heavily dependent, has long been a major government responsibility. And so has the agricultural research that underlies the miracle of

American agricultural productivity (which in turn provides economic benefits for the rest of us).

Agriculture has also benefited from such government measures as road building, and electrification, crop price supports, low-cost loans, tax credits, cost sharing, information on farm improvement, pest control measures, and important restrictions of various kinds. Our banking industry benefits mightily from the Federal Reserve system and the Federal Deposit Insurance Corporation. Our computer industry has likewise benefited from government support, going back to the time in the 1930s when IBM won a big contract with the new Social Security Administration that enabled the company to launch its new punch-card "computer" system.

It should also be pointed out that some of the most dynamic periods of economic growth in this country have coincided with wars—the Civil War, World War I, and World War II—periods when government itself became a major market for the private sector. In World War II, for instance, government spending grew from $6 billion to $87.4 billion, or 40 percent of the GNP. Government control over the economy during the war years was every bit as embracing as in socialist countries.

Conversely, some of our greatest economic debacles have occurred when government did not intervene, or did so in a way that made matters worse. Recall the Great Depression (chapter 4), when the government refused to curb financial speculation and then cut back on spending at the very time when the rest of the economy was plunging into recession.

## GOVERNMENT AS REFEREE

It must also be stressed that a lot of what government does for and to the private sector has been done at the behest of the private sector itself when a referee was needed. In the 1920s, the infant radio industry pleaded with the federal government to bring order to the existing chaos—the negative synergy produced by a competitive scramble and the frequent overlapping of radio frequencies. The upshot was a system of frequency "allocations" administered by a new regulatory agency that in time became what we know today as the FCC.

Furthermore, our entire economy operates within a dense fabric of laws and regulations, rules of the game that have evolved over a long period of time. Most of our building codes, zoning restrictions, health codes, safety regulations, etc., are widely supported (in principle) by the public at large and even by most of the affected businesses; the people who constitute the "marketplace" prefer, by and large, to play by the rules and have others do so as well. Jack Tramiel is wrong; business is more like football than war. The current euphemism is "regulated capitalism."

The Nobel Prize-winning economist Wassily Leontief illustrates with a metaphor, quoted in the *Christian Science Monitor*: "The problem of guiding an economy is like sailing," he says. "You need [both] the wind and a rudder. The wind is the profit motive. The rudder is government influence."

## PREACHING VS. PRACTICE

It is also a fact that capitalists often do not practice what they preach. Though they may extol the virtues of free competition and the free market in after-dinner speeches, in fact they are seldom content to play the role that the model prescribes for them. Instead of welcoming competition, they do everything they can to prevent it, co-opt it, eliminate it, or, if all else fails, strike more or less explicit deals to divide the pie into "market shares," or "territories." Competition is not something capitalists enjoy for its own sake, by and large. It is what they put up with if they have to.

As one of the leading promoters of capitalism, George Gilder, rightly observes in *Wealth and Poverty*: "Capitalist creativity is guided not by any invisible hand, but by the quite visible and aggressive hand of management and entrepreneurship. Businesses continually differentiate their products, their marketing techniques, their advertising, and their retailing strategies in order to find some unique niche in the system from which they can reap, as long as possible, monopoly profits. . . . Without the aid of government, protecting patents, or otherwise excluding competitors, these monopoly positions tend to be short lived. But they are the goal of business strategy. . . ."

Capitalists also characteristically try to manipulate their markets. Rather than responding reflexively to spontaneous "demand," they go to great lengths to create and inflate it, with cunning product designs, seductive packaging, hyperbolic advertising, and worse. Without the outside forces of morality and law, the outcome would more often be "private vices, private benefits," to modify Adam Smith's famous aphorism.

## LOOK AT THE RESULTS

All of these deviations from the theoretical model are only minor embarrassments, though, compared with what "free enterprise" has produced after more than 200 years; as various critics have noted, capitalist theory cannot even explain, much less legitimize, the most important single feature of every industrial economy, capitalist and socialist alike.

Modern societies are dominated by large, synergy-producing organizations, not atomistic individual entrepreneurs. New ventures may start small, but in an age of mass markets—even international markets—they soon get big, or get bought out, or lose out when the "big boys" jump into the game. Not always, of course. But often enough to discredit the nineteenth-century vision of a system in which many small firms are competing on a more or less equal footing in a finely balanced, self-regulating marketplace.

For every successful entrepreneur these days who makes it entirely on his own, there are many other ventures launched as spin-offs by large firms, as joint ventures by two or more firms, or as team efforts backed by venture capital, institutional financing, government loans, and/or state and local government support of various kinds. (Indeed, many states are themselves becoming venture capitalists, using public funds and other forms of support to grubstake homegrown businesses.) Many other new ventures emerge from various corporate "skunk works"; big companies are by no means infertile grounds for old-fashioned enterprise.

## A NEW STAGE

In reality, our corporate leviathans represent a new stage in economic evolution that challenges the theory of capitalism itself.

Nineteenth-century economist Alfred Marshall, in his monumental and still useful text, *Principles of Economics* (1890), showed more appreciation of this change than do some modern practitioners. The fundamental characteristic of modern industrial life, Marshall noted, was not competition but enterprise based on planning and forethought. These activities "may and often do cause people to compete with one another, but on the other hand they may tend, and just now indeed they are tending, in the direction of cooperation and combination of all kinds. . . ."

To put the issue in bold relief, if the trend toward bigness and complexity has not been confined to the private sector in capitalist countries—if it is equally characteristic of socialist economies, nonprofit organizations, and governments as well—then obviously capitalism alone can't account for it. Something else is driving this trend. The something else is, of course, synergy.

But more to the point, modern corporations are not simply examples of capitalism on a grand scale. Leviathan is a different animal—a mutant or, more precisely, a species whose progressive evolution has made it different in important ways from its ancestors. AT&T, IBM, GM, and the like are quasi-public institutions operating in a highly regulated and politically molded marketplace, and it is no longer clear who owns or controls the destiny of Leviathan.

For one thing, ownership and management have effectively become divorced from one another. These days the executives of large corporations seldom own more than a small fraction of the company's stock. Not only is ownership likely to be widely diffused through public stock offerings but many of the stockholders are themselves large institutions—mutual funds, workers' pension funds (management expert Theodore Drucker calls it "pension fund socialism"), insurance companies, universities, and the like. These "owners" do not in any meaningful sense exercise control over the company's operations.

Nowadays, our economy is only partially capitalistic. The term "capitalism" can still serve to identify those aspects of a modern economy that more or less conform to the classic model, but they are only a part of the picture. In addition to the high-risk, cutting-edge ventures and the established industries that are experiencing new competitive pressures due to deregulation or foreign competition, several large "niches" are occupied by very different animals: long-time defense contractors (many of whom are "sole source suppliers"), regulated monopolies like the public utilities, stable old-line companies like Proctor & Gamble, government-run enterprises like NASA and the Tennessee Valley Authority, and, not least, the thousands of neighborhood bars, drugstores, and cleaners that are disciplined, not by competition, but by their dependence on the loyalty (and disposable income) of a local clientele.

"Free enterprise" is fashionable again, and rightly so. But those who have been extolling the role of the entrepreneur in economic change tend to idealize, to credit individuals with heroic accomplishments that are more often the result of several factors—or several actors—in combination. It is the exception rather than the rule when a lone eagle combines the inventiveness, entrepreneurship, capital resources, technical skills, management skills, and marketing skills that are required for almost any successful new venture nowadays. Indeed, many a Steve Jobs (a founder and late chairman of Apple Computers) has been saved by a John Sculley (the former head of Pepsico who is now Apple's president). Even a small business like a local restaurant or clothing store may utilize the services of design, management, financial, and marketing consultants.

## THE ULTIMATE PARADOX

The hallmark of most successful ventures these days is high synergy. Studies of corporate excellence show very clearly that high-synergy organizations almost always rely on motivational factors that have to do with superordinate goals, "teamwork" and service to the customers, and/or society as a whole. Profits (and losses) are still vitally important to Leviathan, of course, but most of the three hundred fifty thousand employees who work for IBM, say, are not motivated by the profit motive alone. Also important are the intrinsic challenges of the work, identification with the company and its objectives, being part of a winning team, opportunities for advancement, the desire for peer and manager approval, recognition for personal achievement, and sometimes just plain fun.

The ultimate paradox of capitalism is that its most successful exemplars also happen to be organizations that depend on social (and spiritual) rewards, as well as material rewards (as a number of recent writers on business management have stressed). Listen to Wanda Smith, the human factors engineer at Hewlett-Packard who designed the ticket system for the Bay Area Rapid Transit district (BART): "At Hewlett-Packard the emphasis is on teamsmanship. . . . You play down one person's involvement. In all the projects at Hewlett-Packard you're totally dependent on your colleagues. It's a great support system." Or listen to Akio Morita, the founder of SONY: "In Japan, we think of a company as a family. The workers and management are in the same boat. . . . It is a fate-sharing body. . . . Management does not treat labor as a tool but as a partner. . . . Without cooperation from all the people, [a manager] cannot be successful. We believe it is important to give everyone a sense of participation." Karl Marx would have been amused by this turn of events.

## CAPITALISM VS. SYNERGISM

In sum, it is not capitalism that explains Leviathan. It is synergy. To repeat what was said earlier, our economic progress has been a synergistic phenomenon—a cooperative effect that has involved, in varying degrees, geographic and ecological factors, technological innovations, capital and other resources, entrepreneurs, a division of labor (and its essential complement, organized cooperation and "management"), vital public services, a compatible economic environment, a supportive political order, reinforcing cultural and religious values, and so on.

One of the most widely used justifications for capitalism is a passage from Walter Lippmann's towering work, *The Good Society*, written in the late 1930s: "For the first time in human history men had come upon a way of producing wealth in which the good fortune of others multiplied their own. . . . They actually felt it to be true that enlightened self-interest promoted the common good. For the first time men could conceive a social order in which the ancient moral aspiration for liberty, equality, and fraternity was consistent with the abolition of poverty and the increase of wealth. . . ."

Lippman is talking about synergy, of course. But more significant is the fact that the context in which this passage occurred had to do with the industrial revolution, not capitalism per se. Lippmann was, in effect, talking about the entire configuration of factors that have made economic progress possible. Lippmann's observations were not an implicit benediction for capitalism but rather for the achievements of complex, technological societies.

## CAPITALISM, SOCIALISM, AND SYNERGISM

The fact is that both capitalist and socialist ideologies have outlived their usefulness. Both of these nineteenth-century models are based on simplistic (and one-sided) premises about "human nature"; both are highly selective about which aspects of reality they choose to stress; both are guilty of serious omissions; and both are equally unworkable by themselves. If it is true, as the critics of socialism charge, that the socialist ideal of a self-regulating community is naive, so is the capitalist ideal of a self-regulating marketplace.

Ideals, like white lies, may have their uses, but neither of our antiquated ideologies provide the kind of conceptual framework that we need for understanding how a modern society works. Like all partial truths, capitalism and socialism are most serviceable when taken with a grain of salt—or, better said, when blended together. Pure capitalism is just as much an unattainable ideal as is pure socialism. Yet elements of both have been evident throughout history, and both can play a vital role in furthering the general welfare.

Every complex society consists of a vast web of synergies. It is synergy, not socialism, which produces Russian cars, TVs, tanks, airliners, and spaceships. It is synergy that has enabled China, North Korea, North Vietnam, India, and Cuba to feed, clothe, house, and defend some two billion people. And it is synergy that underpins such contradictions of capitalist ideology in our own society as national defense, social security, the space program, and public utilities.

## A SYNERGISTIC IDEOLOGY

What are the ideological implications? Every person born into our society can be considered a "stakeholder." Nobody has ever improved on Edmund Burke's classic definition of society in "Reflections on the Revolution in France" as "a partnership not only between those who are living, but between those who are living, those who are dead, and those who are [yet] to be born."

We all share the biological and cultural heritage of our species, as well as the many collective goods that our particular societies provide, from national defense to the "safety net" of the welfare state. In diverse ways, each of us has the potential to serve as a vital link in the living chain that connects past generations with those yet to come. Some of us will contribute our genes and our offspring. Others may contribute ideas, inventions, or works of art. Still others will contribute their acquired skills and productive labor.

On the other hand, some will not contribute at all; for various reasons, some individuals will remain in, or revert to, a state of dependency. Or they may even become socially destructive, in which case society will try to intervene for self-protection. For the most part, though, the various possible outcomes cannot be predicted at the outset. As the great evolutionary biologist Theodosius Dobzhansky expressed it, every human being is "a living experiment in adaptedness."

"Equal opportunity" must obviously be a part of any ideology that is grounded in this perspective. This is certainly not controversial. But what about results? What about the rights and duties of the citizenry? Capitalism (and the liberal philosophy that underpins it) is vociferous about protecting individual political and economic rights, but it is silent about social duties or obligations. Its formula might be stated as follows: From each according to his inclination; to each according to his ability, effort, luck, and, in the final reckoning, his competitive success. The individual has no obligation to society, but, on the other hand, society has no obligation in return.

Socialism takes the opposite tack. It imposes social duties that are weighted according to one's ability while guaranteeing that everyone's material needs are satisfied. Indeed, the communists go so far as to insist on equal shares for everyone. On the other hand, socialism is silent about personal rights.

The synergy principle leads to a formulation that is different from either of these—a middle way. Recognizing that the whole is an interdependent system composed of cooperating parts, the ideology of synergism addresses the needs of both the whole and the parts. It is attentive to the duties that any family, organization, community, or society as a whole must extract from its members in order to preserve the whole and further its purposes. It is mindful of the ancient saying: He who takes from society without giving back is a thief. At the same time, it fully recognizes the needs—material, political, and psychological—that we possess as individual human beings. Most importantly, it attempts to strike a balance between the extremes of guaranteeing equal shares for everyone and a beggar-thy-neighbor policy.

## THE FAIR-SHARES ETHIC

One might call it a "fair-shares" ethic: From each according to his (or her) ability *and* aspiration; to each according to his (or her) need *and* contributions. Everyone is expected to contribute a fair share, if able to do so, and everyone is assured in return that his or her basic needs will be met. The rationale for this is not complicated. The welfare state can rightly be looked upon as an insurance policy for society as a whole. Who can say which individuals among us may, in the long run, have need of the safety net. But there must also be equity—a balancing of rights and duties.

At the same time, a fair-shares ethic recognizes that there is also a profound inequity in giving equal shares to someone who works hard and someone else who loafs on the job. "Free riders" are also exploitative. Thus, beyond providing for everyone's basic needs, the fair-shares ethic also links rewards—material and otherwise—to the individual's performance and contributions.

There is nothing radically new about the fair-shares ethic. In fact, all modern societies adhere to this policy tacitly, though more or less reluctantly and imperfectly. No modern society follows either an equal-shares or a beggar-thy-neighbor policy, whatever may be its ideological posture.

Indeed, the concept underlying the fair-shares ethic has ancient roots. In Plato's *Republic* there is the idea of "justice"; in jurisprudence there is the principle of "equity"; in socialist theory there is "social justice." Only capitalism has no concern about justice per se, a flaw that has been noted by various critics. "Can men live in a free society if they have no reason to believe it is also a just society?" asks Irving Kristol in *Two Cheers for Capitalism*. "I do not think so."

Who determines what is a "fair" share? In fact, we do it for ourselves and for one another all the time; a fair-shares ethic is already widely used but seldom acknowledged, much less justified in ideological terms. Of course, the manner in which we apply it leaves much to be desired. If there were some mathematical formula that could be used, we would long ago have deployed it. But in fact, determining what is a fair share involves a very imprecise art, one which is greatly dependent on the particular context and the perceptions of different actors. Nevertheless, it is a valid concept that can provide us with an explicit guideline for economic and social policy.

For instance, when General Motors made the mistake of declaring fat bonuses for its executives at the very time when it was trying to extract "give-backs" from its production-line workers, the company displayed a remarkable insensitivity to the concept of fair shares. And when a university president recently decreed a 10 percent across-the-board salary cut for the faculty and staff while reducing his own salary by a token $35 per month, he deeply antagonized everyone involved and undermined his authority.

A fair-shares ethic recognizes that those who contribute to the success of an organization are stakeholders, and loyalty upward must be reciprocated with loyalty downward. A company that closes a plant and turns its back on the workers and their community violates the fair-shares ethic. It cannot expect to obtain a maximum effort from its remaining employees.

By contrast, a company like Procter & Gamble, which pioneered profit-sharing, (a tacit acknowledgement of an ownership stake) along with generous fringe benefits and a deep commitment to the well-being of its employees, exhibits a pattern of reciprocal loyalty that in turn has long had a positive effect on that company's productivity and bottom line.

Capitalism cannot deal with such nuances. And neither can socialism. A synergy perspective can. But whatever ideological stance we choose to adopt, the future lies with those who are able to appreciate and make full use of the synergy principle.

# 7. The Art of Synergistic Thinking III: Tools

"We have overbuilt [office buildings] in this country on an unprecedented scale," admits J. McDonald Williams, a partner of Trammel Crow, the largest U.S. developer, in *Time* magazine. In the last year or so, office vacancy rates have shot up across the country, while the construction of new buildings has outpaced the growth in white-collar employment by 50 percent. The result has been much bloodletting and red ink in the commercial building industry.

What's the explanation? Very simple: A lack of synergistic thinking.

Many developers, when they were making their go-ahead decisions, were concerned only about putting the pieces together for their own projects—the financing, insurance, architects, contractors, government approvals, and so forth. What they failed to consider was how many other developers were out there with plans to do the same thing, and how the aggregate of construction activity would affect the delicate relationship between supply and demand.

A lack of synergistic thinking can also be seen in the failure of Victor Technologies, one of the early leaders in the personal computer revolution. The Victor 9000 computer was technically a superior machine. It was faster than the IBM-PC and Apple II, had greater memory capacity, a higher resolution monitor, and a vastly superior keyboard layout. What Victor lacked was (1) a large inventory of software (an indispensable partner in any computer system), (2) a realistic sales strategy, and (3) the financial resources to match its needs.

In launching its computer, the leadership at Victor had not taken sufficient account of all the factors that have to be combined to ensure success in the marketplace. A few months after

the Victor 9000 made its appearance, IBM announced the introduction of its first "PC." The rest is history. (For those who
might be tempted to conclude that no small player can compete
successfully against IBM, it is worth pointing to the success that
Compaq has had in head-to-head competition with "Big Blue.")

What these two examples—among countless others—illustrate
clearly is that there really is something called synergistic thinking, and that its use can make a decisive difference. Synergistic
thinking is the sworn enemy of the kind of linear, one-dimensional thinking we saw in the examples above. But, to repeat,
synergistic thinking is not a gimmick, a formula, or a tactic. It's
a *strategy*—a more sophisticated approach to analyzing and solving problems than many of us are accustomed to. Let's look a
little more closely at this distinction.

## LINEAR THINKING

The victims of linear thinking are all us around us: The farmers who went heavily into debt during the inflation-fueled boom
years; the manufacturers of computer games, who mistook a fad
for a new way of life; the parents who are stunned to find that
raising two children is considerably more than twice as demanding and stressful as raising one; the economists who thought high
interest rates were the primary cause of our mounting trade deficit; the oil-rich OPEC countries that went on a spending spree
when oil prices were sky high; the builders of condominiums,
who once thought that they were the wave of the future in home
building; the thousands of aspiring college professors who, after
several years of graduate school, belatedly discovered that the
baby boom was ending and that they were in a shrinking job
market.

Linear thinking never was a good idea. In an age of turbulent
change, it can be fatal. As Peter Drucker has observed: "Planning
starts out, as a rule, with the trends of yesterday and projects
them into the future. . . . This is no longer going to work."

The hallmark of a linear thinker is that he or she glibly expects
current trends to continue. Linear thinkers do not think deeply
enough about the entire configuration of factors that are re-

sponsible for any trend, and about the many supposed "givens" or "constants" in the equation that may in fact change abruptly. There are, for instance, the economists (and other prophets) who pontificate about what the economy will be like five years from now, or in the year 2000. There are the management consultants who confidently predict the future of, say, the computer industry with quantitative precision. There are the "suede shoe salesmen" for various investment vehicles who project future profits on the basis of past performance. And there are the parents who deduce the adult occupations of their children from youthful interests, or worse, from their own occupational preferences.

Linear thinkers don't like messy, complex, imprecise explanations that are hedged with qualifiers. They also tend to place too much confidence in numbers—in things that can be quantified. They believe, with Anatole France, that "those who won't count, don't count." To a linear thinker, the test of truth is whether or not it can be plotted on a graph. (We are reminded of a colleague, whose credentials as a scientist are above reproach, who likes to say that it is better to be approximately right than exactly wrong.) We are not opposed to careful, rigorous analysis of the numbers. We do it all the time in our business. But we try to avoid spurious precision, or a misplaced confidence in the numbers alone.

You can tell a linear thinker by how he or she phrases questions. A linear thinker asks: "What was the cause of death?" or "what was the secret of her success?" or "where did he go wrong?" or "I'm not interested in providing a service, I want to know: will it make money?" or even "I'm glad he's a hard worker, but what were his grades?"

Linear thinkers tend to be one-dimensional, one-leveled, and, often, mentally lazy. They resent complexity. They want simple answers. They think in terms of prime movers, or of isolated causes that can be lifted out of the systems in which they are embedded. They like to deal with one or two "variables" and treat everything else as a constant.

Linear thinkers also like to focus on the "parts"; they are uncomfortable with complex "wholes." And they like to concentrate on the most direct and immediate consequences of things; they don't show much interest in long-range ramifications, or side effects. Indeed, they don't even know what synergy means.

## SYNERGISTIC THINKING

The first thing to be said about the art of synergistic thinking is that it is extremely demanding—a high art that can only be perfected through self-discipline, and dedication, and practice. It does not seem to come naturally. In outline form, here are some of its major characteristics:

- A focus on *both* the "whole" and the "parts," on the ways in which the parts affect the whole (and vice versa), and the ways in which parts and wholes interact;
- A "gestalt" approach, which stresses the need to see and appreciate all of the parts, or factors, that combine to influence the whole;
- A deep understanding of configural, cooperative, "codetermining" causation—of synergy;
- A multileveled, multidimensional perspective, which stretches our understanding of causation to include, at one extreme, "internal" social and psychological factors and, at the other extreme, the supposedly "external" factors in the "infrastructure" and the "environment" that we are prone to treat as given;
- A keen awareness of how small changes can have large consequences, ranging from the threshold effects discussed earlier to the many systems where a change in one or more parts can have a drastic impact on other parts, or on the whole;
- A receptiveness, based on a willingness to face reality, toward the root fact that everything in life is contingent and that the world is inevitably in flux (in the ancient metaphor, you can never step twice into the same river);
- An acute sensitivity to the symptoms of low synergy or dysergy, and to the hidden dependencies that can become dysergy traps;
- An orientation to finding synergistic solutions—new com-

binations, cooperative ventures, mutually beneficial collaborations, and so on.

## SOME APPLICATIONS

Many examples have already been described, but let's look at a few specific cases in point. First on the negative side:

- It is a scandal, both inside and outside of our military establishment, that we have ordered masses of new hardware—ships, planes, land vehicles, and other expensive items—without making adequate provision for the manpower, training, or maintenance required to make and keep all this hardware operational. At best this situation represents an appalling lack of synergistic thinking; at worst, it involves putting self-interest ahead of the national interest.
- Though the trend toward freestanding, outpatient medical care—from "women's centers" to "surgi-centers"—may offer more convenience and, sometimes, lower costs, there have also been some losses of synergy and even some negative synergy. For lack of the kinds of backup services that a hospital can routinely provide, some of these outpatient facilities have had patients who experienced serious complications. Furthermore, by taking away from hospitals some of their most profitable services, which in the past have often subsidized money-losing services, the trend toward freestanding health facilities threatens the long-run viability of our hospitals. Finally, because many of the freestanding centers are physician-owned, profit-making ventures, there may also be a built-in conflict of interest. Among other things, there may be powerful incentives either for unnecessary treatment or for treatment that should have been done in a hospital.
- The cumulative effect of an income tax code that has been added to and altered almost incessantly over the past fifty years is an administrative monster. It is a perversion of the philosophy behind our tax system when more than 43 percent of American taxpayers must rely on professional assistance in filling out their returns. (And tax reform, we fear, will not affect the paperwork.)

- A well-known local carpet-cleaning service has recently fallen on hard times, though others in the area are doing well. We saw one reason why when this company was engaged by our landlord to clean the carpeting in our office building. The person who came to make the bid neglected to note on his form that the truck should bring a four-hundred-foot vacuum hose. The job was scheduled for a Saturday afternoon, and the work crew arrived late from the previous job, griping and complaining that they didn't have the right equipment and that the job had been underbid. They rushed through the parts of the job they could do without a long hose and arranged to reschedule the rest of the job for the following Wednesday morning using a portable tank instead. When a new crew arrived on Wednesday, they warned that the portable tank could not clean as well and that, in any case, it would take eighteen hours for the carpets to dry. Since this was unacceptable to the tenants, the job was rescheduled again for the following Saturday. This time the crew came with enough hose, but they forgot to clean two of the suites. So the landlord, one of the biggest in town, finally lost patience and found somebody else to finish the job.

- After six years of deregulation, the airlines—a vital part of this nation's infrastructure—are still experiencing heavy turbulence. While it may be true that the industry as a whole is operating more efficiently, in the process airline service has, for many users, markedly declined. Freed from regulatory restrictions, the airlines have concentrated on serving the most profitable routes and time slots, with the result that there may be too many flights between major cities at peak periods and not enough at other times. During peak periods, there may be long delays in taking off (due to system overload) and missed connections at the other end. Or else long layovers because nonstop flights are getting harder to find. At other times, or if you are going to a smaller city, you may not be able to get a flight at all. Or else it will cost you a lot more than in the past, because the most profitable routes are no longer providing subsidies to the less profitable ones. Finally, there is growing concern over possible corner cutting by the airlines to keep costs down, a problem that could be jeopardizing air safety.

## SOME COMMENTS

In all of the cases above, we can see the destructive effects of failing to think synergistically. The problems in our military establishment are symptomatic of both a hardware mentality and a politically driven procurement process. Grown men should know better than to think that hardware alone can win wars. Someday our nation may pay dearly for this shortsightedness.

As for the trend in health care services, hospitals are products of an evolutionary process—they are synergistic systems. When you begin unbundling these systems in the name of competition, you may reduce both the costs and the benefits of the older approach.

The zoo that is the federal tax system is worse than the proverbial camel designed by a committee. It was designed and is constantly being redesigned by several committees and successive administrations; and, of course, a multitude of lobbyists. Each new provision, each complication in the tax code, was added in order to address this or that particular need or problem, or to placate this or that interest group. Individually, each increment has added only a little bit to the whole. But as the tax code has grown from a few pages into a small encyclopedia it has become a forbidding edifice that can only be mastered by tax specialists. Moreover, the tax system has become a major cause of distortions and instability in the economy. (It remains to be seen what the impending tax reform will accomplish.)

In the case of the disorganized carpet cleaners, they clearly violated the first rule of a service business, which is that success depends on having workers who are well motivated, well trained, and well disciplined. Without good workers, all the equipment and advertising in the world won't make it possible to deliver on your promises in an efficient, and profitable, manner.

Finally, there is the case of the airline industry—one example among several in an era of deregulation. We confront here a classic dilemma. Are the airlines at heart a public service—a societal support system in which functional, performance criteria should take precedence, or are they primarily businesses that should respond to, or even manipulate if they can, their "market"?

The answer may lie somewhere in the middle. The airlines are inescapably interdependent parts of a complex system, a system that provides a vital public service. This service can be accomplished either well or poorly, profitably or inefficiently. However, government rules and regulations cannot alone ensure that the system will either meet the public need or be efficient. Sometimes, in fact, a regulated system may fail miserably to meet needs and may only protect the inefficient providers.

But then, free competition can also fail to do the job. Indeed, the airlines provide a prime example of how competition can produce negative synergies while undercutting needed forms of cooperation. In the end, what is required is a commitment by both the airlines and the government to work together toward striking a balance between public service and market forces. At this writing, such a commitment has not yet materialized, and the prediction is that the situation is likely to get much worse before it gets better.

## THE POSITIVE SIDE

The power of synergistic thinking, happily, also has many positive exemplars. Consider just a few:

- At our local Safeway supermarket, night crews routinely spend the wee small hours restocking the shelves. It occurred to the management that it would cost only marginally more to keep the store open twenty-four hours a day, thereby capturing some of the late-night convenience-store shoppers, as well as night-shift workers and others who preferred to shop in an empty store. Even if only few people may use the service, the favorable publicity alone makes the move worthwhile.
- We know two brothers who wanted to invest in some income-producing real estate. One had savings for a down payment, while the other had some surplus income that could be used to cover the expected negative cash flow (the excess of costs

over revenues) for the first two years or so. Acting alone, neither brother could afford to make such an investment. Yet by pooling their resources they were able to close a deal on a duplex apartment building that gave them both immediate tax write-offs and future appreciation.

- In the intensely competitive fast-food business, success often goes to those who think synergistically. Thus McDonald's has begun to branch out with "Mini-Macs" aimed at capturing pedestrian traffic and "McStops" that combine McDonald's restaurants with motels, gas stations, and convenience stores. Meanwhile, one of McDonald's chief competitors, Burger King, has mobilized (literally) a synergy-based response. The company has recently launched a fleet of customized vans that are serving its famous Whoppers, shakes, and fries from on-board kitchens to customers at factory gates, on military bases, and elsewhere.

- Two of the most durable small businesses in our town have been a furniture stripper and a furniture refinisher, who were wise enough to locate next door to each other. Over the years, both businesses have benefitted mightily from being able to offer one-stop service, and from mutual referrals.

- Physicians in this country have traditionally been among the most individualistic of professionals, and in the past the American Medical Association has bitterly opposed and vigorously fought against the establishment of group practices. But now a dramatic change is occurring. Under the combined pressures of increasing costs, increasing competition due to a growing surplus of physicians, and new reimbursement mechanisms for patient care, the incentives for physicians to join a group practice have greatly increased, as have the penalties for not doing so. These incentives include lower costs for such office expenses as staff wages, equipment, and rent, increased revenues from a higher patient volume, the ability to obtain contracts from subscriber groups that wish to purchase health care "packages," and the increased visibility (and referrals) that a group practice can provide for its individual members. The result has been a proliferation of group practices, from about 10 percent of all practicing physicians in 1965 to 30 percent in 1980. It is conservatively estimated that by 1990 over half of all physicians will belong to groups. The potential for synergy has always been there, but only now are its benefits proving to be irresistible.

• Our nearby restaurant arcade recently decided to make a push to attract evening customers for its sixteen eateries. The "bait" that the managers are using: free movies that are shown on a giant TV screen in the common eating area.

## THINKING SYNERGISTICALLY

These examples are only meant to be suggestive. They are not precise "models" because the synergy principle teaches that each problem, and each situation, is different, if not unique. Instead, these examples illustrate an approach to solving your own problems, or achieving your own goals.

Safeway assumed a double life as a late-night convenience store, as well as a midnight grocery store, simply by extending its hours and incurring a marginal increase in costs. Our real estate partners did what the members of close-knit families have always done; the two brothers combined their complementary resources and skills for their mutual benefit.

McDonald's and Burger King have diversified into business areas that are related to what they already do, and know how to do. They are building on their already well-known public images. They already have most of the organizational capabilities in place. They already have economies of scale for many of the needed ingredients, supplies, equipment, etc. And, best of all, the new outlets complement and reinforce the existing outlets, capturing customers that would not otherwise buy Big Macs or Whoppers and, very likely, generating more customers for their regular restaurants.

As our furniture stripper and refinisher recognized, each one performs a part of the complete job of furniture restoration. Because their businesses are naturally complementary, they have been able to gain a competitive edge by, in effect, putting the two businesses together and collaborating closely with one another.

Group medical practice has so many advantages, except in cases of bad management, that the physicians who have joined the growing trend often wonder why the medical establishment could have been opposed to the idea for so long. Group practices are cooperative arrangements in which everybody, including the patients, stands to gain.

Finally, the tactic used by our restaurant arcade is one of the oldest on record—using one attraction to generate business for another.

## HOW TO USE SYNERGY

What's the secret? How can you make use of the synergy principle in your own life? And how can our businessmen and political leaders make better use of it? Where does one begin?

The answer is: with a question. Synergistic thinking begins with questions such as: "How can I use my time more efficiently?" "How can I cut my costs, or increase my profitability?" "What factors am I overlooking in my plan?" "Have I really analyzed carefully all the potential costs and benefits?" "What can I do differently if I want to get better grades, sell more widgets, or win more votes?" The questions themselves are not new, of course. What may be new for many of us is how we think about such questions, and what kinds of solutions emerge.

Perhaps the best way to illustrate the point is by describing some of the ways that we have applied the synergy principle to our own lives, which includes our growing management consulting business (we're partners), some restoration and furnishing of a recently acquired old Victorian house, a family that includes two teenage daughters and a preschool son, and, not least, the writing of this book.

For example, we save up errands as much as possible and cluster them together, or try to combine things like birthday and Christmas shopping. The two "men" in the family both get their hair cut on one trip to the barbershop. We have two adult family members with birthdays a few days apart, so we have always had a combined birthday party for them. When we bake meat loaves, we do a half-dozen at a time and store five away in the freezer.

Likewise, we make our own crunchy granola recipe in batches that are large enough to provide a month's supply.

We also try to do only one big grocery shopping each month and stock up large quantities of such consumables as paper towels, canned goods, bottled juices, etc. The rest of the month we try to get by with a quick stop at the grocery store on the way to or from somewhere else. And recently we've started shopping for full-case discounts as much as possible, first at local retail stores but also at our local wholesale outlet, the Price Club.

Our household bills get paid on one night a month (except for a few mid-month bills that can't wait). We save up household repairs and chores and devote a block of time to them every few weeks. We also practice a "contrarian" approach as much as possible. If we can do something like grocery shopping or taking a vacation when everyone else isn't, we avoid getting caught up in their negative synergies. (We almost never go grocery shopping on Saturdays, but we find Sunday afternoons to be an ideal time during the football season.) It doesn't take us much more time to proceed in this fashion. It is a matter of how we orient our thinking and what we look for in the way of solutions.

We also use the synergy principle in our wardrobe purchases. We often try to buy outfits that complement one another, so we can mix and match and make do with fewer items. But, in any case, we buy everything with an eye to how it will go with our other clothing and accessories. If necessary, we even take with us on shopping trips wardrobe items that we want to tie in with our new purchases.

As we have redecorated and furnished our house, we've taken pains to pick the right combination of paint colors, the right wallpaper, and compatible oriental rugs and upholstery fabrics. Likewise, we've been careful to select furniture items that will fit well into their designated spaces while also becoming an integral part of the entire room and the overall effect. Even the seasonal flowers in our garden are selected to complement the colors of our house.

Of course, we also use the synergy principle in our business. To illustrate: Because our professional staffers are in and out a lot, instead of assigning one desk exclusively to each person we sometimes use a system of flexi-desks. We also share the use of portable computers in addition to our freestanding computer equipment. This makes it possible for any staff person to be set up at any available desk. We also do the bulk of our data entry and report production at night, when moonlight staffers take over our desks, computers, etc. The system requires careful co-ordination and flexibility, but it works well. As a result, our overhead costs for office space and equipment, not to mention our production costs, are less than for many of our competitors.

Our strategic plan for the business has also utilized the synergy principle. Instead of specializing too narrowly in one area and becoming vulnerable to changes in the marketplace, we have diversified the business both in terms of the types of clients we can serve (health care and commercial/nonprofit organizations) and in terms of the kinds of assignments we can undertake.

Finally, the synergy principle is an essential tool in our consulting practice. When we are in the diagnostic phase of a project, we try to identify all of the relevant variables, using an analytical framework that we call the Synergy Model as a guide. We try to look at each part, not only in terms of how it performs but also how it fits into the larger whole. We look not only at the "hard" data (costs, prices, revenues, etc.) but at the "soft" data—the leadership (including personalities), the politics, administrative and decision-making processes, etc. A frequent problem with our clients is that different parts of their organizations, say finance and planning, may be working at cross-purposes. Sometimes the internal conflicts in an organization are so intense that "success" comes to be defined as defeating some other department, even when it detracts from the goals of the organization as a whole.

Likewise, when we develop strategies for our clients, we look for potential synergies: How to reduce conflicts and build a consensus for collective goals; how to make better use of existing resources; how to modify specific parts in such a way as to get better performance from the other parts, and the whole; and how to combine resources to achieve new synergies.

We also find that there are many opportunities for potentially synergistic affiliations between organizations, including joint ventures, sharing of capital equipment that two or more organizations need but only intermittently, sharing of research costs, joint marketing activities, even arrangements that will avoid an unnecessary duplication of effort.

With profit-making organizations, of course, the antitrust laws, for better or worse, restrict what can be done to take advantage of the opportunities for cooperation. We are eagerly awaiting (at this writing) the revisions that the Reagan administration plans to propose in our antiquated antitrust laws. In light of the emerging pattern of worldwide competition, the legal obstacles we frequently encounter when it comes to achieving synergy-based economic efficiencies are no longer justified.

## THE SYNERGY MODEL

Nothing illustrates better, we think, the richness and power of a synergy-oriented analysis than the comparison (and contrast) between other analytical approaches and our own Synergy Model.

The most sophisticated of the recent New Testaments on the art of management have been touting McKinsey & Co.'s "7–S" model as a mind-stretching tool. Distilled from an extensive research program on "excellent" companies, the 7–S framework (so named for the first letter in each of its seven component elements, or variables) is designed to provide specific guidelines for business success. The seven S's are:

1. *Strategy*: The plan or course of action by which resources are mobilized and used to achieve overarching goals;
2. *Structure*: The organization and distribution of functions, responsibilities, and authority;
3. *Systems*: Administrative and communications mechanisms, procedures, and processes;
4. *Staff*: Personnel resources;
5. *Style*: The *modus operandi* of the key personnel and the organization's internal "culture";
6. *Skills*: Distinctive capabilities of key personnel, or of the organization as a whole;
7. *Shared Values*: Guiding concepts and objectives that can inspire and motivate the members of an organization, sometimes referred to as superordinate goals.

The authors of the 7–S framework admit that it is a bit procrustean and oversimplifying; in order to provide potential users with memory hooks, the seven variables were cut and trimmed so they would all start with the letter S. Nevertheless, the model is an important step forward conceptually in that it broadens the traditional business school emphasis on "hard," objective, rational factors and allows for the often neglected "soft" factors that have to do with human motivations, human skills, and human relations.

Advocates of the 7–S framework emphasize that business success depends on each of these factors being fully and effectively utilized. As Richard Tanner Pascale and Anthony G. Athos put it in their book, *The Art of Japanese Management* (1981): "Addressing oneself to one or two of the S's is generally not sufficient."

American managers have generally tended to put more weight on the hard S's (Strategy, Structure, Systems), whereas Japanese managers put equal weight on the soft S's (Staff, Style, Skills, Shared Values). The employees' creed at Matsushita Electric, for example, includes this tribute to the synergy principle: "Progress and development can be realized only through the combined efforts and cooperation of each member of our Company. Each of us, therefore, shall keep this idea constantly in mind as we devote ourselves to the continuous improvement of our Company."

Thomas J. Peters and Robert H. Waterman, Jr., point out in their book, *In Search of Excellence* (1982), that the best American companies, like their Japanese counterparts, are successful in part because they too stress the soft S's. They are able to elicit extraordinary efforts from ordinary people and create corporate cultures in which everyone is both encouraged and motivated to contribute.

Equally important, all of the factors in the 7–S framework are treated as parts of an interdependent, mutually reinforcing network. As Pascale and Athos observe: "Unless there is an overall *fit* of all the managerial parts across time, there will be little sustained leverage and few results." In successful companies, they note, the "synch" among the seven S's is very good (i.e., there is high synergy). They illustrate the point with a diagram of the

# THE SEVEN-S MODEL

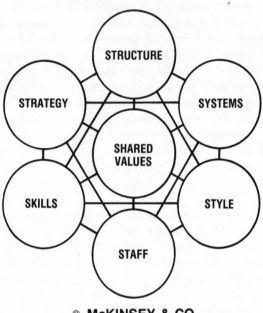

© McKINSEY & CO.

*Figure 3*

7–S's developed for McKinsey & Co., (figure 3) which also happens to be suggestive of another kind of synergistic system—a
molecule composed of seven interconnected atoms.

The virtue of the 7–S model is that it calls for a more balanced
"parts-in-wholes" approach. It is a teaching and analytical tool
that can help a manager think about the various parts of his or
her job and how the parts fit together. In essence, the 7–S model
provides a partial job description for top managers.

However, its proponents concede that it is not exhaustive; the
model leaves out many of the concrete technological, economic,
financial, and market factors that are also of vital importance to
business success.

For instance, the 7–S model does not instruct managers to

study closely what the competition is doing, something that even General Motors has forgotten to do from time to time, to its regret. Nor does it direct managers to pay close attention to government actions that might greatly affect the fortunes of their firms, ranging from new regulations to tax policies and manipulation of interest rates. Nor does it remind managers to keep a weather eye out for any new technology on the horizon that might either improve their company's products or render them obsolete. Indeed, many of the mundane problems relating to production costs, cash flow, debt service, inventory control, and a host of other factors are not even alluded to in the 7–S model.

The synergy principle teaches that, in addition to the 7–S's, there are many other factors which an entrepreneur or manager would be foolhardy to overlook. Some of these additional factors are common to all businesses and some depend on the context. In any event, these factors must also be included in any managerial framework.

Accordingly, Corning & Associates has developed a more encompassing analytical framework. Like the McKinsey model, our Synergy Model has an inner core of "soft," organizational, human factors, which we have oriented around organizational goals. However, we have also added an outer ring of more objective factors, both internal and external. Our two-ring molecule is illustrated in figure 4.

The first thing to be noted about the Synergy Model is that it is much more complicated than the 7–S framework, but so is the real world. Indeed, the Synergy Model explicitly directs attention to the relationship between "internal" factors and the many "external" factors that may also determine business success or failure. One can do all the "soft," core things right and yet still be clobbered by one or more of the factors in the outer ring of the Synergy Model.

In reality, these outer-ring factors drive many of the things organizations and their managers actually do on a day-to-day basis: financial performance evaluations, research and information gathering, planning processes, production planning and management, marketing activities, interactions of various kinds with financial institutions, government agencies, the press, private organizations, and much more.

## THE SYNERGY MODEL

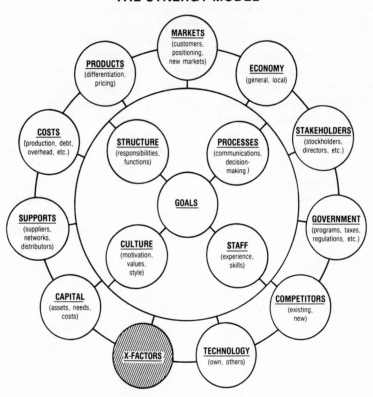

© **CORNING & ASSOCIATES**

*Figure 4*

To some extent, the factors that we have included in the Synergy Model are self-explanatory, if not obvious—though many a manager has been guilty of neglecting one or more of them. However, some words of explanation are necessary in a few cases.

Take the "stakeholders" in an organization. These may include the directors, the stockholders, the community in which it is located, the government, our society as a whole, and, not least, the employees. Likewise, the "marketplace" can include, among other things, the expectations, needs, and wants of one's customers, the informal rules of the game of the local business community, or various cultural norms and taboos. "Supports" refer to suppliers, subcontractors, "affiliates," joint venture partners, and the like.

"Capital" includes not only assets but also capital requirements and the cost of acquiring it (fees and interest charges). Finally, the catchall category labeled "x-factors" (for extras) allows for the fact that many businesses have to be concerned about problems which are idiosyncratic. Weather conditions are vitally important to ski resort operators, for instance, while farmers must also be concerned with soil conditions, animal diseases, and insect pests, among many other things.

For this reason, the Synergy Model provides only a general guideline, not a detailed roadmap; it is ultimately the responsibility of the individual business operator (and his or her consultants) to think through and specify exactly which factors are important in a given context, as well as how these factors interact with one another and how they affect the fortunes of the whole.

## FILLING IN THE BLANKS

A similar approach can also be used as a means for analyzing various specific problems, or goals, either business or personal. The distinctive feature of any synergy-oriented analysis is that it both stretches your thinking about a given problem and encourages you to organize the results in a systematic way. In order to facilitate this objective, we frequently employ two do-it-yourself thinking tools: diagrams that can be used to help identify and visualize the various component parts, factors, or elements of a problem as well as the interdependencies among them. Our approach represents a simplification of the technique that professional systems analysts use.

The first tool, which we call a "Systematizer" (figure 5) looks somewhat like the Synergy Model, and with good reason. The Systematizer is simply a more generalized version of the Synergy Model. In effect, the systematizer is a blank slate that allows each person to define his or her particular goal or problem and then fill in the blanks in each of the "factor circles" with what are

## SYSTEMATIZER

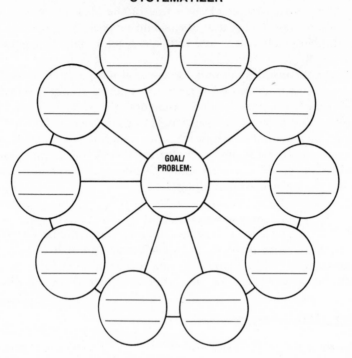

GOAL/
PROBLEM:

© CORNING & ASSOCIATES

*Figure 5*

identified as the most important factors. The number of factor circles will vary with the problem, of course, but we make use of a preprinted form with ten blank circles. In our experience, ten circles will suffice for most analyses, but there is always the option of adding more circles to the model, or even another ring.

It is important to stress that the results of this exercise cannot be any better than the problem solver's imagination, mental discipline and, not least, knowledge, and experience. It doesn't provide a substitute for hard mental labor, only a facilitator. This is one reason why such analyses are generally better done as team efforts.

The second tool we use is designed to help analyze the interdependencies and synergies (positive and negative) among the various factors identified in step one. It can aid in addressing the question of how the various factors interact—how they affect one another. We call this tool a "Factor Analyzer," and it involves a freehand diagraming exercise using two or more factor circles connected by arrows labeled with ( + ) or ( − ) to represent positive synergies, negative synergies, or both (figure 6).

In addition, we use dotted arrows in the Factor Analyzer to identify "feedback" relationships—interactions where the effects that one factor has on a second may induce a reciprocal effect on the first. Feedback can be either negative or positive. The classic example of a negative feedback system is a thermostat. When the heat put out by a furnace warms a room to a preset temperature, the thermostat sends a signal (negative feedback) instructing the furnace to shut down. Positive feedback, on the other hand, serves as encouragement to do more of the same.

When only two or three factors are involved, the analysis is fairly straightforward (A) and (B). When many factors and many interdependencies are analyzed simultaneously, the result can look something like (C). In any case, these diagrams are, again, only aids to systematic thinking. The precise nature and magnitude of the synergies, or feedback effects, must be determined separately.

Of course, diagraming exercises are not a substitute for the creativity that is essential to finding synergistic solutions to our problems. The good news, though, is that, like any other kind of creativity, high-synergy ideas tend to come to the prepared mind.

## PREPARED MINDS

One example, among the many we could have chosen, involves a recent client assignment. We were engaged by a hospital that had spent seven years debating a new strategic direction and that wanted our help in finding a way out of its deadlock. Due to changing demographics in the region where the hospital was located, its core area was not growing. However, a contiguous area was experiencing rapid growth, and many of the hospital's phy-

# FACTOR ANALYZER

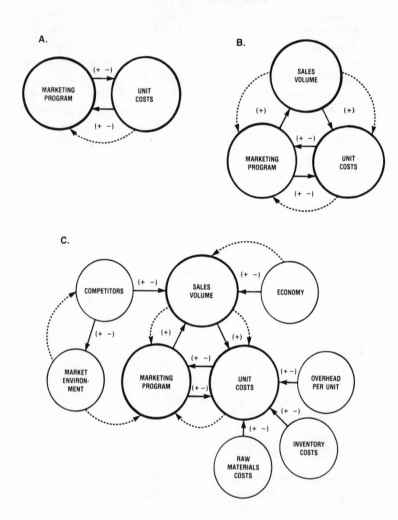

*Figure 6*

sicians were drawing an increasing number of their patients from this high-growth area.

The proposal that had been on the table for several years involved shutting down the old hospital, which was aging and in need of renovation anyway, and building a brand-new facility in the high-growth area. The problem was that many members of the board of directors, as well as the community, were opposed to shutting down and relocating the old hospital. What forced the issue, finally, was that a point had been reached where the old hospital was losing patients. Unless something was done soon, the hospital might eventually be forced out of business.

The solution we worked out with the hospital's top managers, and which the board finally approved unanimously (to its great surprise), involved a win-win strategy. Instead of either preserving (and renovating) the old hospital or building a new hospital, the decision was to do both. This was not a new idea, but it had previously been rejected as too risky, a course of action in which the organization could easily get overextended. The synergy-oriented idea that broke the logjam and made the two-hospital solution acceptable was the proposal that the new hospital be constructed and operated as a joint venture with one of the other hospitals in the region, which meant that the risk and responsibility could be shared.

## THE BOTTOM LINE

Both in the business world and in our personal lives, the bottom line is synergy—making all the parts, or factors, or facets come together into a harmonious, productive, profitable whole.

A major distinction between synergistic thinkers and the rest of us is that their "cognitive maps" are more complex and detailed. They think more deeply, more systematically, and more exhaustively about their problems, and they are acutely aware of interdependencies. They are not necessarily more cautious, only more thorough. Though they are wary of impulsive gambles, they are not afraid of innovation or of well-calculated risks. Indeed, they welcome synergy-producing innovations. They are, at heart, neither conservative nor liberal, neither capitalist nor socialist. Rather, they have clearly defined goals and a realistic sense of what it takes to achieve them. They are prepared to compete or cooperate as the need and opportunity may arise, and they fully appreciate the complicated interplay between synergy and dysergy.

This orientation, this strategic approach, is applicable across the board—to families, communities, businesses, the arts, the professions, sports, the military, government, and much more. But most important, it is applicable to the challenges we face as a nation and to the problems that were described in chapter 1. Let's turn, then, to the task of applying it.

# 8. Synergy (and Dysergy) in Families

The nuclear family has an ancient history and an important purpose, as we noted earlier. It was a key to the success of our early ancestors because it provided for a sharing of responsibility and a division of labor (thus increased effectiveness) in reproducing, feeding, training, and protecting the offspring. Indeed, it would have been impossible, literally, for our early ancestors to prosper as they did without the intense social cooperation that arose very early in our evolution.

Even today, the synergies associated with the nuclear family give it a clear advantage, by and large, over child-rearing in an institution or by a single parent. It matters a lot whether or not there are two parents in the home to share the burden of producing the next generation, as many a divorced parent and unwed mother will attest; child rearing is best played as a team sport.

## ECONOMIC ADVANTAGES

What are the synergies that modern families enjoy? Some are obvious, like the economic advantages in being able to share a household. By cohabiting, two or more people can generally save on the costs per person of housing, food, fuel, and the like. Indeed, a recent eleven-city study found that singles spend almost twice as much per person at the grocery store, on the average, as couples. A major reason is that most food packaging is designed for two or more portions. Another reason is that single persons buy more prepared foods, which are higher priced.

A division of labor and sharing of various household tasks (cooking, repairs, cleaning, gardening, finances, sewing, laundry, taxes, etc.) can also be synergistic—if everyone does their share. Cooking for two does not take twice as long as cooking for one, and one big load of laundry does not require twice as much time, energy, or hot water as do two small loads. There can even be synergies in sharing simple tasks like making the beds or washing dishes, where two people can generally do the job in less than half the time it takes one person alone.

No one should underestimate the potential savings. A 1978 study conducted by the Institute for Social Research estimated that the average family contributes to household upkeep the equivalent (at prevailing labor rates) of about $59,000 a year. Sometimes the savings from doing it yourself may be indirect, but not always. Take the case of the Twilleys, of Kensington, Maryland. One of the more than 1 million American families where both parents work but on different shifts, the Twilleys were able to save on costly outside care for their three young children by dividing up the parenting responsibilities. "It's ideal for child care," says Susan Twilley, "because we only pay for three hours of babysitting a day."

Families can also economize on the "hardware" associated with modern living. Two or more people are often able to share one automobile, telephone, TV, dishwasher, washing machine, refrigerator, stove, and so on. By the same token, when two family cars are insured on one policy or two family members are insured on one health policy, there are usually savings over the cost for two individuals. There are also some advantages in vacationing together. Double-occupancy rooms and shared car rentals mean savings over the cost for two individuals.

## SYNERGISTIC DECISIONS

Two heads may not always be better than one when it comes to job hunting, house searches, parenting decisions, career choices, and the like, but a key to the success of the 60 percent of all marriages that do *not* end in divorce is the fact that each spouse highly values the other's "inputs" and strongly prefers to do things by consensus. (Recall also the research cited earlier showing that groups, by and large, make better decisions than do individuals by themselves.) Indeed, a recent study conducted jointly by researchers at U.C. Berkeley and Stanford of more than two hundred small business owners in the Midwest found that 61 percent of the respondents relied most for business information and advice on their spouses, not their bankers, accountants, lawyers, trade publications, or business colleagues. This is especially true of the many mom-and-pop businesses in the U.S.—of which there are several million in all.

## EMOTIONAL SYNERGIES

Then there are the psychological and emotional advantages of a strong marriage (or a close friendship, for that matter). We are social animals. Our needs for companionship and emotional attachments are of primary importance, as shown by the depressing effects of loneliness and the elevated death rate among widowers. In fact, total life expectancy is lower for both single men and single women; married couples live longer. Not all marriages provide these benefits, obviously. But all our experience teaches that the best marriages are mutually satisfying. They are the ones where each partner is happy and where each fulfills the other's needs.

Spouses, relatives, and close friends can also be a source of mutual strength in coping with stressful or even life-threatening events. Studies of cancer victims indicate clearly that a "significant other" can play a critical role in determining whether or not a person is able to conquer the disease. In Curtis Bill Pepper's recent book about cancer patients, *We the Victors* (1984), one of the "victors" affirms: "It's having the caring and loving around you that helps you make it." It can truly be said in such situations that survival is a synergistic effect.

Less dramatic but equally important are the innumerable ways in which supportive family members can encourage and support one another when it comes to meeting challenges and coping with the problems of living. Most of us can think of examples from our own daily lives.

By the same token, there is positive synergy when a prospective father plays an active, supportive role in the childbirth process, as in "natural childbirth." Testimony from a generation of couples who have broken with the older tradition of excluding the male from the birthing process indicates that, in general, both partners are rewarded by sharing the experience. It also brings them closer together.

## SUBTLE SYNERGIES

There are also many more subtle advantages to family life. It has been said that the art of entertaining consists of knowing how to juggle at least two things at all times, and a dinner party tends to go more smoothly when two people can divide up and share the various tasks, from conversation to pouring the wine. Likewise, when each partner is plugged into a different information "grapevine," both may benefit from what each one of them learns. On long trips, it is usually advantageous to have two drivers in the car, so that the driving responsibility can be shared. Equally important, when there are young children in the car one parent can attend to the children's needs while the other does the driving.

When a family is "extended," meaning that there is a close-knit relationship among a number of relatives, the kinds of synergies mentioned above can be augmented. Large families can provide a safety net for one another and can spread the burden of helping individual members in times of need. They may also collaborate directly in various activities, from real estate investments to family business ventures. They may provide networks of information for each other. They may exchange hand-me-down children's clothes, toys, and furnishings. With the high cost of housing, they may even share living arrangements; a significant recent trend has been for young families to move back in with their parents.

## TWO-CAREER SYNERGIES

Today, of course, the traditional division of labor, with the male serving as the breadwinner, no longer applies to some 65 percent of all families. There are currently some 18 million mothers who also hold down jobs, as well as many more millions of women in childless two-career households. Accordingly, many aspects of family life, from the sending of Christmas cards to sit-down meals, have suffered.

Yet this new pattern of family life has many compensating synergies. Income security is one of the most obvious. During the recent recession, two-income families suffered much less income loss due to unemployment, on the average. The chances of both spouses losing their jobs were far less than for the bread-winner in a one-income family.

Two incomes not only provide a higher standard of living for the family as a whole but they may open up career choices and opportunities that would not otherwise be possible. Many wives have helped put their husbands through school (and vice versa) for the ultimate benefit of the family as a whole. By the same token, a wife can risk starting a business of her own if her husband's income is secure. In effect, he can subsidize some of her start-up costs. If a new mother wants to spend more time at home while her child is still of preschool age, she can switch from full- to part-time work, or to a less demanding career track. Or, a couple may even want to arrange for job sharing, with both partners working less than full time in order to enjoy more home life.

There may also be psychological synergies in a two-career family. Many women aver that having a career makes them better wives and homemakers. Holding down a job enhances their feelings of self-worth and their attitudes toward the homemaker role. Often too, having a career of their own enables them to relate more closely to their husbands' work. A major survey of the attitudes of working mothers versus stay-at-homes and career women without children found that, by a substantial margin, the women who had both children and a career were happiest with their lives; the two roles together provided satisfactions that each alone could not.

## NEGATIVE SYNERGY

Of course there can also be negative synergies in a two-career family. Divergent career demands may create difficult choices and unsatisfactory solutions; what may be a very good move for one partner's career could be disastrous for the other's.

Parenting can be a full-time job in itself, and the problem of juggling a career and family may create intense time pressures (and psychological stresses). And, if everyone doesn't do their share of the housework, the inequities may become a cause of conflict. In a recent survey of women with families by *Redbook Magazine*, a large majority reported they did most of the housework. And a *Ladies Home Journal* poll of eighty-six thousand women identified as the greatest source of anger in their lives the lingering "tradition" of leaving the housework to mom. (Harmonious families, on the other hand, stress shared responsibility and "teamwork.")

Indeed, for every synergistic marriage there is at least one in which the predominant effect is dysergy, as the divorce statistics testify. As noted earlier, over 40 percent of all U.S. marriages end in divorce, and about 21 percent of the 31.5 million households with children are headed by a single parent.

Beyond that, many nominally intact families are actually engaged in internal warfare. It has been estimated that about 2 million children each year are victims of child abuse and that perhaps 10 million battered children are in serious need of outside help.

Wife abuse has also shown an alarming rise in recent years. It has been said, and with some reason, that "a marriage license is a hitting license." Though there are no reliable statistics on the subject, one suggestive study among college students in the Midwest produced the startling (and perhaps atypical) finding that there had been at least one violent quarrel among roughly one out of every five regularly dating couples. And polls have revealed that as many as one-third of American adults condone domestic violence.

Does all this dysergy matter? Does the evident turmoil in many American families make a difference? To be sure, many divorces may be preferable to continuing a destructive or exploitative marriage. (Domestic violence figures as a cause in about one-quarter of middle-class divorces.) But not all divorcing couples calculate the relative costs and benefits very well beforehand. The cost of a marriage, good or bad, comes before the fact of a divorce; the cost of a divorce comes after the fact.

## SOME OF THE COSTS

Thus behind the divorce statistics lie millions of serious personal traumas that can exact a heavy toll in terms of lives disrupted, work effectiveness and productivity lost, personal conflict, lawyer's fees, and even health problems. The family's standard of living also declines when one household splits in two, unless one or both partners quickly remarry.

The children of a divorce may also suffer in various ways. Some are economic. In the early 1980s, fully half of all divorced mothers in the U.S. were receiving only part or none of their mandated child support payments—a shocking statistic.

Other costs are emotional and psychological. Recent, careful studies of children who have been in the middle of a divorce reveal, according to Linda Bird Franke in *Growing Up Divorced*, that the damage can be greater than was previously believed—not always but in many, many cases. One side effect for a child caught in a wrenching divorce can be a loss of self-confidence and a weakening of personal motivation and a sense of direction. School grades may suffer. The child may drop out of various activities and become withdrawn. Some 7 million "latch-key" children come home to an empty house after school each day. Self-destructive behavior patterns and difficulties with various personal relationships are common. And later on, as teenagers, these children may join the alienated, drug-using, "punk" subculture.

The long-term consequences of the recent divorce epidemic have yet to be assessed, but some preliminary shorter-range findings suggest that the effects are more severe for boys than for girls. For reasons that are not well understood, girls seem to have better recuperative powers.

## POSITIVE SYNERGIES

In contrast, there is good evidence that a synergistic marriage and family life have positive effects for all concerned, including especially the children. The life histories of outstanding people have, with rare exceptions, identified a strong, close family as a major contributing factor. Likewise, the remarkable success of Jewish Americans as an ethnic group has been attributed, in part, to their strong family traditions.

The same applies to Italian-Americans, who have recently "emerged" as leaders in many areas of our society. If there is a single thread that runs through the culture of these people, it is the strong propensity for families to stick together and support each other. "A sense of respect and loyalty, a respect for family members, the cohesiveness of the family—I think of these values as fundamental to our interactions with other people," observed Aileen Riotto Sirey, a psychotherapist and president of a national organization of Italian-American women, in a *New York Times* article by Stephen Hall.

In the same article, Governor Mario Cuomo of New York, who applies the notion of family to the larger community that he currently serves, describes to Hall how his family roots affect his attitude toward his job: "With us, it's going from small family to big family, the state of New York. Everything I do revolves around the notion of sharing benefits and burdens in the community. And that's family."

## DYSERGIES

On the other side of the coin, strong family bonds may sometimes work to the detriment of the community. An extreme example is the Mafia, whose "families" (both biological and honorific) are responsible for a large share of the $25 billion a year that the Justice Department estimates as the annual "take" by organized crime from gambling, loansharking, hijacking, prostitution, drugs, and the like. Indeed, it has been estimated that 80 percent of the heroin entering this country comes from Sicilian processing labs under Mafia control, while most of the cocaine brought into the U.S. is said to be controlled by a handful of tight-knit Colombian families.

The destructive consequences of this illicit activity are incalculable. As former Secretary of Health, Education and Welfare Joseph Califano points out in the *New York Times*: "[Heroin] holds users in a tenacious grip of physical dependence. Heroin addiction spreads through urban areas like a malignant cancer. . . . No other drug has demonstrated the same capacity to rip up a neighborhood, and with it the pride and aspirations of the people who live there."

## FAMILY BUSINESSES

As one might expect, the combination of family and business sometimes produces positive synergy—along with positive effects on the bottom line—and sometimes not. In the annals of business history, there are many examples of families that have provided effective leadership for family-owned businesses over many generations. Some are famous, like the Rothschilds, the Du Ponts, the Hearsts, and the Heinzes. Others are more obscure—the many thousands of multigeneration farm families, the multitude of third-generation neighborhood businesses, the family-owned wineries, the skilled craftsmen who pass the business on from father to son. Indeed, sometimes the family-business nexus is institutionalized, as in the close-knit Hutterite and Amish colonies.

On the other hand, family discord, or even power struggles, have ruined more than one business. A case in point is Superior Oil, where family feuding so weakened the company that it became vulnerable to a takeover bid by Mobil Oil. Similarly, the heirs of Omaha frozen-dinner pioneer C. A. Swanson were so busy battling one another that they allowed the company to decline to the point where the family was forced to sell out to the Campbell Soup Company.

## FAMILIES AND COMPETITION

What about competition in families? Granted that the very basis of family life is cooperation, nevertheless, competition is a major subplot. For starters there is competition (tacit or otherwise) for mates. And many a marriage has been threatened, or destroyed, by competition from another woman, or man. There may be more or less explicit competition between families, ranging from innocuous efforts to "keep up with the Joneses" to the sometimes bloody competition between "clans," or Mafia "families." The Kennedys were at one time intensely competitive with the Lodges; at various times the Rockefellers, Du Ponts, Roosevelts, Fords, and other prominent families have felt the sting of competition with one another; and, mythology aside, there was a real-life family feud between the Hatfields and the McCoys.

There may also be professional competition between husbands and wives; professional jealousies have been a factor in many a divorce, even though such feelings may be short sighted and possibly self-defeating.

Then there is sibling rivalry, the apparently inescapable dynamic, symbolized by the biblical story of Cain and Abel, that can be mitigated but probably never eliminated completely. Experienced families know that raising two children is considerably more than twice as hard as raising one; it's a classic example of negative synergy. Yet in strong families sibling rivalry is subordinated to family loyalties. (Much depends on how the parents handle it, according to the child psychologists, and on how well the parents do in providing a model of family solidarity and cooperation.)

AN OLYMPIC SYMBOL

A symbol, perhaps, of family synergy can be found in the recent winter Olympics. What are the odds that two of your children will become Olympic medal-winners? Considerably better than average if you raise a dedicated brother-and-sister figure-skating pair like Kitty and Peter Carruthers. Peter summed it up to a reporter for the *New York Times*: "We're in business together. We fight. We argue. But when you're real close to somebody, you know you have to come back and work with each other. I think that is what love is all about. She understands me; I understand her. I don't think anyone else could tolerate me."

In sum, the basis of a synergistic family is, quite simply, cooperation and *equity*—a set of relationships in which the members are doing their part and getting their share of the benefits in return. Close families tend to revolve around a sense of common purpose, mutual support, and respect for each member's needs. You must pay your dues to the family (in various ways), but in the long run you will get back more than you paid in. That's synergy.

# 9. Synergy in Communities

There is no law of nature dictating that we should live together in villages, towns, and cities. Yet we do. George Murdoch, the prominent anthropologist who directed an exhaustive survey of some two hundred fifty human cultures, drew this conclusion in *A Modern Introduction to the Family*: "The community and the nuclear family are the only social groups that are genuinely universal. They occur in every known society."

How come? Why is it that we are such a communal species? The answer, of course, is synergy. Only the functional advantages—the synergies—can explain it, and these synergies, it turns out, are many.

## ORIGIN OF COMMUNITIES

Some synergies go back to the very roots of civilization. More than three hundred thousand years ago at places like Torralba in Spain, Terra Amata on what is now the French Riviera, Tatzhikstan in Central Asia, and Choukoutien in China, large numbers of protohuman hunters camped together for several weeks or months each year while they combined forces to pursue large herds of migrating game animals. Sometimes the animals were driven into gullies where they could be killed en masse. Sometimes fire was used to drive the animals over cliffs. And sometimes they were stalked in ones and twos by organized hunting parties. In any case, food procurement was a "communal" activity, at least part of the time.

Buried remains found at these and other sites also suggest the beginnings of a larger division and sharing of labor for such activities as shelter building, food preparation, and toolmaking. There is even evidence of communal rituals involving the use of ochre as a body paint.

Beyond that, we can surmise that these prehistoric communities (probably several related families) benefited from being able to share vitally important information about their environment; they were also able to imitate and thus quickly spread new inventions or skills; and they exchanged various artifacts and tools among themselves. Equally important, these primordial communities were able to protect themselves and their favored hunting sites from various animal and human competitors. Collective security was doubtless a major unifying factor back then, just as it is today.

More synergies were added to communal living by the permanent villages that almost everywhere provided a hub for the earliest agricultural settlements. For one thing, the villagers shared in the protection and use of common water and fuel supplies and, most likely, a communal system for waste removal. The village also served as a marketplace for an expanded division of labor. Besides the farmers and herdsmen, there were craftsmen of various kinds and, sometimes, full-time soldiers, priests, and headmen. Often too, these settlements became "central places" in a larger trade network that gave each village access to vital raw materials, to finished products that could not be made locally, and to markets for the villagers' surplus produce.

## AGGLOMERATION EFFECTS

When the populations and the trading networks of these emergent villages reached a sufficient size, they began to experience what economists call "agglomeration effects"—a critical mass of people, resources, and economic activities. Only when there is a large enough market for various goods and services does a full-blown division of labor make sense; as Adam Smith first pointed out, the size of the market sets an upper limit on any potential economies of scale. At the same time, the specialization of roles that occurs in a more complex economy depends on having a large enough labor pool.

Equally important, as the division of labor becomes more complex, it becomes increasingly dependent on a supporting network of people who can provide raw materials, component parts, transportation, and other services. Among other things, a full-time potter needs to have a reliable supply of potting clays, a water supply, a dependable source of fuel for his kiln, a means for getting his products to market, and, preferably, a generalized medium of exchange such as money to facilitate economic exchanges.

The "magic number" for such agglomeration effects, based on the evidence amassed by various anthropologists, seems to be about five hundred people. This is about the average size of the autonomous agricultural villages that have survived to modern times.

## ECONOMIC SYMBIOSIS

Thus economic development is a symbiotic process involving the resources and capabilities of the community as a whole. One reason why success breeds success, economically, is that new breakthroughs depend upon those that came before and upon resources and skills that only a large, successful community possesses.

Furthermore, a growing community tends to attract more growth, so long as the means are there to sustain it. Historically, most large cities began life as marketplaces, trade depots, fortresses, or all three. However, their further growth over the course of time has been sustained primarily by in-migration rather than by internal population increases. The cities have been magnets, partly because they have offered security, partly because they have been the dynamic centers of economic growth, but also because they have been the incubators of civilization; the primitive societies with the richest cultures, anthropologists have found, also tend to be the ones whose populations are the largest and most closely knit. As the master urban planner James Rouse puts it: "Cities are where the action is. Without them we would have none of the things we associate with a modern society. No arts, no education, no culture, no commerce."

## ARE CITIES COMMUNITIES?

Can we really call the dense masses of humans who inhabit modern cities "communities"? Yes and no.

In reality, the modern metropolis is at once an inclusive community for some purposes and a conglomeration of many smaller communities for many other purposes. Homeless drifters, the prisoners in the city jail, and penthouse dwellers alike benefit from public services such as fire protection and basic utilities. And, despite recent calls for a greater private-sector role in providing public services, it is generally much less expensive for government (or a regulated private monopoly like our public utility companies) to provide these services on a communitywide basis. Up to a point, there are economies of scale.

Consider the case of Runaway Point, an unincorporated subdivision just outside of Savannah, Georgia. In Savannah, monthly garbage collection fees charged by the city were running $2.50 a month a couple of years ago. In Runaway Point, where various private companies do the job, the monthly fees averaged about $12.00. When the city manager of Savannah, Arthur Mendonsa, was asked if it might be better to let private companies take over the city's services, he replied: "That's garbage. Only if a city is very poorly run would it save money." Indeed, the advantages of citywide services are such that Runaway Point has been seeking annexation (so far unsuccessfully). It is part of what seems to be a national trend toward regional integration.

Or consider the situation in New York City, where private sanitation companies cart off commercial garbage and trash. In one fourteen-block area of midtown Manhattan, it has been determined that fourteen different sanitation companies are providing removal services. Not only is this system inefficient and more costly for everyone but the frequent presence of fourteen different sanitation trucks in the area adds to an already monumental traffic problem.

## GOVERNMENT'S ROLE

George Santayana's warning that "those who cannot remember the past are condemned to repeat it" is nowhere more applicable than to our attitude toward government (or quasi-government) services. Most of the things government does nowadays for the community "as a whole," from fighting fires to mass transit, have at one time or another been provided by freely competing private companies. It has generally been the case in this country that only when voluntary or private approaches have proven unsatisfactory does government take over a public service.

To be sure, an inept, inefficient government can be as bad as, or worse than, the competitive free-for-all of private enterprise. When it comes to providing public services, exorbitant wage scales, incompetent management, or indifferent, sloppy work on the part of civil servants can easily nullify any potential economies of scale, or any advantages of centralized organization. (Of course, private enterprise can suffer from these problems too.) In fact, local governments frequently do find it desirable for one reason or another to bid out various jobs, from streetlight maintenance to road construction, repairs of city-owned vehicles, or the upkeep of city parks. And with government at all levels currently looking for ways to cut costs, there is a growing trend toward "privatizing" even more public services these days, where money can be saved. Nevertheless, the potential for synergy is there, regardless of who does the job.

Our mutual dependence on such communitywide synergies is dramatized when one of them fails. The great New York City power blackout of 1977 was a horrifying example. The consequences included a night of fear, chaos, and rampant crime, numerous deaths and injuries, 3,000 arrests, roughly $250 million in property losses, an equal amount of "excess" expenses incurred by the city, plus some $50 million in uncompensated wage losses in the private sector and $100 million for new utility equipment.

The big blackout was a deeply disruptive event, but there have also been countless smaller breakdowns of synergy—police strikes, transit strikes, sanitation strikes, floods, epidemics, water shortages, blizzards, you name it. Sometimes almost everyone in the community is adversely affected. At other times, only a part of the community suffers. Sometimes the consequences are mild—some inconvenience perhaps. At other times, tens or hundreds of thousands may die.

## AGGREGATING DEMAND

Of course, public services are not the only forms of communal synergy. Cities also "aggregate demand," as the economists put it, for various cost-shared private services, from taxicabs to grand opera. Because of their tax bases, cities can also support cultural institutions such as zoos and art museums, amenities that few small towns can afford.

Cities as corporate entities also initiate many actions that affect the community as a whole, from lobbying for state or federal aid to building subways and promoting business development. Indeed, as the national economic pie has begun to shrink, towns, cities, states, and even entire regions of the country have found it necessary to engage in sometimes ferocious competition with one another.

Thus Boston did battle with New York to become the home port for an aircraft carrier and its support ships, and so did Seattle and Everett, Washington. In Syracuse, New York, 248 local companies cooperated in pledging $3.2 million for a four-year campaign to woo high-tech companies away from other areas in the Northeast and the Sun Belt. Almost every major city, in fact, has an office and a budget for business development.

Likewise, at the state level, South Dakota (to cite one example) has been systematically raiding Minnesota companies with lucrative relocation offers, and more than sixty have moved across state lines during the past few years. (One reporter characterized the competition as "another war between the states.") At least 36 states also have high-tech promotion programs.

## THE GOLDEN CORRIDOR

Even at the regional level, the Council for Northeast Economic Action has launched a bold effort to promote the revival of what it calls America's Golden Corridor. "Does the Sunbelt have all the good news?" asks the council in a recent advertising supplement. "Fifty-four million Northeasterners ... don't think so."

Is the Golden Corridor really a "community"? The Council's response: "There is the recognition that the time has come to meet head-on the common problems surrounding infrastructure, taxation, the retraining of the workforce, and the balance of the public and private sectors. That recognition has already released tremendous energies and sparked considerable reform. Far more than geography, it is welding the Golden Corridor into a region."

## INFORMAL COMMUNITIES

Beyond such communitywide synergies, most large urban areas these days embrace a myriad of smaller communities. Some are tacit and informal. There are the neighbors who keep an eye on one another's homes or water the plants and feed the cat when someone is out of town. (According to police studies, neighborhoods where the residents look out for one another have significantly lower crime rates.)

There are also the young singles who start their careers in the big city by sharing an apartment, which may provide both economic and social benefits. The "regulars" at a neighborhood bar may provide companionship, exchange information, and sometimes help one another out. In addition, there are tens of thousands of baby-sitting pools, cheese-buying clubs, and ad hoc committees to "save our park" or badger the city into installing a stop sign at the corner. Even the street people and drug addicts may form social networks, and so, unfortunately, do street gangs and organized crime syndicates.

## CRIME PATROLS

One of the most publicized of these grass-roots communal activities has been the neighborhood crime patrols. These consist of citizens who walk their own neighborhoods in teams of two or more during the high-crime hours, mainly to provide extra sets of eyes and ears for the police department. There are now perhaps ten thousand crime patrols in all, and New York City alone is reported to have some two hundred fifty of them.

When these patrols are well organized and make their presence felt, the synergy can be dramatic. In the early 1980s, the Community Safety Patrol teams in Oakland, California, wore yellow jackets and carried walkie-talkies, which made them visible and kept them in touch with a home base (and the police if needed) at all times. The result was a significant reduction in street crime in the neighborhoods that were being patrolled regularly. One high-crime precinct in Oakland dropped from second to fifth place.

Equally important, the presence of the crime patrol serves to lessen fears and increase the residents' sense of security. Now, when an elderly lady needs to go out to the drugstore at night, she can arrange for an escort.

The rewards for the members of these crime patrols are companionship, satisfaction from the contribution they are making to the community, and the recognition and status that they acquire in their neighborhoods.

A commercial variation on this theme is the crime-fighting arrangement that the parent company for the all-night 7-Eleven stores has worked out with cab companies in a number of cities. At 3 A.M., a 7-Eleven clerk, working alone, can be very vulnerable. And so can a cab driver waiting at a dark street corner for his next fare. An alternative is to let the cabbies wait at the 7-Eleven stores, where they and the clerks can keep an eye on each other. The drivers also get a warm, well-lighted place to wait, complete with a bathroom and hot beverages, while the store clerks have the benefit of being, in effect, in touch with the police via the driver's dispatcher. As a 7-Eleven company spokesman put it, few late-night clerks need to be convinced that the plan is a good idea.

## FORMAL ORGANIZATIONS

Modern cities are also thickly planted with formal community organizations—mini-communities for almost every imaginable purpose. And in each case these organizations produce synergistic effects that would not otherwise be attainable.

Take a city like Baltimore, Maryland, for instance, with a population of about 780,000. Baltimore has no less than 100 neighborhood associations that do everything from mounting local festivals to lobbying for better garbage removal service. There are also sixteen ethnic organizations that sponsor various activities, along with some 15,000 business firms, 700 churches, 125 labor organizations, and several hundred community organizations. These include such national social/service organizations as the Shriners, Kiwanis, Knights of Columbus, Masons, and Veterans of Foreign Wars.

In addition, Baltimore, like most other large cities, has a plethora of special-purpose organizations: Democratic and Republican party clubhouses, social clubs, chess clubs, yacht clubs, computer clubs, tennis clubs, the Legal Aid Society, senior centers, Boy Scouts, Girl Scouts, parent-teacher associations, Little League baseball, and much more. Most impressive, perhaps, has been the Greater Baltimore Committee, a civic group of nine hundred local businessmen who have provided the leadership for Baltimore's remarkable urban revival over the past twenty-five years, including the construction of the world-renowned commercial/social/tourist center, Harborplace.

Baltimore also has a rich cultural life, which is heavily dependent on organized community support. There are three city-wide social events each year, including the city fair, the state fair, and the Preakness Festival Week. There is a symphony orchestra, a ballet company, an opera company, three theater groups, nine museums and art galleries, libraries, an active historical society, a zoo, and the striking new National Aquarium.

The three professional sports teams that until recently called Baltimore home (one moved away very suddenly)—are also dependent on organized local support of various kinds, as are the numerous high school, college, and community athletic teams.

Higher education also thrives in Maryland. There are no less than 42 colleges and universities in the Baltimore area, each a community in itself, including Johns Hopkins University, the University of Maryland, the Peabody Conservatory of Music, and the Naval Academy at Annapolis.

Thus, contrary to sociologist David Riesmann's image of the "lonely crowd," Baltimore is a city in which most of the residents belong to one or more mini- or micro-communities. And Baltimore is hardly unique.

## NONPROFIT ORGANIZATIONS

Nationwide, there are some 800,000 nonprofit organizations that depend on roughly 80 million volunteers each year. Church membership in this country is conservatively estimated to be 140 million, of whom perhaps one-half are actively involved. And one partial listing of national associations and societies contains 1,120 names. At the front end of the alphabet there are organizations such as the Aaron Burr Association (500 members), the Air Force Sergeants Association (128,000), and the American Federation of Astrologers (4,000). And, at the tail end, there is Zero Population Growth (10,000), the Ziegfield Club (300), and the American Society of Zoologists (4,500).

## COOPERATIVES

At least 71 million Americans also belong to cooperatives. Credit unions alone have over 50 million members. Farmers' coops (tractor pools, grain elevators, even cooperatively owned dairies) count some 1.5 million members. Health care cooperatives include about 6 million people. Electricity cooperatives have 7 million members. And there are an estimated 10,000 food cooperatives, ranging from neighborhood cheese clubs to entire grocery store chains.

Consumer oil cooperatives, for example, are typically able to negotiate a blanket rate reduction for their members ranging from 10 to 20 cents a gallon below the retail price. The synergy is mutual, however. The advantage to the dealer is that a consumer cooperative provides an efficient way to gain access to (and communicate with) a large number of customers who are concentrated in one area.

## SOCIAL ACTION

Then there are the social action organizations, many of which have local chapters around the country. MADD (Mothers Against Drunk Drivers), NOW (National Organization for Women), PUSH (People United to Serve Humanity), and PECOS (Parents for Enforcement of Court-Ordered Support) are only a few of the recent entries on a long honor roll of collective efforts to deal with consumer issues, environmental problems, tenants' rights, nuclear war, teenage drug abuse, animal abuse, utility bills, and many more.

The synergies associated with such organized, collective efforts have been demonstrated time and again. An organization can pool individual resources, financial and otherwise, and use these resources to retain skilled leadership, engage in research, mount publicity campaigns, undertake lobbying efforts, gain media exposure, recruit additional supporters, and do a host of other things that individuals alone cannot do as well. Indeed, even so visible a consumer activist as Ralph Nader has found that organization is an essential tool. He is credited with having launched or inspired some 120 different consumer groups, ranging from the Public Interest Research Groups that dot college campuses in 23 states to lobbying groups with names such as the Center for Auto Safety, the Health Research Group, and Congress Watch.

## LATENT COMMUNITIES

Finally, many of our towns and cities contain what might be called "latent communities"—a sense of identification and a predisposition to provide mutual aid or collective effort when the need arises. When a family's house burns down, the neighbors may take them in and in various ways help them to cope with the initial crisis. When one block of homes is devastated in a tornado, neighbors on other blocks, as well as various community organizations, may provide help for the survivors.

Even more impressive are the occasions when the community as a whole mobilizes to meet an emergency. In what the residents of Fort Wayne, Indiana, remember as "the flood of 1982," practically the entire city pitched in to make sandbags, build dikes, help flooded-out victims, set up emergency shelters, and make food for workers and victims alike. Most important, perhaps, was the role of the high schools, which organized a heroic teacher-student effort. More than half the city's 12,000 students and 2,000 school personnel were involved. Seventy-four school buses drove 10,500 miles carrying 41,000 volunteer workers on 658 trips, while 100 food-service personnel worked 400 hours to supply emergency food. "The kids of Fort Wayne saved the city," says the mayor. "There is no doubt about it."

If communities display many different kinds of positive synergy, they may also be breeding grounds for negative synergy.

As urbanist Edward Boorstein notes, "For a city to work well, many things have to mesh—its economy, population, housing, transportation system, schools, hospitals, and finances." Unfortunately, many cities these days do not work very well.

Let's start by considering the issue of size. Do large cities necessarily offer greater synergies than smaller ones? Is bigger necessarily better? The answer, most students of urban life seem to agree, is no. Despite the fact that there are seventy-two cities in the United States with populations of more than 200,000, the "optimum" size seems to be smaller, somewhere between 50,000 and 200,000.

When a city gets too large, many of the advantages of community life may actually diminish. In effect, an ill-defined threshold may be crossed, beyond which more growth may produce negative synergies of various kinds. Just as our stereotypes suggest, big cities seem to be more violent, congested, unhealthy, and anomic places to live, as well as being less efficient at providing recreation, education, and other public services.

## SOME EVIDENCE

Consider some of the evidence compiled by Kirkpatrick Sale in his illuminating book, *Human Scale* (1982):

*Crime.* Crime rates increase generally with increasing population size, but there is a sharp jump when a city gets larger than 100,000. In one recent year, cities of 25,000 to 50,000 reported about 340 violent crimes per 100,000 people, whereas cities of more than 250,000 reported about 1,160 per 100,000.

Of course, some large cities do better than others, most notably cities in other countries. In 1982, the death rate for violent crimes in Chicago was more than three times as high as the rate in Montreal, Canada, and similar contrasts can be made between other large American and Canadian cities.

*Health.* While infant mortality rates are slightly better in large urban areas where the most sophisticated medical technology tends to be concentrated, the death rates for cancer, heart disease, and diabetes, and the incidence of ulcers, alcoholism, and drug addiction, among others, is significantly higher in large cities.

*Mental Health.* Schizophrenia, acute paranoia, suicide rates, and rates of admission to mental hospitals all are higher in larger metropolitan areas. Some sociologists blame the differences on a tendency for large cities to attract people with mental problems. That's debatable, and the fact remains that large cities haves proportionately more cases.

*Education.* Public education expenditures per pupil run higher in larger cities and with less favorable results, as measured by standardized tests, school dropout rates, and the like.

*Recreation.* It has been shown that the public recreation facilities—parks, pools, playing fields, etc.—are generally better maintained, safer to use, and easier to get to in smaller cities than in large ones.

*Economic well-being.* Big cities have not had a notably better record in the past few years with regard to inflation and recession. If anything, the big cities have been harder hit than elsewhere. A recent *New York Times* survey of the eighteen largest U.S. cities detected a significant "decline" in the quality of life due to economic stresses. Indeed, the cost of such basic essentials as housing, food, and utilities is substantially higher in our large cities than in other parts of the country. And, contrary to the conventional wisdom, smaller cities are able to provide public services at a much lower cost per capita than large cities. Some calculations were prepared for a 1975 study by the Urban Institute:

*Table One*

| The Cost of Public Services | |
| --- | --- |
| City Size | Per Capita Expenses |
| 50,000–100,000 | $229 |
| 100,000–200,000 | $280 |
| 500,000–1 million | $426 |
| more than 1 million | $681 |

Copyright 1975 by The Urban Institute

*Political participation.* One of the most consistent findings by political scientists is that people in large cities are less likely to participate directly in city affairs and feel less able as individuals to influence city hall than the residents of smaller ones.

*Personal satisfaction.* Perhaps the most telling data on our big cities relate to how people feel about living in them. One major survey published in the journal *Demography* in 1975 reported the following breakdown of residential preferences:

### Table Two

| Residential Preferences | |
|---|---|
| Community Size | Preference (percent) |
| over 500,000 | 9 |
| 50,000–500,000 | 16 |
| 10,000–50,000 | 22 |
| under 10,000 | 19 |
| Rural areas | 33 |

*Source: Based on data from a National Opinion Research Center Amalgam Survey.*

## DISECONOMIES OF SCALE

Huge cities are a relatively recent phenomenon. They are a product (mostly) of the Industrial Revolution, and their growth was powered by factors other than efficiency in delivering public services, or the quality of life. As a result, many cities are unmanageable monstrosities. This is why the developers of the New Towns in Europe and of such instant communities in this country as Reston, Virginia, and Columbia, Maryland, have pointedly kept them small, by modern-day standards. (Reston has about 35,000 residents and Columbia has 43,000.) This is also one reason, among many others, why there has been a reversal over the past thirty years of the historic U.S. trend toward larger cities.

Some of the other codetermining reasons for the shift include: new transportation and communications technologies (and infrastructures) that have permitted greater dispersion of industry without a corresponding increase in freight costs and travel times; the flight of white-collar workers to the suburbs after World War II; and the flight of industry to join the white collar workers in the suburbs when faced with disincentives like high rents, burdensome city taxes, ever-increasing urban congestion, escalating prices for city land, and rocketing costs for urban construction. It has been estimated that the cost of doing business in a large city these days runs 20 to 30 percent higher than elsewhere.

In fact, modern cities are rife with dysergy: noise pollution, air pollution, and people pollution that create personal stresses and contribute to health problems; disease viruses that are able to spread more quickly (and widely) in such densely populated areas; aging roads, sewers, and buildings that are much more costly to repair or replace because they are located in a crowded urban environment; masses of cars and trucks that add up to choking congestion, pollution, and heavy taxes to pay for the roads, streetlights, parking meters, traffic cops, traffic courts, etc.; and public parks that are overcrowded, littered, and very often dangerous—which defeats their very purpose.

## SOME EXAMPLES

Let's consider a few specific examples:
- The graffiti on, and in, New York City subways and buses. This "scourge," as Mayor Edward Koch calls it, cost the city about $3.4 million in cleanup expenses in 1982. It's an assault on both the pocketbooks and the sensibilities of most of the city's residents. And, to the discouraged visitors (or potential visitors) whose trips to New York are important to the city's economy, it conveys a sense of anarchy and menace to match the city's notorious crime statistics.
- "Wino Park" (officially People's Park) in San Francisco, a well-intentioned effort by the Glide Memorial Church to give some of the city's homeless alcoholics a safe haven where they could drink in peace in a downtown "pocket park." In fact, the park became a magnet for drug pushers, thieves, muggers, and hardened ex-convicts. Crime in the area greatly increased; unruly crowds, trash, and noise accumulated at the site; residents of the area were victimized; alcohol treatment program officials felt their efforts were being sabotaged; property owners felt their efforts to rehabilitate the neighborhood were being undermined; and the winos, instead of finding a haven, were unwittingly set up to become victims.

- Atlantic City, where legalized gambling was supposed to spark a rejuvenation in what was once an elegant seaside resort. Instead, the casinos have had the opposite effect. Since ground was broken for the first casino in 1977, the city has become ever seedier, its slums have expanded, its unemployment has remained high, and its local politics have degenerated into open racial hostility. Said one official: "We no longer have a community. We're a city of parking lots and casinos." This despite the fact that Atlantic City's nine huge casinos draw some twenty-seven million visitors a year, making it the nation's most popular tourist attraction. The reason for this paradox is that the casinos are oases. People are bused in, spend their money almost exclusively inside these self-contained Taj Mahals, and then are bused home. The wherewithal to build and support the casinos has also been trucked in from outside, while most of the 30,000 new jobs created by the casinos have gone to nonresidents. To top it off, the building of the casinos triggered feverish land speculation, which resulted in escalating prices, widespread dislocation of the poor, and further deterioration of the city's housing stock.
- Times Square, at once the entertainment heart of New York City and the epicenter of the nation, perhaps, for sleaze, smut, and urban decay. Says Mayor Koch: "We have the scum of the earth here." By one recent count, 42nd Street between Seventh and Eighth Avenues—sometimes referred to as the "meanest street in America"—boasted twenty-six sex emporia. It is a block on which pedestrians run a gauntlet of trash, panhandlers, drug pushers, addicts, and prostitutes, and it has defied innumerable campaigns over the past forty years to clean it up and rebuild the area. A major effort to do so is now underway, but, as one observer noted, a project of such magnitude has to move forward on many fronts at once; unless it gets to the roots of the problem, the sleaze will simply ooze into some contiguous area.
- Miami, the most crime-ridden city in America despite its relatively small size (350,000). Once the vacation and retirement capital of the East Coast, if not America, Miami has

been overwhelmed in recent years by the combined effects of (1) a decline in tourism (partly due to the effects of inflation and recession and partly due to competition from other parts of the country), (2) a wave of Central American immigrants, including the "Marielitos," that Fidel Castro dumped on this country back in 1980 (many of whom were hard-core criminals), and (3) criminal activities associated with the drug traffic (an estimated 70 percent of the cocaine and marijuana coming into the U.S. passes through South Florida).

## COMMUNITY DECLINE

Such dysergies are only small tumors, though, compared to the negative synergy that spreads through a community when its underlying economy declines.

Detroit, Michigan, can serve as an example. No city in America has more nearly typified our industrial dynamism and material progress as a nation, historically, and no city has been harder hit by the recent decline in our blue-collar, smokestack industries. The roots of Detroit's economic decay, however, go much deeper and much further back in time.

Some of the causes were part of the national trend described above. The decline began with the flight of the middle class to the suburbs after World War II, an out-migration that was heavily subsidized by various well-meaning government programs. As middle-class whites left Detroit—taking their jobs with them— poor blacks from the rural South and elsewhere moved in to replace them, and in time this population shift set up a vicious circle of negative synergies.

As the tax base began to shrink, the burden of welfare costs began to increase. The result was highter taxes for those who remained in Detroit, coupled with a deterioration of such vital public services as mass transit, the schools, sanitation, police, and fire protection. Housing also began to decline as an increasing number of vacancies were filled with poor blacks. As property values and rental income sagged, an increasing number of landlords began to neglect or even abandon their buildings, while the banks began to "redline" or quarantine decaying neighborhoods; loan money for the purchase or rehabilitation of buildings in redlined areas dried up.

## MURDER CITY

All this had the effect of driving more middle-class whites out of the city, along with more local industries. Incoming blacks found it increasingly difficult to get jobs. Welfare costs continued to climb. The tax base continued to decline. Crime rates shot up. (For a while Detroit was known as "murder city".) Racial tensions mounted. And in 1967, at the height of the racial troubles in this country, Detroit exploded. In a traumatic outburst of rioting that lasted for several days, whole areas of the city were "trashed" and/or burned. There were forty-three deaths and many more injuries.

Shocked by what had happened, various industry and civic leaders rallied behind a downtown renewal effort called "Renaissance Center," but this showcase of hotels, shopping, and recreation facilities did little for the economy and the damage from the riots far outweighed such positive actions. In fact, the riots accelerated the flight to the suburbs. Despite the influx of blacks, Detroit lost 155,000 residents in the 1960s and another 310,000 in the 1970s, along with an increasing number of local industries.

Some recent figures tell the story. Detroit is now 63 percent black, and more than 25 percent of the residents receive some form of public assistance. Unemployment probably exceeds the official figure that in the past few years has ranged from 15 to 20 percent. (Over 60 percent of those in the eighteen- to twenty-four-year-old age group are unemployed.)

All told, about 80 percent of the city's factory jobs have been lost, and during the 1970s the number of city employees declined by 25 percent. Some 50,000 housing units have also been totally lost. Of the remainder, about 30 percent are "deteriorated" and 60,000 do not meet the minimum standards for habitation. Property values in Detroit declined slightly during the 1970s and early 1980s, at a time when values in the rest of the three-county metropolitan area increased by 116 percent and the consumer price index increased by 130 percent. (In other words,

Detroit's property values actually declined by more than 50 percent in real terms.)

After touring Detroit a few years ago, a visiting journalist wrote in dismay that the city "may in a real sense be dead—the first dead large city in the nation." Although there has been some improvement since the recent recession, Mayor Coleman Young admits that "this city is fighting for its economic life."

## A POSITIVE MODEL

If Detroit provides a model of negative synergy, the city of Baltimore provides a model of what positive synergy can do. Baltimore too has had economic troubles and a shrinking population. Baltimore too experienced a middle-class flight to the suburbs and a shift in its racial composition. (By 1980, some 55 percent of the population was black.) Baltimore too had race riots in the latter 1960s, which left the city badly scarred. But for Baltimore the response was much different, and so was the result.

Baltimore is "an old pumpkin turned into a magnificent carriage," as *New York Times* reporter Roberta Reinhold put it. "The once moribund downtown hums with vitality, its renovated waterfront draws throngs every weekend, and its old ethnic neighborhoods, formerly the butt of derision, are now viewed as a source of cultural richness." Indeed, Baltimore is enveloped by regeneration and growth; it is often cited as a national model.

How did this stunning turnabout occur? To begin with, Baltimore had some natural advantages. Because it was a large city that dominated a small, middle-class state, it was in a good position to tap the ample economic and human resources of the rest of the state. It also had an excellent waterfront, however decrepit, that awaited only a bold vision of how it could be converted into a commercial, recreational, and tourist center which, in turn, could become a magnet for other business investments.

Equally important, Baltimore and its seaport were strategically located in the Northeast Corridor—within overnight freight delivery of 67 million people and 44 percent of the nation's industries. Moreover, Baltimore is 75 to 150 miles closer to the Midwest than any other East Coast port (which translates into

7 to 12 percent lower freight rates). Baltimore also had ready access to major transportation arteries: interstate highways, Conrail, AMTRAK, and a nearby airport.

Another of Baltimore's natural advantages was its large number of vacant, though solidly built, row houses that were ideally suited for urban homesteading—renovation by young, middle-class families using "sweat equity" and their own financial resources. By the same token, many of the city's older commercial buildings, being solidly built, were suitable for conversion to new uses.

The most important single ingredient, though, was leadership—in part by urban planner James Rouse, who mobilized the business community to support the renovation of the downtown area, including his grand plan for Harborplace, but also by the active, sustained commitment of local business leaders, including the 900-member Greater Baltimore Committee.

In addition, Baltimore has been blessed with a remarkably dedicated, hard-working, and effective mayor, William Donald Schaefer, who has been carrying the ball for the city with great energy and skill for more than sixteen years. Not only has the Schaefer administration been a model of fiscal integrity and sound management (the city's bonds are top rated), but the mayor himself has been the city's most aggressive and persuasive salesman, both with government agencies and private investors. *Quest* magazine has called Schaefer "the best mayor in America."

## IMPRESSIVE RESULTS

The results to date have been impressive. Revitalization of the downtown area began in the 1950s and is not done yet. It includes new high-rise office buildings, the conversion or refurbishing of many older buildings, new hotels and restaurants, a new World Trade Center, a new convention center, new museums, both new and renovated theaters, a new outdoor concert pavilion, a spanking new subway, and, of course, a transformed inner harbor whose glittering centerpiece is Harborplace.

Indeed, with its rich history and its many cultural and recreational facilities, Baltimore has become a major tourist attraction, which has also aided the local economy. (Harborplace alone boasts annual sales of over $60 million and more visitor traffic than Disney World.)

Nor has the city's infrastructure been neglected. The seaport has been modernized, the railroad station has been refurbished, the airport has been completely rebuilt, major improvements have been made in the city's key thoroughfares (including a new eight-lane tunnel under the harbor to reroute interstate traffic), while new electrical utility construction has ensured an ample supply of low-cost energy.

The total cost to date for the public sector alone has been put at more than $1.5 billion, of which about $300 million has come from Washington. (Thanks largely to Mayor Schaefer's efforts, Baltimore is third in the nation in winning federal discretionary money for urban renewal.) The rest has come from the state and the city and from donations by the business community. Of course, there have also been large investments by private developers and banks. Among other things, Baltimore provides a model of cooperation between the public and private sectors.

So successful has this revival been that Baltimore has experienced a significant business influx over the past ten years. Among the immigrants are such heavyweights as General Motors, Bethlehem Steel, Bank of America, Equitable Life, Control Data, and Hyatt Corporation.

## "SHOPSTEADING"

The rejuvenation of Baltimore's business environment has also been aided by the city's unique "shopsteading" program, through which numerous small businesses have been launched without recourse to the massive and expensive urban renewal projects of the 1950s and 1960s. The way it works is that derelict stores are sold for $100 to businessmen who are willing to salvage and refurbish them, with the added incentives of low-cost city financing to help get the job done and a city pledge to renovate sidewalks, streetlights, roadbeds, and so forth.

Another priority in the overall plan has been revival of the residential neighborhoods. As much as possible, this has been done by renovation rather than demolition, especially in some of the old ethnic sections. Not only was Baltimore the first to try urban homesteading but the city continues to lead the country, with over 6,500 restored homes on scores of city blocks as of 1980. In the process, the city has been careful to give equal weight to housing for the poor. The city itself took on the responsibility for renovating some 3,800 homes itself, 1,000 of which it has sold at low cost while the rest have been rented to low-income families. In addition, there has recently been a boom in new apartment and condominium construction, as more middle-class families are attracted back into the city.

To be sure, Baltimore has had its share of problems over the years. Crime rates are relatively high, and so is unemployment. Much more remains to be done to provide enough jobs and adequate housing. But the trend is in the right direction; the underlying economy has been steadily gaining strength (in the past five years, the city's tax base has increased by a remarkable 58 percent), and with it has come a revival of confidence and a revitalization of community life. As Equitable's president, John B. Carter, observes: "The place has a great feeling."

## THE EXPLANATION

No one factor was responsible for this impressive achievement. It was a synergistic phenomenon—a compound of vision, new ideas, skillful leadership, sound management, active support by the business community, a favorable business environment that has been marketed aggressively, full exploitation of the available federal assistance, major investments by the state and the city, targeted aid to small businesses, a concerted effort to revitalize residential neighborhoods using an effective new approach, strong support by the city for its cultural and recreational amenities, attention to city's infrastructure, and much more.

It is hard to imagine that the result could have been achieved with any less holistic approach. Certainly, to date no other city has been quite so successful in reversing the forces of decline. Once again, the process has been synergistic.

# 10. Synergy on the Bottom Line

If "the business of America is business," in Calvin Coolidge's sage observation, it is equally the case that the business of America is synergy. Though it often travels disguised as "innovation," "technology," "organization," "teamwork," "cooperation," "economies of scale," and the like, by any other name synergy is still a vital part of our economic life. Consider just a few variations on the synergy theme.

- *Retail emporiums*, where a number of small dealers—say in antique furniture—each rent a portion of the display space and pay the store operator a commission on any items that are sold. The dealers benefit from having their items on display along with many others (an "aggregation of supply," in economic terms) in a prominent location that they could not afford to rent individually. Many more potential customers are likely to be attracted to a large, well-stocked, well-located storefront, in much the same way that people flock to trade fairs, crafts fairs, shopping malls, and the like. Plus the store manager takes care of arranging and paying for the lease, licenses, insurance, utilities, cleaning, bookkeeping, advertising, and, most often, the sales personnel as well.

- *Multi-cinemas*, where the total cost for the box office, popcorn stand, projectionist, restrooms, office staff, newspaper advertisements, telephone lines, and so on are spread among several theaters. The use of multiple screens also gives the theater owner flexibility. A blockbuster movie like *Raiders of the Lost Ark* or *E.T.* can be shown on more than one screen; movies with only limited drawing power can be rotated quickly on one screen while those with more staying ability can be held over; and if the theater operator has one loser out of six, say, the "dogs" only take small bites out of the overall profits. So successful is this strategy that the Cana-

dian firm Cineplex has recently been building movie com-
plexes with ten, fifteen and even twenty screens.
- *Generic advertising*, a one-time exception that is becoming the
  rule, with an annual advertising bill that has been estimated
  at more than $100 million. Instead of making a pitch for a
  brand-name product, generic ads try to sell a type of product
  (or service): orange juice, milk, canned goods, potatoes, avo-
  cadoes, beef, poultry products, cotton, wool, rice, nuts, coffee, and even the military services (join the "army, navy, air
  force, marines" goes the slogan). Generic advertising represents a cost-sharing device, of course. But equally important, it can do some jobs that brand-name ads can't, namely:
  (1) countering competition from other types of products, (2)
  increasing public awareness of the product, (3) improving
  consumer knowledge about the product's features, and (4)
  highlighting new or unusual product uses. Thus, thanks to
  generic advertising we now know that eggs are a low-cost
  source of protein, that orange juice can be consumed any
  time, and that potatoes have lots of nutrients and are not all
  that fattening.
- *Mergers.* Many mergers in recent years have been predatory
  bloodbaths with sometimes disastrous results. A notable exception, however, was the merger between Nabisco and Standard Brands. The reason is that the marriage was mutually
  advantageous and was handled by both sides as a union between equals. The two partners had complementary product
  lines, but they marketed their products to the same customers with the same kind of advertising and promotions. By
  combining forces they were able to pool their marketing efforts in various ways. They also brought complementary
  sales strengths to the partnership. In the U.S., Nabisco had
  a direct sales force of some 3,000 people, while Standard
  Brands relied on food brokers. Now both partners are strong
  in both sales approaches. Overseas, Standard Brands was
  pre-eminent in Latin America and South Africa, while Nabisco was well entrenched in Europe and Japan. Thus, the
  merger gave each partner a quick leg up in new markets.
  New product introductions have also benefited from com-

plementary strengths. Standard Brands has always had an outstanding market research arm but lacked a direct sales force to aid with new introductions. The merged organization now has both. Finally, the combined balance sheet of the merged company provided the resources needed to expand more aggressively. (As this book was going to press, Nabisco Brands was in turn bought out by the tobacco conglomerate, R. J. Reynolds.)

- *Shared office suites*, a common practice among lawyers, doctors, dentists, and other professionals. Sometimes an entire building may be jointly owned or leased. At other times only a suite of offices may be involved. In addition to the advantage of cost-sharing, a "professional" office complex can provide higher visibility and status for all of the participants. So popular are these cooperative arrangements that there are now chains that specialize in providing office-sharing arrangements. For instance, the International Office Network (ION) will provide you with your choice of furnished or unfurnished offices (rents are higher for large multi-room suites with exterior views), complete with free parking spaces, paid utilities, janitorial service, a security patrol, a "beautifully furnished" reception area with a trained receptionist, a conference room, a telephone answering service, mail service (with monthly bills), a copying service (6 cents per page), and a word processing service (including one free hour each month).

- *Cogeneration.* "Two Plus Two Equals Five," reads an ad for GE's cogeneration equipment. If an industrial plant, say, needs electricity for its machinery plus steam heat or hot water for various human needs, a cogeneration system can do both jobs at once with results that are synergistic. A central power plant alone has an efficiency that rarely exceeds forty percent. A conventional hot water heater has an efficiency of about sixty-five percent. In both cases, the unused energy goes to waste. By combining the two processes, however, efficiencies as high as ninety-six percent can be achieved.

- *The telephone system*, one of the everyday miracles of modern living. Because telephones are not linked directly with one another but pass through centralized switching systems (an electronic "commons"), each telephone unit requires only one set of interconnecting lines. And because we all share the cost of keeping the entire system in operation twenty-four hours a day, every day, we are able to make use of the system for our limited needs more or less at our convenience and can call almost any other unit in the system.

- *Networking*, ranging from luncheon groups that provide forums for sharing information to more formal relationships among professionals in different fields who refer business to one another and combine forces on "multidisciplinary" jobs. Thus a management consulting firm such as ours might team up with such "affiliates" as a law firm, an architectural firm, a firm specializing in market surveys, or an industrial engineering firm, depending on the nature of the assignment.

- *Superstores*, which aggregate in one location a broad range of grocery and household items that might once have been purchased from a number of specialized outlets. In addition to the items found in most supermarkets, the superstores offer such add-ons as on-premises bakeries, delicatessens, liquor stores, pharmacies, book and magazine stands, financial services, and flower shops. The latest wrinkle, though, is a hybrid between a supermarket and a warehouse called the "superwarehouse." The basic formula is age-old: Vast selection, extremely high volume, very low prices, tightly controlled costs, and some important operating efficiencies as well. A typical Cub Foods store, for example, is four times the size of a conventional supermarket and may stock 25,000 items—double the selection of most supermarkets. More important, Cub's prices are fifteen to twenty percent lower than elsewhere. In part this is due to high volume and lower handling costs. For instance, sugar can be purchased in 50-pound bags and canned fruit by the case. Likewise, by getting produce by the trailer-load directly from the farms, Cub stores can eliminate middlemen, reduce warehouse and handling costs, and, at the same time, save days of freshness and cut down on wastage. Cub stores also get shoppers to bag their own groceries, which results in significant savings on labor costs. And because Cub stores rely on word of mouth, their advertising budgets are about one-quarter of what other stores spend.

- *Joint ventures*, the countless temporary partnerships where two (or more) parties combine resources or skills that neither alone possesses to achieve an objective that would otherwise be unattainable. Thus National Steel and a Japanese steelmaker, Nippon Kokan, recently formed a joint venture to produce and sell certain kinds of specialty steel products in the U.S. Nippon wanted access into the protected U.S. steel market, and National wanted access to Nippon's advanced technology, without which it could not remain competitive. In the same way, Chrysler has recently teamed up with Mitsubishi to build small cars in the U.S., and GM has hooked up with Fujitsu Fanuc to produce robots.

- *Financial supermarkets*, a name being applied to the trend toward combining financial services that were once divided up among commercial banks, savings and loans, stock brokerage firms, commodity brokers, real estate investment firms, mutual funds, money market funds, and the like. Though there are potential drawbacks to this trend, one appeal to the general public is that it offers one-stop shopping in an age when people have interlocking and fast-changing financial and investment needs, and precious little time to shop around. For the financial institutions, a major advantage is that their business is more diversified and less dependent on a particular economic climate; they can leverage themselves against bad times and bear markets.

- *Rental services*, which enable us to reap the benefits from cooperation without having to know, much less like, the people on whom we mutually depend. Next time you rent a car, hotel room, tuxedo, TV, boat, computer, storage space, work of art, movie, piece of furniture, safe-deposit box, airplane, or rototiller, just ponder how many other people may have used that item before you and, by their actions, made it possible for you to have access to it when you needed it at a relatively low cost.

- *Cooperatives*, such as the Nanny Goat Hill Gallery run by a group of artists in the Russian Hill section of San Francisco. Some eighteen "members" (some memberships are divided among two or more artists) share the rental costs plus management and upkeep of the gallery in return for the privilege of one month-long show per member every eighteen months.

- *Mainstreet merchant associations*, such as the Downtown Business Improvement Districts mandated by the State of California, which arrange for joint advertising campaigns, coordinated sidewalk sales, holiday decorations, downtown shopping maps, beautification, and a variety of other business promotion activities, often with an eye to counteracting the competition from nearby shopping centers.

- *Timesharing*, an ownership- and use-sharing mechanism that has been applied successfully to, among other things, vacation condominiums, boats, airplanes, computers, exclusive mini-hotels, factories and even offices. For instance, many physicians have their practices spread out in different parts of a city, often in conjunction with the hospitals where they have admitting privileges. Because of the combined economic pinch of new ceilings on health insurance reimbursement formulas plus an oversupply of doctors in some areas, more physicians are showing an interest in timeshared offices that they can use (and pay for) only as needed.

- *Group rates*, which have been applied to everything from life insurance to theater tickets. For example, packaged travel tours are designed to get people to travel together in groups on a prearranged schedule so as to take advantage of joint bookings for airline flights, hotels, limousines, meals, etc. Economists call it "aggregating demand."

- *Spin-off technologies*. Lumber companies in the Northwest used to burn their sawdust in huge metal tepees called "hogs" that shot towering streams of sparks into the night sky all over western Oregon and Washington. But now the hogs are mostly dead, rusting monuments to a bygone era. The reason is that somebody invented pressed fiber logs and, later, pressed fiber boards, which resulted in lower costs, higher profits, and more efficient use of our natural resources.

American business runs on synergy. Competition obviously plays an important role, but synergy deserves equal billing; almost every time a story appears in the business section of the newspaper these days regarding some promising new venture, the chances are that synergy lies at the heart of it.

## COPY MATS

Take the Copy Mat stores, for instance. Commercial copy shops have been around for several years now, and their success provides yet another example of synergy—namely, cost-sharing by many occasional users of high-speed, high-quality copy machines that provide, in addition to relatively low prices, such "bells and whistles" as reductions, double-sided copying, color transparencies, automatic collating and stapling, special bindings, and so forth.

However, the Copy Mat stores have added still more synergy to the formula. To save on labor costs (and copying charges), Copy Mats emphasize do-it-yourself service on fast, high-quality machines with automatic counters that feed the tallies to a console next to the cash register.

In addition, Copy Mats offer their customers an array of related services: rental mailboxes, rental typewriter booths, a professional typist on premises (in some cases), passport photo service, and a generous supply of staplers, glue sticks, scissors, paper clips, and work space, all in pleasant, well-furnished surroundings. Not suprisingly, our nearby Copy Mat is doing a land-office business, seven days a week from early morning until late in the evening.

## PROFESSIONAL MANAGERS

Consider also the growing number of companies that specialize in managing professional and trade associations under contract. Smith, Bucklin & Associates in Chicago, for example, provides its clients with trade show and convention planning, public relations, financial management, statistical services, and even a telephone-answering service. In addition, Smith, Bucklin maintains twelve Washington lobbyists who share the job of looking out for client interests, ranging from fisheries to futures trading to safety regulations.

For most of Smith, Bucklin's 130-odd clients, the payoff is far greater expertise in the management of their associations at a far lower cost. Furthermore, observes New York association manager Jules Schwimmer, "we enable association officers to devote their time to their own business."

## LEASE-A-STAFF

Californian John Schmelzer, a health-care consultant, has so far signed up more than eighty-five medical and dental practitioners for his lease-a-staff service, an idea that has recently begun to take hold in various parts of the country.

Schmelzer can offer his clients several advantages. First, he spares a busy doctor or dentist the trouble of finding, screening, and doing the paperwork and tax forms for competent staffers. Second, he uses the combined purchasing power of his 450-odd leased employees to get much more attractive fringe benefits at a relatively low cost. The average cost of such add-ons for a physician these days is about $47.98 per $100 in salary, Schmelzer reports; he can offer significantly better benefits at about $31 per $100, or 17 percent less. Staff turnover is also much lower for his clients (10 percent versus 25 percent).

No wonder that the number of leased employees has grown from a handful to over 100,000 in just a few years. As leasing consultant Carmen Arno aptly observes, employee leasing is "an awakening giant."

## HARDWARE

Sometimes the synergy involved in a new business venture is rooted in the hardware. We like to use an invention of our own, for which a patent is being sought, as an example. The product is called a "Pacifier Leash," and it is really nothing more than a new wrinkle on the old practice of securing a pacifier to an infant's clothing to prevent it from going astray or falling to the ground.

There are two advantages to the Pacifier Leash. One is that it is readily adjustable, so that it can be attached variously to strollers, infant carriers, or an infant's clothing. The other advantage is that the Pacifier Leash employs a strip of Velcro fastening material to provide an automatic safety release feature. Should the leash become entangled in any way the Velcro strip will pull apart at approximately 5.2 pounds of force and release the pacifier and leash from its attachment pin.

Now the point is that every component of the Pacifier Leash is an off-the-shelf item. In making the prototypes, all the parts were purchased locally in sporting goods stores, hobby shops, sewing supply stores, and hardware stores. What is "new" about this invention is that various familiar parts (grommets, braided cordage, Velcro, lanyard hooks, cord locks, binder rings, baby pins) have been combined in a new way so that all of the parts function together (synergistically) to produce a novel result.

## SUBTLER SYNERGIES

Though such hardware synergies can be very dramatic, especially when a cutting-edge technology is involved, synergy often contributes to the bottom line in more subtle and unobtrusive ways.

Consider this gambit: A retail clothing store in our area was about to go out of business. It had declining sales, a mountain of debts, and a bad credit rating. Meanwhile, another clothing store in the area was offered an opportunity to acquire $300,000 worth of stock from an outside distributor at fire-sale prices, which the store wanted to sell at a deep discount for a quick profit. The problem was that the second store had no extra floor space and didn't want to tarnish its upscale image. So the two stores got together and made a deal. The upscale store sold its new merchandise through a going-out-of-business sale at the other store. It also paid for advertising the sale and agreed to give the other store a cut of the profits. Among the results: The sale was a success; the creditors were paid; and there was a tidy profit to boot.

## UPGRADING WALGREEN'S

Positive synergy may also occur when an anemic (low-synergy) operation is revitalized. Take the case of a nearby Walgreen's

Drugstore, which recently undertook a remodeling and modernization program. Some of the changes, while seemingly superficial, were nevertheless important: brighter lighting, a fresh coat of paint in attractive colors, colorful new floor tiles, better labeling of displays, etc. More significant, though, was the replacement of the old display cabinets in favor of a much more efficient design that permitted a 50-percent increase in the number of items on the floor while, at the same time, allowing for wider aisles.

To take advantage of the extra space, some of the existing product lines were augmented, from cosmetics to consumer electronics. Several new product lines were added, including grocery items, wines, and liquors. More checkout counters and advanced electronic cash registers were installed to speed up the checkout process. And several new sales personnel were added to handle the expected increase in volume and a plan to greatly extend store hours.

Finally, all these improvements were linked to an aggressive marketing campaign that included discounting, frequent splashy sales, and a policy aimed at making Walgreen's' prescription drug department the lowest priced in town. The bottom line, according to the manager, was that the store's sales volume tripled in three months. What had been a marginally profitable store had been turned into a volume and profit leader.

## A TURNAROUND

An even more dramatic example of what synergy can do is the turnaround that occurred at Rockford Headed Products, a small midwestern manufacturer of screws, bolts, and fasteners, which in 1978 seemed destined to suffer the same fate as many other smokestack companies in this country.

When Frank Taylor bought Rockford, the firm was failing, the victim of bad management, a sour economy, and competition from cheap imports. But Taylor knew exactly what he was doing; having specialized in reviving faltering operations for big companies before going into business for himself, he had a well-prepared plan.

Taylor's research had shown that the way out of the ruthless price-cutting competition which was driving Rockford out of business was to move the company away from standard fasteners, which are sold mainly to wholesale distributors strictly on price, and into special-purpose fasteners, which are sold mainly to end-users who pick suppliers on the basis of quality, on-time delivery, and, last of all, price. Standard screws may sell for $5 a thousand, whereas special items might fetch $50 to $100 a thousand.

When Taylor took over the company, only 15 percent of its business was special-purpose fasteners. This was so despite the fact that the former owner had invented some highly marketable products, such as self-threading screws that could speed assembly time or hold better in certain types of materials. Taylor also had some ideas of his own, like a new notched bolt that could replace three pieces in electric terminals and save manufacturers assembly time and parts costs.

In order to make the shift, however, Taylor would first have to transform the business internally, from the bookkeeping office to the manufacturing floor. Accounts receivable had been running fifty days late, so Taylor began a push to make them current. Half of the company's shipments had been going out late, so Taylor began insisting that they all go out on time.

## CUTTING OVERHEAD

More important, after studying the operational side of the business for several months, Taylor began a major drive to slash overhead and improve quality. For instance, due to sloppy production practices, 20 percent of the raw materials purchased by Rockford was ending up as scrap. "You pay 40 cents a pound for it," Taylor told the *Wall Street Journal*, "and you sell it for 2 cents" as scrap.

Quality is an attitude, as Taylor points out, and it takes a long educational process to change attitudes. Nevertheless, the company has managed to reduce the scrap rate to less than 8 percent, along with such other cost-containment measures as a strict cost-accounting system for his managers.

Rockford was also hampered by its physical plant—a one hundred-year-old leased factory containing an odd mix of incompatible machines that needlessly increased production costs.

"We had to rationalize the equipment if we were ever to bring down overhead costs," notes Taylor. So one of Taylor's major objectives was to build a modern plant with up-to-date equipment. The design was paid for with federal assistance, and a local bank bought a $1.25 million bond issue for the construction and furnishing of a new 44,000-square-foot facility.

Finally, the marketing of Rockford's high quality, special-purpose fasteners required a sales force; for this kind of business the traditional middlemen would not do. So Taylor signed up twenty-five manufacturer's representatives to drum up business for a 5 percent commission on sales. The strategy paid off when Rockford began to win contracts away from other suppliers who had let their quality or delivery commitments slip.

The bottom line? Rockford has been transformed into a highly profitable company that has been growing steadily and setting new year-to-year sales records. Today, some 120 production workers tend sixty-five machines in Rockford's efficient new factory, turning out millions of special-purpose fasteners.

What accounts for Rockford's turnaround? In a word, synergy. Take away any one of the major changes that were made and the outcome would have been very different.

## SYNERGISTIC TRENDS

If synergy is what fuels the processes of innovation and entrepreneurship in this country, it is equally the case that synergy has been the energizing force behind some of our major business trends.

Take diversification, for example. When an outfit like American Express with its vast resources, experience, and worldwide organization adds a highly compatible "new" business like a travel service to its traditional service line, the result is a multiplication of synergies.

Likewise, it was a logical move for Rubbermaid to add a line of plastic office products to its traditional line of high-quality plastic kitchenware. It was a natural for Hallmark to begin producing party goods, candles, albums, and small gift items for sale through its card shops. Polaroid was well qualified to move into instant passport photography and medical diagnostic photography. Kodak has been highly successful with office copiers, audiovisual equipment, and chemicals. Campbell Soups, which long ago began diversifying into areas of the food business with greater growth potential (e.g., Swanson's frozen dinners and Pepperidge Farms' prepared baked goods), has recently reinforced this strategy by purchasing Snow King (frozen meats), Mrs. Paul's Kitchens (frozen fish), Vlasic Foods (pickles and relish), German Village (pasta), and several others. And when the *New York Times* began offering a computerized information service a few years ago, this was simply another way of exploiting its already formidable capabilities as a collector, packager, disseminator, and, not least, repository of information.

When car dealers were squeezed by the recent recession and foreign competition, they too began diversifying. Some added car rental franchises; others offered lines from two or more car manufacturers, or added lines of trucks, recreational vehicles, or motorcycles; still others sought out contracts for servicing city-owned vehicles; some are even doing things that would have been unthinkable only a few years ago—such as sharing the cost of providing a "courtesy van" with other dealers who happen to be located close by.

## FRANCHISING

Franchising is another synergy-driven trend. According to legend, the franchising idea was developed by the Singer Sewing Machine Company after the Civil War, and more than a century later the trend shows no signs of abating. Today there are some 466,000 franchised business establishments in this country, accounting for close to 15 percent of the total GNP. These range from such traditional product-oriented franchises as gas stations, car dealerships, muffler shops, and fast-food outlets to the new wave of service-oriented businesses such as do-it-yourself picture-framing shops and low-cost legal services.

At its best, franchising combines the strengths of both small and big businesses. A franchise owner usually has a substantial degree of autonomy and responsibility for managing the business, along with such built-in incentives for hard work as the risk of failure (and, most often, the loss of a substantial cash investment) and the opportunity to retain a large share of the profits. Yet, at the same time, the franchiser may contribute resources that are equally crucial to gaining a competitive edge: proven new ideas, proprietary products, financial resources, marketing clout, business experience, and management skills. The advantages of this blend are reflected on the bottom line with great consistency. Whereas the failure rate for small businesses generally is 65 percent, according to the Department of Commerce, the rate for franchise outlets is only 4 percent.

## MR. BUILD

Take for example "Mr. Build." Mr. Build is the brainchild of Art Bartlett, the man who cut his teeth on the Century 21 real estate mega-franchise. Bartlett developed Century 21 from a single office in 1971 into a colossus with 7,600 offices coast to coast and $20 billion in annual sales, and now he is out to repeat his success with the home remodeling business.

Like Century 21, Mr. Build involves what is called conversion franchising, which entails persuading many already established local businesses to join under a national banner. What Mr. Build offers in return for a $7,900 up-front training fee and a schedule of monthly fees, which vary with the size of the franchisee, is a fast path to growth: training in marketing and business management that many small businesses desperately need, a national sales campaign, the right to use the Mr. Build name and image, access to group discounts for everything from building materials to insurance and, not least, a company-backed guarantee in the form of a performance bond for up to $100,000 assuring that the work will be completed on time and to the customer's specifications (no small benefit for a business such as home remodeling).

As one of Mr. Build's trainers puts it to his trainees: "The whole goal of the system is to increase sales for each and every one of you. We won't succeed unless you succeed. But as each of you grow, we'll all grow together. That's the marvel of synergy."

Does it work? After a little more than a year as a Mr. Build franchisee, New England remodeler Skip Kelley saw his marketing costs cut in half and his sales increase by 50 percent. He closes deals with a much higher percentage of his prospects, the average size of his jobs is significantly larger, and he now manages his business with greater skill, self-confidence, and, not least, time off that he never had before. "As far as I'm concerned," Kelley told *Inc.* magazine, "Mr. Build is the only way to fly."


## COLOSSAL CORPORATIONS

If some businesses have grown larger by diversifying or franchising their services or product lines, others have expanded by acquiring or eliminating competitors ("horizontal" growth), or by building cost-efficient organizations that encompass all of the steps from raw materials to the final consumer ("vertical" integration), or both. In any case, the emergence of the colossal corporation has been another synergy-based trend.

The granddaddy of them all is the Great Atlantic and Pacific Tea Company, whose long dominance in the grocery business (15,000 stores in 1934) was achieved in part by purchasing directly from the food producers or shippers ("eliminating the middleman") and by building and/or operating company-owned food-processing plants, fisheries, and fleets of trucks. At the same time, A&P pioneered the no-frills, high-volume, low-margin approach to the grocery business. The combined result was that A&P was able to undercut and/or buy out many of its competitors.

Likewise, Standard Oil of New Jersey (the forerunner of EXXON) bought oil fields, built drilling rigs, operated fleets of tankers and trucks, built oil refineries, and franchised tens of thousands of gas stations, all the while gobbling up competitors as fast as it could. At the turn of the century, the company controlled four-fifths of all the oil refining and marketing operations in the country. And when it was finally dismembered by the Supreme Court in 1911, it was divided into thirty-four separate companies. Even so, EXXON remains a giant, with revenues of close to $100 billion, some 800,000 stockholders, 180,000 employees, and 65,000 gas stations, among other things.

## IS BIGGER BETTER?

Bigger is not necessarily better, of course. But it is not mere coincidence that an economy built on rugged individualism today rests on foundations that include such corporate megaliths as IBM, GE, GM, AT&T, ITT, and EXXON. Other things being equal, bigness may provide a number of advantages. As that great capitalist and synergist John D. Rockefeller pointed out: "The day of the combination is here to stay. Individualism is gone, never to return."

The advantages that big, diversified companies may enjoy over smaller competitors include economies of scale, greater financial and human resources (and skills) in such vital areas as marketing, sales, and service, more resources for research and development, the ability to attract and remunerate top-flight managerial talent, greater visibility in the marketplace, greater ability to raise capital for expansion or innovation (either lines of credit or internal financing), and the ability to weather bad times in one region, or in one part of the business. For instance, the cost of marketing a new product may involve a huge investment for a start-up company, but for a large company with a big sales force already in being the cost may only be incremental.

## HOSPITAL SYSTEMS

One of the latest recruits to the bigger-is-better movement is hospitals. Multi-hospital systems grew 36 percent between 1978 and 1983, to about 34 percent of all community hospitals, and the trend is, if anything, accelerating. One reason why: Hospitals have voracious appetites for capital, and multi-hospital systems tend to get higher credit ratings, which means lower interest costs and the ability to float bonds even when the market is soft. Not only do multi-hospital systems have more assets to pledge and the ability to spread the risk over a broader financial base but they are viewed by lenders as having more management expertise and more political muscle.

Long ago economist John Kenneth Galbraith observed that the modern corporation at its best embodies a kind of institution-alized genius. The invention, development, and marketing of a new product by IBM, say, involves a vast array of specialized knowledge and skills, far beyond the reach of any modern Renaissance man, and these must be combined effectively to achieve the final result. Such synergy-producing cooperative efforts are so commonplace these days that we often take them for granted, or lose sight of the relationship between the parts and the whole; if we are only foot soldiers down in the trenches, the larger battle plan may be obscure to us. Indeed, organizations like IBM or Lucasfilms make a point of keeping people who are working on the parts from being privy to the whole.

Nevertheless, such huge industrial ventures as a new airliner, a new automobile, a new computer, or even a movie such as *Star Wars* ultimately requires big organizations with big corporate brains and big bucks. Most new businesses start small, of course, and many a breakthrough begins in the garage, or in a small corporate "skunk works." But even a shooting star like Apple Computers had to "get big or get out."

## SMALL IS BEAUTIFUL

On the other hand, sometimes even in the business world "small is beautiful." The appropriate size for a particular business depends on the nature and size of its niche. Many businesses purposely remain small because they cater to a specialized clientele or provide a specialized function in the marketplace that is better served, or at least more efficiently served, by a smaller organization. Yet small businesses are no less dependent on synergy than are the corporate giants.

Rockford Headed Products is a case in point. In its new guise as an innovative producer of specialty items for the fastener market, Rockford's advantages lie in being able to stay ahead of the competition while maintaining a reputation for high quality and personalized, responsive service. Taylor is not worried about competing against the big boys. "We can move quicker. We design and produce a part before they get the paperwork done."

Other examples include: The so-called micro-brewers and specialty food companies that produce consumables for special tastes or local markets (such as the Henry Weinhard brewery in Portland, Oregon); distinctive one-of-a-kind clothing stores that cater to a particular kind of clientele (like Bergdorf Goodman in New York); small circulation magazines that are targeted to a relatively specialized readership (such as *Runner's World*); manufacturers of unique products (such as the Snugli infant carrier); solo professionals whose businesses depend on their particular talents and skills, and on the word of mouth of satisfied clients; and the tens of thousands of local merchants whose businesses are oriented to serving a particular neighborhood.

## EIGHT JOHNNY VAUGHNS

Small businesses can be very adept at using the synergy principle. Take Johnny Vaughn, a well-regarded bandleader in the San Francisco Bay Area (who just recently retired). On any given Saturday night, Johnny's band typically would be playing in six or eight different locations at once, from Vallejo to Monterey. How did he do it? In fact, Johnny's musicians were almost all moonlighters; instrumentalists and singers who held other jobs during the week and did "gigs" on weekends and other special occasions under the Johnny Vaughn label. Johnny himself was the booking agent, personnel director, arranger, coordinator, and business manager, with the help of a small office staff. Some weekends Johnny didn't personally perform at all.

## THE CARAVANSARY

Another synergy-using small business in our area is the Caravansary, a novel retail store that combines several related functions in such a way that they reinforce one another. In part it is an upscale cafeteria featuring quiches, stuffed brioches, croissant sandwiches, fancy salads, cheeses, pastries, wines, and the like that are supplied by several local specialty food companies. Because the Caravansary puts heavy promotional stress on takeout foods, it is also partly a delicatessen and picnic supplier. Catering is also a major part of its business, a service for which its distinctive menu is especially well suited. In addition, the Caravansary offers cooking classes in a model kitchen and lecture area on premises, most of which doubles as a dining area during mealtimes. Finally, the Caravansary sells a line of gourmet kitchen, dining, and picnic utensils that are targeted to its epicurean clientele.

## ONE-HOUR PHOTOS

Consider also the one-hour photo processing services that have been sprouting in every part of the country since a fast, compact film-processing machine appeared on the market. Some of these quickie film developers are being located in shopping centers, ideal places for capturing walk-in shoppers. Others are being squeezed into traditional camera shops, which are then able to add a one-hour processing service to their existing mix. Still others are joining forces with copy shops. In any case, the location of choice is likely to be one where synergies are possible.

## COMBINED MARKETING

As a final example, consider how some small firms are using synergy to compete with bigger companies. Big firms often have the advantage when it comes to bidding for government contracts because it is both a costly and time-consuming process. Less than 20 percent of all government contracts in 1983 went to small businesses. So, in an effort to offset their disadvantage, eight small high-tech companies in the Boston area recently formed a joint venture called Small Business Technology Group, Inc., to perform marketing, bidding, and administrative functions on behalf all of the member companies. What the umbrella organization attempts to do is to assess Defense Department needs and then tap one or more of the eight companies to bid either on research and development projects or on product procurement contracts. Fear of antitrust suits is often a roadblock to business cooperation, but in this case the move was sanctioned by a little-used law.

## LESS IS MORE

As the current wave of "divestitures" indicates, sometimes even big businesses may find that less is more. Back in the 1960s and 1970s there seemed to be an irresistible rush toward huge "conglomerates," vast corporate umbrellas that might embrace dozens of totally unrelated companies. Thus aircraft manufacturers bought boat builders; food companies bought electronics manufacturers, soft-drink makers bought movie studios—and ITT bought anything and everything.

The conventional wisdom at the time was that the merger mania was synergistic: Corporate growth and diversification were assumed automatically to be advantageous. The rationale was that diversification would buffer the company as a whole against a down cycle in a particular industry, as well as giving each of the parts access to a larger pool of capital and other resources. Accordingly, synergy became a buzzword on Wall Street, and conglomerate stocks did relatively well.

These were also the days when some big management consulting firms were going around promoting the idea that growth-minded companies should use their traditional businesses as "cash cows." A cash cow could be milked to obtain the resources for buying out more glamorous, high-growth companies.

## NEGATIVE SYNERGIES

The problem was that, often as not, the conglomerate trend also produced some serious negative synergies as well. Top management was often spread too thin and knew little about the businesses for which they were responsible, and as time went on such management deficiencies began to take a toll. Worse yet, the new owners often precipitated an exodus of the people who did know how to run their acquisitions.

A study by McKinsey & Co. found that of three types of businesses (conglomerates, companies comprised of closely related businesses, and one-product specialty companies) the conglomerates generally do the poorest by most measures of business performance, while multiproduct companies such as Proctor & Gamble, which stick to the businesses they know, do the best. McKinsey director John Patience told the *New York Times*: "Conglomerate managements have shown they cannot manage new businesses well."

A second problem was that the "cash cows" were often cynically neglected by the managers, who were preoccupied with higher strategic goals. In time, the performance of these bread-and-butter industries began to suffer; many of them became easy targets for the competition.

Another form of negative synergy became evident during the recent recession, when poor showings by some of the parts had the effect of dragging down the stock price and financial ratings of the whole organization. This was especially common in cases where foreign competition was involved, or where inflated market prices collapsed (as in the mining industry). When the weakness in some part was perceived to be structural rather than only a cyclical dip, the result was a whole that was less than the sum of its parts.

Finally, it has recently become apparent that some mergers may be doomed from the start. Ideally a merger benefits both partners; each gains from the strengths of the other, and there is some logic to the move. But so-called hostile takeovers are another matter. As Peter Drucker points out, most of the companies bought out in predatory mergers do worse financially afterward. And so do many of the victors, whose increased indebtedness and demoralized acquisitions can become albatrosses. One recent study of fifty-eight recently merged companies, using two different financial success criteria, concluded that twenty-eight failed on both criteria and six more failed on one.

## THE SYNERGY TRAP

In 1984, there were no less than 2,500 corporate amalgamations. Yet, in the same year there were also 900 divestitures— uncouplings of corporate marriages that didn't work. "Synergy is a trap unless it's very well defined," says Charles M. Harper in a *Business Week* feature. Harper is chief executive of ConAgra Inc., a company that has a long record of successful acquisitions.

So why does the takeover game continue? Sometimes for very good reasons—for potential synergies that are waiting to be tapped. But in many other cases, the underlying motives are more crass. Uppermost is the greed of a new class of takeover lawyers and investment bankers (and many stockholders too), who are looking for quick profits. Our tax laws also provide substantial incentives for such buyouts. In addition, the takeover game has created a kind of Pac Man business climate in which almost everyone is forced to adopt an eat-or-get-eaten strategy.

Nevertheless, there is now a clear countertrend toward the divestiture of unrelated or poorly performing parts, along with better integration among the parts that remain. So when Gulf & Western, Coca-Cola, Quaker Oats, Beatrice Foods, Time, Inc., ITT, RCA, Playboy, and Esmark announce plans to streamline their operations, these days Wall Street loves it.

## ONLY AN APPETIZER

The dysergy produced by America's corporate feeding frenzy is, unfortunately, only the appetizer, for negative synergy is rampant in our business environment these days.

Sometimes the dysergy may be the result of forces that are beyond anyone's personal control. Today there are about 30 percent fewer printers in the U.S. than there were 10 years ago. Why such a high attrition rate? Because the cost of paper, inks, and other supplies went up at least 200 percent; warehousing costs went up 400 percent; trucking costs likewise went up 400 percent; fire insurance rates climbed 300 percent; the cost of new equipment and plant modernization more than doubled. And all this was in addition to the inexorable upward push of labor costs and taxes.

Under these circumstances, the printers had no choice but to raise their prices and hope for the best. The predictable result was that their customers began to economize on their printing costs, especially since most of them were themselves being squeezed by inflation. Some customers simply cut back on their printing needs: Here a planned brochure might be canceled; there a rubber stamp might be used to "update" a company's stationery when it moved to new quarters; elsewhere unused copies of an old report might be recycled with a new appendix section. Other customers ordered smaller quantities, or opted for a lower quality paper stock, or for a one- or two-color print job instead of a multicolored job. Or worse, they took their jobs to less expensive overseas printers.

For many small printers, the combination of rapidly escalating costs and lower revenues proved fatal. No one factor was responsible; it was a synergistic effect.

## BAD MANAGEMENT

Sometimes, however, negative synergy can be the result of bad management. The Mesta Machine Company bankruptcy provides a sad illustration (described in a *Wall Street Journal* piece) from a long list of recent business failures.

Though not well known to most Americans, Mesta Machines was for several generations America's premier mill machinery manufacturer, one of the giant concerns that helped to underpin our industrial prowess. It was Mesta that made the 16-inch naval guns for our battleships, as well as the ship propeller shafts, artillery carriages, 155-millimeter canon, and other heavy weapons that were used in World War II. And in peacetime it was Mesta that made the lion's share of our giant forging presses, turbine shafts, and steel-rolling mills. In its heyday, Mesta employed over 4,000 workers, and the cavernous foundries and machine shops at its West Homestead, Pennsylvania, plant sprawled for more than a mile and a half along the banks of the Monongahela River.

No one factor was responsible for Mesta's ultimate decline and fall, but human factors were overriding. In the 1960s, a new steel-forging method called continuous casting was beginning to be introduced overseas. The new method would soon prove to be a much more efficient way of making steel. Yet American steel companies for the most part decided to stick with the older rolling-mill technology, and so did Mesta (whose longtime head, Lorenz Iversen, had died only a few years earlier). In so doing, both the U.S. steel industry and Mesta lost their engineering and competitive edge, and in time foreign producers were able to seize the leadership.

The other major factor was Mesta's labor costs, which were skyrocketing. Iversen had been an inspiring manager who always kept in close touch with his workers and treated them generously. Indeed, because Mesta maintained excessively high mill-manning levels and provided high wages coupled with a lavish incentive pay system, it had the highest labor costs in the industry. But this had been more than offset in the past by Mesta's reputation for engineering excellence and high quality, and as long as Iversen was in charge Mesta's workers resisted unionization.

## NEW MANAGEMENT

After Iversen's retirement, however, a new breed of managers was brought in from the business schools. In time these newcomers developed a top-heavy bureaucracy that succeeded in alienating the workers, and in the late 1960s Mesta was unionized. Thus, at the very time when foreign competition was becoming a more potent threat, the union sought to institutionalize Mesta's bloated mill-manning levels and high wage scale. Management, on the other hand, was belatedly responding to the competitive challenge and sought to reduce labor costs.

The inevitable confrontation resulted in a crippling five-month strike. The union finally won, but it was a pyrrhic victory. Burdened by high labor costs, low morale, outdated technology, and sharply increased indebtedness due to the strike, the company never recovered.

## DYSERGY TRAPS

In the business world as elsewhere, synergy often depends on a delicate balance of forces; what starts out producing positive synergy can have the opposite effect when conditions change. Mesta's unusually high manning levels and generous wage scale were what gave the company an edge during the World War II era when quality and on-time delivery were all important. But when Mesta was faced with more efficient competitors in a price-sensitive market, its one-time advantages became liabilities that helped to seal the company's doom.

A business operator who does not fully appreciate the workings of the synergy principle can easily fall into such dysergy traps. Nolan Bushnell's Pizza Time Theatre chain provides a recent example.

Bushnell is the entrepreneurial genius who cofounded Atari, the company that pioneered video games. But Bushnell is a self-described "bad executive," and despite Atari's early success the company nearly went broke in the mid-1970s, before it was rescued by Warner Communications (which recently sold the company again when faced with a sagging video game market and new financial troubles).

After Bushnell was finally ousted from Atari in 1977, he began developing a new idea for a chain of restaurants that would combine fast food and "family" entertainment. The result was the Chuck E. Cheese Pizza Time Theatre, with its boisterous mixture of pizzas, video games, and "live" robot entertainment.

At first, the idea proved to be phenomenally successful. In five years the company grew from zero to 260 stores. Annual sales reached $99 million and by the end of 1982 the "roll-out rate," as chain developers put it, was two new stores a week.

Yet one year later the company was in deep trouble. Sales volume at many of the restaurants had been declining for months. Costs had been increasing. The company had to report substantial losses, and its stock plummeted from a high of 32 1/2 to 4 3/8. Once again Bushnell was forced to resign under fire, and several months later his successors filed for bankruptcy.

What went wrong? One business writer blamed the collapse on "a discredited concept: that kids will continue to be amused by repetitive video games and robot entertainers and their parents will put up with crummy pizza."

That wasn't the concept, of course. That was only the reality. A good idea had been poorly executed, and when the novelty wore off the weaknesses began to outweigh the strengths. First, the entertainment base was too narrow—too dependent on a short-term fad. Second, the quality of the food and the service left a great deal to be desired, and Bushnell had been cavalier about the numerous customer complaints. Equally important, by offering a *combination* of food and entertainment, Pizza Time incurred overhead costs that were considerably higher than for competing pizza parlors. Thus, what had originally been a source of strength ultimately became a liability.

Why do some businesses succeed phenomenally well while others with great promise stumble and fall by the wayside? This is a perennial issue, of course, one that has occupied legions of economists, management experts, and writers of business school textbooks, not to mention the countless business operators who have actually been on the firing line. However, the issue has taken on increasing urgency in the past few years: Businesses of all kinds have been battered by inflation, recession, and the effects (direct or indirect) of foreign competition; not since the Great Depression have there been so many business failures, or so much economic devastation.

Of course the odds of success have never been very good to begin with. Roughly four out of every five new businesses are destined to fail within the first few years, and less than 10 percent of all new product introductions succeed in the marketplace. Even successful businesses do not usually outlast the lifetime of their founders; the average business in this country has a life expectancy of about twenty-five years, and businesses that have been around for one hundred years or more are the exception rather than the rule.

## THE ANSWER

What the synergy principle teaches is that long-term survival, in the business world as in nature, depends on continuing to do everything right (or all the important things, anyway), whereas failures can and do occur as a result of doing just one thing wrong.

Many a bold new venture fails for lack of simple things like a good location, or good timing, or sufficient start-up capital, or a realistic relationship between production costs and pricing. And many a successful family business has expired with the founder because "the old man" didn't take the trouble to groom his son or daughter (or anyone else) to take over, or else resisted giving up control when the time had come.

Likewise, many a successful big business has failed because it got complacent, greedy, or arrogant. While Japanese companies during the 1960s and 1970s were busily figuring out how to produce goods with higher quality at lower cost by using more efficient production methods, many American companies were figuring out how to cut corners on product quality in order to save on production costs and increase short-term profits. This simple difference in business "philosophies" has had profound economic consequences for both countries.

A good, practicable idea is an indispensable first step when it comes to launching a successful new business venture, but it is almost never sufficient. Many more factors are normally involved, and only if all the factors are combined effectively will a good idea succeed in the marketplace. For every Mrs. Fields (gourmet cookies), Compaq (computers), or Creative Closets (yes, closets), there are countless Pizza Times, Osborne Computers, and De Lorean automobiles. Nolan Bushnell did many things right and a few big things wrong. And so did Adam Osborne and John De Lorean.

## THE McDONALD'S MODEL

Recall the Synergy Model. What our analytical framework stresses is that there is usually much more to a business success story than meets the eye—more in fact than the owners and managers themselves may recognize.

One of the best-documented examples of an organization that has put all the pieces together is McDonald's. By far the largest food service organization in the world, the McDonald's chain operates more than 9,000 restaurants with an estimated 150,000 employees in all fifty states and forty-one foreign countries, and in 1985 the company racked up sales of over $11 billion. Whatever one's personal food preferences, McDonald's is indisputably a high-synergy organization.

The story behind the McDonald's legend has been retold many times, and numerous explanations have been advanced to account for founder Ray Kroc's late-blooming success (he was fifty-two when he launched the chain). Yet most of these explanations fall short of the mark, for they usually leave out one or more important factors.

In a nutshell, the phenomenal success of McDonald's is due to the fact that it does everything right, by and large. The end result is a consistently superior performance: A level of efficiency, high quality, and low prices coupled with a degree of consistency, cleanliness, and courtesy that was previously unheard of in the service industry.

Virtually every McDonald's restaurant (except where there are deliberate variations) offers the same array of products served in a spotlessly clean, modern, and friendly atmosphere. Usually your order will be filled within a minute after entering the store. You can also be assured that your french fries were cooked within the past seven minutes and your hamburger within the past ten. And nobody does a better job of preparing and cooking fast foods.

## McDONALD'S' STRATEGY

McDonald's' underlying business strategy is also an important factor. The textbooks say that there are two basic approaches to being an effective competitor. One is to be the low-priced producer. The other is to be the high-quality producer. Some businesses, McDonald's included, have been able to do both. If you can carry it off, it's an unbeatable combination.

McDonald's' almost fanatical devotion to the "soft," core factors in the Synergy Model has had a lot to do with its success. Its basic structure relies on the strengths of the franchise model—and the synergy principle. "My belief was that I had to help individual operators succeed in every way I could," Kroc has said. "Their success would ensure my success."

McDonald's' corporate style, or culture (which borders on being a religion), provides the company with a strongly supportive value system; its slogan stresses "Quality, Service, Cleanliness, and Value." The company is also highly selective in choosing its personnel and has a well-developed system for staying close to them, ranging from regular inspections to frequent performance evaluations.

McDonald's is also renowned for its employee training program, by far the best in the industry (more than 30,000 managers have been trained at "Hamburger U."), while its elaborate system of employee incentives and rewards helps to ensure that the company's underlying values are actually adhered to. In addition, the top managers try to be responsive to the employees and their needs. (The Big Mac was an employee idea, while the new McD.L.T. was dreamed up by a store manager.)

Employee loyalty and pride in the company are further enhanced by the company's civic mindedness and philanthropy, which also serve to burnish its public image as a caring member of the community. For instance, immediately after the recent, tragic massacre at McDonald's' San Ysidro, California, store, Ray Kroc's widow established a fund to which she personally contributed $100,000, while the company donated an additional $1 million in an effort to help the survivors pay their medical bills and get counseling. In response to the feelings of a grieving community, McDonald's also decided to close the San Ysidro store and offered its seventy-odd employees positions in other nearby outlets.

## SWEATING THE DETAILS

What makes the system work, though, is McDonald's' equally fanatical attentiveness to the factors listed in the outer ring of the Synergy Model. According to General Motors in its advertising, "nobody sweats the details like GM." Well, McDonald's does, for one.

Nothing is left to chance. Over the years the company's planners and industrial engineers have sweated over a myriad of details: How best to store potatoes to enhance their flavor; how high hamburger buns can be stacked without affecting their shape and texture; how to ensure that each customer gets precisely the same portion size; the optimal cooking temperature for french fries; the most efficient way to package ingredients.

Before any new product or other innovation is introduced by McDonald's, it undergoes exhaustive testing. The breakfast menu, which greatly improved its operating performance and now accounts for 20 percent of its total sales volume, took four years to develop and test market. Its chicken offering took six years to evolve. And the drive-in window that is now standard at McDonald's restaurants around the country was extensively tested and tinkered with beforehand.

McDonald's is equally careful about how it picks locations for its restaurants and how it designs, builds, and decorates them. Some chains stick doggedly to a single formula, but McDonald's is constantly experimenting with new kinds of locations and different designs. For instance, one of its innovative market research studies showed that about three-quarters of the customers make their trips to McDonald's in conjunction with some other activity. So, instead of "siting" stores on the basis of local population size, the company now locates them in relation to the residents' activity patterns.

Technological innovation has been another of McDonald's' strong points, and once again nobody has done it better. In fact, McDonald's' engineers have been responsible for a whole new generation of labor-saving food-service equipment, ranging from french fry scoops and computerized french fry cookers to a computerized food-ordering system.

McDonald's has also been shrewd about making capital investments. Many years ago the company began plowing its profits into the purchase of vacant land in areas where future McDonald's restaurants might be located. Today the company owns over 50 percent of its restaurant sites, inclusive of the buildings, making it the second largest private owner of real estate in the U.S. (after Sears Roebuck). As a result, McDonald's is able to collect rent from many of its stores, in addition to royalties.

McDonald's' marketing and advertising have, over the years, also been extraordinary. Its golden arches are recognized throughout the world. Its friendly clown/mascot, Ronald McDonald, "ranks right up there with Santa Claus," as one competitor ruefully conceded. And its annual advertising budget, at over $550 million, is the highest in the food service industry, both absolutely and in proportion to sales.

## HIGH SYNERGY

That's the only way to describe it: High synergy. One statistic sums it up. In 1979 the average daily sales for each McDonald's restaurant was $2,416. That figure was 30 percent higher than the daily average for any of its competitors among the fast-food chains and twice as high as its lowest ranking competitor. (By 1985, McDonald's' daily average had risen to $3,560.) Such a remarkable competitive edge is the result of an outstanding performance in relation to every one of the factors listed in the Synergy Model. It is the combined effect of doing a great many things right.

By the same token, high synergy is the reason why Japanese auto manufacturers, with labor costs that are only slightly lower

*Table Three*

| The Japanese Advantage | | |
|---|---|---|
| | Japan | U.S. |
| Parts stamped per hour | 550 | 325 |
| Manpower per press line | 1 | 7–13 |
| Time needed to change dies | 5 minutes | 4–6 hours |
| Average production run | 2 days | 10 days |
| Total work force, per plant | 2360 | 4250 |
| Average absentee rate, per plant | 8.3 percent | 11.8 percent |
| Total time needed to build a small car | 30.8 hours | 59.9 hours |

*Source: Harbour & Associates. Data are for 1982. They include all Japanese and all American companies.*

than ours, can produce cars for about $1,500 less on average than Detroit can using essentially the same technology, as is evidenced in table three above.

High synergy—that's the underlying explanation for the enduring success of such diverse business ventures as American Airlines, L. L. Bean's, Proctor & Gamble, and the Hyatt Hotels. The bottom line for these and many other companies is the combined product of an enormously complex structure of well-integrated cooperative effects.

To reiterate what was said earlier, in our economic life as in nature the fittest competitors may also happen to be the most effective cooperators. Competition via cooperation has been a basic strategy in evolution. Economic Darwinism, properly understood, invites us to use the synergy principle to full advantage. McDonald's is no less "Darwinian" than any other fast-food chain. The good news is that high synergy often has high survival value. Furthermore, what is most adaptive for our economic survival may also be compatible with what makes for a civilized, humane, and equitable—not to mention personally rewarding—work environment.

# 11. The Synergistic Society

In one way or another we are all practitioners of synergy, whether we realize it or not. Look at the two-year-olds who are struggling to master the "precision grip." Or the three- and four-year-olds who build fanciful creations out of Lego Blocks, Tinker Toys, and Lincoln Logs. Or the teenagers who sing in the high school chorus, play in the band, or participate in team sports.

One of the songs in *Meemyself the Wicked Elf*, an original musical comedy that is performed from time to time at our local children's theater, is rendered in a quavery voice by "the only free musical note," a character named "So." So has become separated from her close companions, Do, Re, Mi, Fa, La, and Ti, because they were kidnapped by the wicked elf. So is sad because she realizes that she cannot make music alone; all she can do is hum.

Or consider the house painters who routinely transform the appearance of a run-down house with the application of a fresh coat of "coordinated" paint colors, or the ministers who strive to weave the various parts of their Sunday services into integrated "wholes," or the army drill instructors who try to instill in their recruits the need for "teamwork," or the parents who agonize over the many details that combine to make for a successful wedding, or the political "advance men" who orchestrate every seemingly spontaneous aspect of their candidates' campaign appearances.

In almost every field of human endeavor, from aircraft design to zoo management, the ability to make effective use of the synergy principle is a key to success. To illustrate, let's take a brief, snapshot look at some of the more common ways in which people earn their livings—or otherwise pursue happiness.

## SPORTS

Listen to hockey great Wayne Gretzky, quoted by a reporter for the Associated Press: "When a hockey team is playing well, we look better as individuals," he says. "The goal-scorers receive all the glamor, but it takes twenty guys going all out all the time to make a team. This is a real team. Certain guys do certain jobs. We all know the importance of each other."

Listen to Olympic skier Steve Mahre, speaking for himself and his twin brother Phil in the *San Francisco Chronicle*: "I never would have hiked and run and endured all that drudgery if I didn't have Phil doing it with me. I would have worked out, sure, but not as hard or as often as I did."

Listen to Heismann Trophy winner Hershel Walker in his awards dinner speech in 1982: "Life is a team, life is a group, and you have to play together."

Consider also such great moments in team sports as the gold medal-winning victory of the underdog American hockey team over the top-rated Russians in the 1980 Olympics. Or the Cinderella performance of the San Francisco 49ers in the 1981 season, when they went from cellar of the league to the Superbowl in one inspired season and then beat the favored Cincinati Bengals for the championship.

## GREAT TEAMS

If synergy is involved in the making of great athletes, and great-moments sports, it is even more vital to the making of a great team. The general consensus is that the Baltimore Orioles have had the best overall record in major league baseball over the past two decades. Since 1966, they've won more games and more pennants (six) than any other team, as well as three World Series. Yet they get lower salaries, overall, than about half of the other major league teams. Moreover, the Orioles pointedly avoid superstars with big salaries and big egos.

What is the key to the Orioles' success? In a nutshell, it involves the triumph of a dedicated team over assorted collections of individual players. Baltimore may not have the best players in baseball, but it has the best team (and the best leadership). "They're a damn good organization," concedes a spokesman for the rival New York Yankees. "They just do it right."

How do they do it? In a profession that systematically undermines the qualities that make for a close-knit team, either by treating players as commodities or by showing favoritism and paying sky-high salaries to individual players, the Orioles have succeeded in bucking the trend.

They build loyalty to the team by developing talent as much as possible through their own farm system. They also strive to be scrupulously fair about individual salaries, so as not to create jealousies among the players. And they prefer to sign their players to long-term contracts. General manager Hank Peters explained to a reporter for the *New York Times*: "I believe in consistency, patience, and fairness. We don't just bring people in and out. We tinker with the machine, but we don't overhaul it. Every time the season opens we have a chance to win something."

The Orioles' management also picks players who will fit in and be strong team players. Says former infielder Lenn Sakata in the *Wall Street Journal*: "There aren't any bad eggs on this club. They tend to get rid of them."

Consistent with this philosophy, on the field the Orioles stress team play and doing what it takes to win, rather than amassing individual statistics. Thus players are "platooned" to a greater extent than on any other club; more players get to play on a given day. Pitcher Scott McGregor observes: "Each guy feels like he is doing his part." Also, it keeps everyone sharp.

The result of this management style is a team whose members have strong bonds of personal loyalty, to one another and to the team. "We know each other very, very well," says McGregor. The players maintain that they play better as a result. They are also more likely to help one another out. Pitcher Mike Boddicker claims: "There's no jealousy on this team—honest."

Of course, the Orioles' formula is not confined to the "soft," core factors discussed in chapter 7. Unlike some other teams that do things such as weight lifting, the Orioles stress the fundamentals and relentlessly practice running, fielding, and hitting throughout the season.

Baltimore is also a well-managed team financially. Though it has always had a solid base of extremely loyal fans, the management has made some shrewd moves in recent years to increase attendance. The result has been even greater public support—and profits on the bottom line—which has served to further strengthen the organization as a whole.

In defiance of the cynics, Baltimore players express a strong preference for playing on a close-knit, winning team over the possibility of earning even hundreds of thousands of dollars more. Says retired pitcher Jim Palmer in the *New York Times*: "Who would want to leave an organization like this?"

## REAL ESTATE

How is the selling price of a property, say a single-family dwelling, determined? The answer, in most cases, is that it is the combined result of many factors.

Among realtors it is axiomatic that three criteria are important when you are looking for a home: location, location, and location. This is an exaggeration, of course. But location is very important. The price tag for a house situated in one of the "better" neighborhoods may be substantially higher than for a similar house on the wrong side of the tracks. Conversely, a few eyesores in a good neighborhood can quickly erode the values of the surrounding houses, as was amply demonstrated by the "blockbusters" (predatory developers) of the 1950s and 1960s.

In some localities, neighborhood quality (and property values) can vary radically from one block to the next, even though the houses are all of similar age and construction. Such sharp differences are often a reflection of whether the houses are predominantly owner-occupied (and thus well maintained) or rentals.

In other localities, changing trends among home buyers can produce some strange anomalies. In New York City, for instance, the "brownstone" residential buildings on the upper west side of Manhattan are generally more spacious and of better construction than those on the upper east side. Nevertheless, it was the upper east side that in recent decades became New York's "Gilded Ghetto" (in Theodore White's characterization). Only recently has there been a revitalization of the upper west side.

To take advantage of such locational synergies, smart "starter home" buyers with limited budgets have long followed the practice of buying a smaller house in a better neighborhood, rather than a larger house in a less desirable area; the better the neighborhood, by and large, the less risk there will be of a decline in property values and the greater will be the potential for appreciation.

Though the synergies associated with location are obviously important in real estate, the locational factor may itself be the combined result of many other factors: proximity to various amenities, access to mass transit and shopping, the quality of the schools, local taxes, and, not least, who else is living there already.

## OTHER FACTORS

Moreover, location is only one of the factors that influence the price of a given house. Also important are such things as the size, style, and condition of the house, how well (and tastefully) it has been maintained and furnished, the selling prices of various "comparables" that were sold in the area recently, and, of course, "supply" and "demand"—market forces that may in turn be influenced by such global factors as interest rates, inflation, and the state of the economy.

Finally, the evaluations and decisions made by appraisers, listing agents, buyers, and sellers also affect the actual selling price. Some sellers are eager to sell. Others want to get top dollar for their homes. Some buyers try for the best deal they can get, while others, searching perhaps for a sought-after old Victorian, might be willing to pay more than the asking price. In any event, it is synergy that makes the buying and selling of real estate an art rather than a science.

## DEVELOPERS

Some of the most highly skilled synergists in real estate are the developers, for there are many factors involved in a successful (and profitable) construction venture: the economic climate, local economic conditions and trends, adequate planning, land acquisition, architectural and interior design, financing, insurance, government approvals and (often) government assistance, construction, landscaping, marketing, property management, even weather conditions.

Given all of these factors, some of the biggest and most successful real estate firms today employ a synergy-based strategy pioneered by billionaire developer Harry Helmsley back in the 1930s. The strategy involves combining traditional real estate brokerage with sideline businesses that specialize in property insurance, property management, the syndication of financing packages, and even maintenance and construction.

The limited partnerships that finance many real estate developments these days are also examples of synergy. The general partner, who is usually a developer (or developers), generally controls and manages the project while the financing is provided by the limited partners—individual investors (ranging in number from a handful to several thousand) who mainly contribute their capital in the expectation that there will be tax write-offs and ultimate profits.

Developers are also the builders of most single-family housing units these days, with good reason. Many synergies (economies of scale) are involved in the "tract" housing developments that rim most of our major cities. Savings can be realized in the purchase of land, design work, insurance costs, dealings with government agencies, the cost of materials, labor costs, even in publicity and marketing expenses. The result is housing that is significantly more affordable than the traditional alternative.

## NOVEL SYNERGIES

To these and other more or less commonplace synergies in the real estate field, new forms of synergy are being added all the time. Some involve collaboration between the public and private sector. For example, a developer in our community persuaded the city to grant him the use of the "air rights" over a city-owned parking lot for the purpose of building moderate income housing, in return for which he agreed to include in his plan two levels of underground public parking. Thus the city nearly doubled the capacity of its parking lot at no cost while the developer got a title from the city that enabled him to avoid land acquisition costs.

Or consider this unique high-rise sharing arrangement in Chicago: a Marriott Hotel occupies the first seventeen floors, with an entrance facing North Michigan Avenue. The top twenty-two floors are occupied by Arco, which has its own side entrance and elevators. And both Marriott and Arco make use of the ground-floor shops and restaurants.

Equity sharing is another synergistic real estate innovation, and there are now firms that specialize in arranging equity-sharing contracts. Typically these agreements involve putting a would-be home buyer who has a substantial income but little or no down payment money together with an investor who is seeking tax write-offs, interest income, and a share of the appreciation on a property that somebody else will be responsible for maintaining. If the agreement is well thought out and carefully drafted, the result can be a mutually beneficial arrangement.

## CONDOMINIUMS

Condominiums are, of course, an old but increasingly popular form of synergy in the real estate field. Some of the synergies are obvious. They include, among other things, economies in development costs, land acquisition costs, and construction costs, as well as (often) cost-sharing among the owners for such amenities as swimming pools, garden areas, and security systems.

In addition, there are such little-appreciated synergies as condo insurance, which is usually cheaper than insurance on a single family dwelling. The reason: all of the units are usually insured together on one policy, and insurance companies typically insure less than the full replacement cost of the entire project. Since it is unlikely that all of the units in a given project would be completely destroyed in a fire, the risk can be pooled.

One of the latest wrinkles in condo construction in effect multiplies the synergy. It involves two-owner condo units that include two master bedrooms and baths, along with shared living, kitchen-dining, and utility areas.

Time-shared vacation condos, another recent trend, can also multiply the synergies. By combining the economies of condo construction with shared ownership of each unit, a family can buy a piece of a place in the country for a few thousand dollars. Perhaps the most elaborate variation on this theme is the thousand-acre Vacation Ranch in California, which offers prospective owners a choice of campsites, cabins, or a trailer park, along with such recreational amenities as a lake, a swimming pool, horse-back riding, water skiing, fishing, tennis, and a social hall.

Another synergy-based real estate trend is associated with the "Yuppies," young professionals who are trying to establish a foot-hold in home ownership. In some cases, these urban entre-preneurs are buying multistory residences, say a New York brownstone or a San Francisco Victorian, and renting out all but one or two floors. By being part-time landlords, the owners earn additional income to help pay the mortgage, as well as getting favorable tax treatment and potential appreciation.

For those Yuppies who prefer not to become landlords, there is the increasingly popular alternative of combining forces with other potential owners to jointly purchase and divide up the space in an urban dwelling. Provided that the partnership is carefully planned and executed, such ad hoc condominium ar-rangements can be very successful.

## ONE REALTOR'S EXPERIENCE

Finally, we can observe in the real estate field the same par-adoxical relationship between competition and cooperation that we have noted elsewhere. An acquaintance with many years of experience as a real estate agent described her business as fol-lows: "Of course realtors are in competition with one another. When you're on commissions, there is always a lot riding on a sale. In some organizations the atmosphere is so thick you can feel it. I once worked in an office where I was warned, in all seriousness, not to throw a piece of paper with a client's name and phone number into the wastebasket.

"In the company I'm with now, things are very different. I've had some nice experiences. People are more willing to share in-formation and expertise. We have weekly seminars at our sales meetings, for instance. People are also more willing to trade off 'floor time' or take an 'open house' for one another. There is the feeling that if we help build the business for the company as a whole it will help generate more clients for each of us.

"We're a large company, and that has advantages too. We all benefit from having a big advertising budget. We have several offices, so we get referrals. We have a full-time, in-house legal counsel. The company also has the internal resources to provide 'bridge loans' [for prospective buyers who must also sell their old house], and this means we can close many more deals. Our name and reputation are also helpful when it comes to getting mortgage money from the banks (and that's the name of the game these days). People often ask me why I don't go out on my own. I tell them I'd have more to lose than I'd gain."

## THEATER

Says Dustin Hoffman, in *People* magazine, of his *Death of a Salesman* costar John Malkovich: "When you work with John the synergy is terrific." What Hoffman is talking about is the effect, in this instance positive but sometimes negative, that actors can have on one another's performances.

During the years when they were doing improvisational theater as a duo, Mike Nichols and Elaine May had a remarkably synergistic relationship. Nichols remembers in a *New York Times Magazine* profile: "She'd fill things, I'd shape them. She had endless capacity for invention. . . . When Elaine and I split up—that was a shattering year for me. . . . I was the leftover half of something."

In the same vein, Mikhail Baryshnikov speaks in the *New York Times* of the changes that have occurred in the American Ballet Theater since he became its director. "I feel there is a nice, fresh feeling about the company . . . a healthy atmosphere for creative work."

## THEATER LEGENDS

Rapport and mutually supportive relationships among the performers are only the beginning, of course. Though it may still be possible to have good theater with one of the major pieces missing—say, a mediocre script, weak performances, heavy-handed direction, amateurish staging, or a poorly designed theater—when all the pieces mesh the results can be magical, and memorable; they become theater legends.

Mike Nichols remembers the late Lee Strasberg, longtime director of the Actors' Studio, using this metaphor to describe the process of creating a great theatrical event. "Do you know how to make fruit salad?" he would ask. After pressing his listener for a detailed description, he would say: "That's right . . . until you pick up each piece of fruit, one at a time, peel it, and cut it into slices, you don't have a fruit salad. You can run over it with a steamroller, but you won't have a fruit salad. Or you can sit in front of the fruit all night, saying 'O.K., fruit salad.' Nothing will happen, though, until you pick up each piece and peel it and cut it up." One piece at a time, but with many pieces carefully prepared and blended to produce the desired end result.

## BROADWAY THEATER

Of course live theater also depends on "bread." Even the school play and the community theater require financial support for the thousand and one things—auditoriums, tickets, lighting, costumes, sets, even janitors—that are needed to make the synergy happen. This is especially the case on Broadway, a not-so-fabulous invalid these days, where money is the mother's milk. The forty-odd legitimate theaters that are clustered in midtown Manhattan (there are some synergies in that too) entertain more than 200,000 people every week during a good season, and box office receipts exceed $215 million a year.

However, financial success does not necessarily mean good theater. Producer Alexander Cohen states bluntly in Margaret Croyden's *Lunatics, Lovers, and Poets*: "Let's face it, Broadway is a business. Making bucks is the bottom line." Another producer, James Nederlander, concurs: "I'm in business and I can't afford to have my houses dark." In the judgment of veteran producer Robert Whitehead, quoted in the *New York Times*: "Culturally, Broadway is impoverished. We have a bunch of girlie-girlie shows and no plays dealing with our lives. . . . The balance has gone over entirely to show biz."

It seems to be more true than ever before these days that new playwrights and serious theater are more likely to be found off Broadway, or in the regional theaters. Says Gordon Davidson, artistic director of Los Angeles's Mark Taper Forum, in Croyden's book: "The plays we do could never originate on Broadway, where a play has to be a big hit or nothing. Broadway deals with numbers of dollars, numbers of people who attend. It's a business, not an art form." Croyden quotes the Phoenix Theater's longtime producer, T. Edward Hambleton: "Serious plays take tender love and care, and when you are working in an atmosphere where it is a thousand dollars a minute, it's very difficult to correct mistakes." Pulitzer Prize-winning playwright Lanford Wilson deplores this state of affairs: "Everything is judged by money. People lose all perspective. The system is not conducive to creating."

Broadway has always been a profit-oriented business, of course, but in recent years the negative synergies that have pushed up production costs and ticket prices have doomed many a fine play and prevented many others from being mounted at all. The average cost of producing a show has risen almost 200 percent during the past decade, and a major musical may carry a price tag of several million dollars. Given such inflated costs, and the pressure to show a profit, orchestra tickets can go for close to $50.

## LOW SYNERGY

From a synergy perspective, Broadway theater involves a remarkably inefficient (low-synergy) system. For each production, one must start from scratch (or nearly so), raising the money, developing an organization, doing the casting, building sets, promoting, advertising, selling tickets, etc. It is a very labor-intensive business. And New York City is a very expensive place to do all those things.

Moreover, because of the nature of live theater, the producers have a very difficult job: to generate many small audiences on successive days in a single locality over a period of many months or years in order to recover the initial outlays, meet ongoing expenses, and, hopefully, show a profit. This is a heavy burden for any one play to carry. (Of course, some shows go on tour or become movies.)

Finally, a system that depends on a combination of highly paid stars plus supporting casts that are assembled more or less off the street and have no job security is not, most close observers agree, conducive to top-quality performances.

Given its economic base, and the structure of the system, it is not surprising that Broadway has become primarily an entertainment vehicle for big spenders, or for the big night out. It may be unrealistic to expect otherwise, especially given the competition from other entertainment media. In any event, the result is bland, safe entertainment that will appeal to the broadest possible audience.

For better or worse, off-Broadway and regional theaters are, more and more, playing the role of farm teams: developing talented young actors, providing launching pads for promising new playwrights and directors, and pretesting new plays before they are sent up to the majors.

## REPERTORY THEATER

Compare this system with repertory theater companies. The pioneer and still a model for other repertory groups in this country was Great Britain's Old Vic. Named for its famous theater, which dated back to 1818, the Old Vic Company was the training ground for many of Britain's most illustrious actors: John Gielgud, Ralph Richardson, Laurence Olivier, Alec Guinness, Michael Redgrave, Richard Burton, Edith Evans, Flora Robson, Peggy Ashcroft, Claire Bloom, and many others. For more than two generations, from 1914 to 1963 (when it was succeeded by the National Theater Company), the Old Vic Company maintained a worldwide reputation as the home of great acting and great performances, particularly of Shakespeare plays.

From the beginning with the Old Vic, the emphasis was on the group, not individual stars. The Old Vic itself was the star, as one former member observes. The aim was to build an "ensemble" that had stability, so that the emphasis could be put on achieving from each of the "parts" a high-quality whole. Though many of its actors were paid only seasonally, and were never paid very well, the challenges and rewards associated with being involved in the Old Vic's productions were sufficient to assure great continuity. Even the actors who moved on to achieve stardom in other arenas often returned for a brief stint, which helped to attract new talent and burnish the Company's image.

## SAN FRANCISCO'S A.C.T.

The closest approximation to the Old Vic in this country is San Francisco's American Conservatory Theater (A.C.T.). For more than two decades, A.C.T. has been a major contributor to American theater. Like the Old Vic, it has been a training ground for some of America's best-known actors. Michael Learned, Marsha Mason, Peter Donat, Harry Hamlin, John Schuck, and Ellen Geer come to mind. It has also been an innovator and has won numerous theater awards. Former director Bill Ball has called A.C.T. a "communal enterprise," and it is generally agreed that A.C.T. is one of the strongest ensembles in the country.

The continuities, and the bonds, that can develop in a close-knit repertory group, says the *Nation*'s theater critic Harold Clurman, can give it a distinct artistic "identity." And this, in turn, can translate itself into better performances. Critic Steven Winn asserts that repertory actors "can accomplish a depth of texture and realism that jobbed-in actors who rehearse together for a month at most simply cannot." The *esprit* and sense of teamwork in a repertory company can turn a lackluster script into a dynamic production simply because of the energy and coherence that the actors can bring to their performances.

Equally important, a repertory group can operate from a different, more synergistic economic base. Instead of relying on the drawing power of a single "hit" play, or a big-name star, a repertory group may produce ten or a dozen different plays a year. If one play bombs, the others may be able to cover the losses. Repertory theater also makes possible such things as season tickets, or series tickets. At the same time, as a permanent cultural fixture in a community, like a symphony orchestra or a ballet company, a repertory theater may be able to attract subsidies— public, private, or both. This can free the company from the Broadway syndrome of having to produce quick results for profit-oriented "investors."

Does repertory theater depend on subsidies? The spectacular

success, on Broadway, of *Nicholas Nickleby*, an import mounted by Britain's Royal Shakespeare Company, suggests that repertory theater can also be profitable. Elizabeth McCann, one of the show's producers, made this telling comment to a *New York Times* reviewer: "The great lesson to be learned from *Nicholas* is that New York desperately needs a repertory company." While conceding that the old saw remains true, "theater must succeed as a business or it will fail as an art," Ms. McCann suggested that it may nevertheless be possible to succeed at both.

## GARDENING AND FARMING

To be a successful garden designer one must be a synergist—skilled in achieving an overall effect that combines many variables: climate, season of the year, setting, soil conditions, nutrients, light conditions, the properties of various plants, the ability to use space effectively, and, not least, the tastes and sensibilities of the garden owner.

To cite one example, we recently had a "woodland" bed installed in a somewhat shaded area behind our house. The setting included a brown wooden fence in back of the bed along with a loquat tree at one end and a Japanese maple at the other. We wanted a bed that would be neat in appearance and somewhat formal, yet also "interesting" and able to provide some fall-winter-spring color, if possible.

Our garden designer first examined and measured the bed. Then he retired to develop a detailed plan, complete with a drawing, which we readily approved. Next he carefully prepared the bed. He cleared out the weeds, dug up and turned over the soil to loosen it up, and added soil amendments to enrich the bed and give it a slightly acid pH.

Some of the lower branches of the loquat tree were pruned to raise the canopy over the bed, and adjustments were made to the automatic sprinkler system to accommodate the water needs of the new plants. Three different nurseries were visited to find the right combination of high-quality plants—rhododendrons, camelias, azaleas, hellebores, bergenia, dwarf pittisporums, and dwarf ferns. These our designer planted not at random but in a subtly contrived pattern that was variegated yet had an overall symmetry and balance. Finally, a redwood mulch was laid on top of the bed to inhibit the growth of weeds, to aid in water retention, and to protect the soil from rapid temperature changes.

Had our designer neglected any one of these factors, or had he tried to please himself rather than his customers, he would not be in such great demand.

## BIODYNAMIC/FRENCH INTENSIVE

Synergy in the gardening field reaches its apex, perhaps, in what has come to be known as the Biodynamic/French Intensive method. This cumbersome title refers to a system of mini-farming developed on the West Coast during the past two decades that combines a number of earlier horticultural innovations.

So powerful is this system that the Biodynamic/French Intensive method is revolutionizing small-scale agriculture. John Jeavons, the guru of "the method," has demonstrated with experimental garden plots and on his own mini-farm that it is possible to produce sustained yields that average four to six times greater than those of conventional agriculture and sometimes ten or twenty times greater. A mini-farmer with a half acre of land can, in some circumstances, earn $20,000 a year from cash crops. Moreover, the techniques are simple to learn, they work in varied climates and soils, and they don't require large capital outlays.

The key to the method is that there is no key. Instead, every aspect of the complex combination of factors that make for healthy plant growth are carefully controlled and managed to achieve an optimum result. The philosophy behind the method, in Jeavons's words, is that "nothing happens in living nature except in relation to the whole."

Instead of using conventional garden rows, the Biodynamic/French Intensive garden is based on the use of large, raised beds. Raised beds have a number of advantages. They provide more surface area and make more efficient use of limited garden space. They also reduce soil erosion and compaction and moderate soil temperature changes during the day-night cycle. They are more convenient for hand watering. They facilitate weeding and pest control. In addition, they allow plants to be clustered together to create mini-climates and "companion plant" relationships which, in many cases, can aid in plant growth, inhibit the growth of weeds, and discourage pests (yet another form of synergy).

## SOIL PREPARATION

Soil preparation also differs from the conventional methods. Instead of hoeing the garden site to loosen up a few inches of topsoil, or even plowing to a depth of perhaps a foot, each bed is carefully "double-dug" with hand tools to a depth of three feet or more, so that water, air, warmth, and nutrients can freely circulate, and so that root systems can penetrate easily and deeply.

Even the bed width (six feet at the maximum) is carefully designed to allow it to be worked, planted, watered, weeded, and harvested without, for the most part, having to step on the bed and compact the soil. If the gardener does have to step on a bed, the prescribed method involves using a large, plywood board to distribute the weight.

Much attention is given to the arrangement of the beds and to planning the garden, in order to make the most efficient use of space and create the optimum growing environment for various plants. Thus if the beds face south, corn should be planted on the northernmost bed so as to avoid blocking sunlight from the tomatoes and zucchini. Shade-loving plants like cucumbers, though, can be interspersed among the corn stalks. Some practitioners grow corn and beans together, using the corn stalks as bean poles. The beans pay back the favor by fixing nitrogen for the corn. Similarly, green beans and strawberries tend to do better when they are grown together. On the other hand, onions stunt the growth of green beans.

"Interplanting," as this method is called, is also used by practitioners as a strategy for preventing the depletion of soil nutrients (for instance, by planting nitrogen-fixing sweet clover together with nitrogen-loving wheat), and for creating natural barriers against vegetable pests. Nasturtiums, for example, can protect vine crops against their insect enemies, and marigolds can help rid the soil of the nematodes that feed on the roots of tomatoes, eggplants, strawberries, and various ornamentals.

## SOIL QUALITY

Practitioners of the method also emphasize the importance of soil quality. Chemical fertilizers can be hard on the soil, especially on the various microorganisms that are important to soil conditioning and plant growth. For this reason, chemical fertilizers are eschewed in favor of compost (which has many desirable qualities), as well as aged manure and a variety of exotic soil amendments. Depending on what soil tests reveal, the soil amendments might include blood meal, bone meal, horn and hoof meal, fish meal, kelp, sand, phosphate rock, dolomite lime, gypsum, eggshells, wood ashes, and more.

All this is prelude, though, to the actual process of planting and nurturing the beds. Carefully developed techniques are prescribed for everything from how (and when) to prepare and transplant flats (shallow wooden trays in which many plant seeds can be given a head start in an enriched environment) to the proper spacing of seedlings (much closer than with conventional methods). Likewise, watering is done with a hand sprinkler so as to minimize erosion, provide better control over the watering process, and "approximate rainfall." Even weeding has become a science, since some weeds, it turns out, have desirable properties and should not be removed from the garden.

The Biodynamic/French Intensive method is ideally suited to the backyard vegetable garden. It is also helping to stimulate a revival of mini-farms. And it is being tried with great interest in underdeveloped countries that are short of arable land but have plenty of labor. However, it is not likely to replace American agribusiness, where the focus, for better or worse, is on technology and the yield per farmer, not per acre.

## MAINSTREAM AGRICULTURE

Mainstream American agriculture can be viewed as a giant, sometimes cruel paradox: a continuing revolution that mixes positive and negative synergies seemingly in equal measure. In

1800, some 90 percent of our population lived in rural areas. In 1910, when the number of farms in this country was nearing its peak, one-third of the population were farmers. Today, the figure is about 2.5 percent. Of the 2.4 million farms in 1983, 30 percent took in over 80 percent of all cash receipts. In farming as elsewhere in our society, the trend is to get big or get out.

Coupled with this bigness is relentless pressure for increasing efficiency. One farmer in the U.S. produces enough to feed about sixty people. The world average is about 5.1 people, and even Western European farmers are only one-third as productive. As a result, Americans pay a smaller percentage of their income for food than any other major nation—23 percent versus 27 percent in West Germany and 52 percent in Russia.

## TECHNOLOGY

One reason is technology. Americans have always led the way in technological innovation, from the McCormick reaper to barbed wire, hybrid corn, center pivot irrigation, and now "no-till" planting. Consider a few recent examples:

- The "total confinement" method of pig production, which has taken pigs entirely out of the old-fashioned pigpen and into a highly controlled environment in which the average pig can be raised from a 2-pound newborn piglet to a market weight of about 220 pounds in five to six months (representing a weight gain of up to 1.2 pounds per day). Each year some 90 million pigs go to market in this country.
- The "big round baler," which produces huge cylindrical bundles of hay that are more than ten times as large as the old-fashioned rectangular kind. One of these new baling machines allows one worker to do a part of the haying operation that used to require several workers, and do it faster to boot (though it is also more dangerous).
- William Spence's remarkable Quadractor, an ungainly tractor on stilts that operates with a gas-sipping 8-horsepower Briggs & Stratton engine and features four-wheel drive and independent four-wheel steering on a unique vertical axle system. The Quadractor can climb a 42-percent grade, tra-

verse rocky terrain with ease and, most important, haul several times its own weight (among other tasks), all for a price tag of a few thousand dollars, a pittance in the farm machinery business.

- High-precision irrigation, where moisture mixed with plant nutrients can be monitored by computer and doled out to the plants through watering tubes. An Arizona cotton farmer using precision irrigation needs only one-half to one-third as much water as with traditional irrigation methods, yet his cotton yields will be 30 to 50 percent higher.

- "Dairy parlor" operations in which genetically improved cows are totally confined from birth and given specially formulated diets. (Pastureland is turned over to the production of feed.) When calves are desired under this regime, a highly technical program of artificial insemination is used to control the timing and reinforce the quality of the herd. Though the nation's dairy herd is only 3 percent larger than it was fifteen years ago, it is producing 16 percent more milk.

## GOVERNMENT PROGRAMS

Of course, technology is only part of the story. Government programs have also played a role, ranging from agricultural research and education to price supports, farm credit programs, rural electrification, soil conservation, and direct subsidies for farm improvements. Since the 1930s, the federal government has spent more than $115 billion just to prop up farm prices, along with $15 billion for soil conservation measures. In 1983 alone, the total federal outlay for farm aid was $7.3 billion, one of the biggest items in the federal budget.

Developments in the nation's infrastructure have also benefited farmers: railroads, paved roads, automobiles, electric power, refrigeration, telephones, antibiotics, etc.

Technological innovations in agriculture get the headlines, but most of the major developments have involved new synergistic combinations, or augmentation of an existing combination. Modern pig farming, for instance, would not be possible without advances in pig genetics, veterinary medicine, the science of pig nutrition, cheap electric power, and an efficient transportation system, among other things.

## SUNFLOWER OIL

One of the more striking illustrations of the role that synergy plays in agricultural innovation is the case of sunflower oil. A patent for extracting vegetable oil from sunflower seeds was granted to an Englishman, Arthur Bunyan, in 1716, but there was little interest in growing sunflowers commercially until well into the nineteenth century. The first country to do so was Russia, and the reason was political, not economic. The Church had forbidden the consumption during Lent of foods that were rich in oil. Sunflower oil escaped the ban because it had not previously been exploited in Russia. Russian farmers took advantage of the loophole and for many years they were virtually alone in growing sunflowers for oil.

In the United States, peanut oil, cottonseed oil, and, more recently, soybean oil predominated. Sunflowers were not competitive with these other oil-bearing crops: Their yields were not high enough; the oil content of the seeds was too low; they matured too slowly and erratically (which frustrated mechanical harvesting); and they were susceptible to rust and other plant diseases.

In the 1890s, American agricultural researchers began a breeding program designed to improve the commercial potential of sunflowers. The program continued, with many false starts and setbacks, for seventy years. Finally, in the late 1960s a hybrid was tested that had all the requisite properties: It matured rapidly; it was resistant to disease; its yields were 20 percent higher than those of nonhybrids; its seeds had twice the oil content of its ancestors; and it could readily be harvested with combines or the sheller-pickers used for corn. The plant even has a deep taproot that makes it resistant to drought. In addition, its residues can be sold for use as a high-protein meal, as roughage for livestock, or as a constituent in pressed wood logs and fiber board. Some producers also see a potential for using sunflower oil as a diesel fuel.

This genetic (and economic) breakthrough coincided with a

rapid growth in demand for vegetable oils, first from the European market and then in relation to a shift in U.S. consumption patterns toward polyunsaturated fats. The result of this synergistic combination has been a dramatic increase in sunflower agriculture in the U.S. In ten years sunflower production rose from negligible levels to become the second most important oil-producing crop, after soybeans. Agricultural experts project that production will increase further, from about 5.6 million tons in 1980 to 10 million tons before the end of this decade.

## NEGATIVE SYNERGIES

The paradox in our remarkable agricultural system is that it also produces some serious negative synergies: an alarming loss of topsoil to erosion, rapid depletion of underground water supplies in some areas, severe water and air pollution due to ever-increasing use of chemical pesticides and herbicides, and extreme vulnerability to such "externals" as interest rates and the value of the dollar overseas.

Indeed, there has been a vicious circle in recent years whereby the government has encouraged greater production (in part to generate exports that could offset a negative trade balance), which has resulted in heavy farm indebtedness for land purchases and new technology, which has led to groaning surpluses that require huge government subsidies, which has inflated the federal deficit, which has helped keep interest rates high, which has added to the farmers' debt burden and helped to increase the exchange rate of the dollar, which has discouraged farm exports (by making American farm products more expensive abroad), which has depressed farm prices and added to the burden of government subsidies, which has reduced farm income and produced a tidal wave of farm foreclosures, which has increased the pressures for greater efficiency and augmented the trend toward bigness.

If bigger were always better, this trend would not be worrisome (though the cost to many farmers and their families has been great). But in fact there seems to be a threshold effect similar to those we have noted earlier. A recent study by the Department of Agriculture has revealed that the biggest farms in this country tend not to be the most efficient. In the Corn Belt, the most efficient farms averaged about 640 acres. Furthermore, 90 percent of these efficiencies could be achieved with about 300 acres. Similarly, on wheat farms of the Northern Plains states, maximum efficiencies were achieved on farms of about 1,475 acres. Again, 90 percent of those efficiencies could be realized on farms of only 230 acres.

Equally significant was the finding that very large-scale corporate farming operations, both in this country and elsewhere, generally fail, or else perform relatively poorly.

The results of a grand, if unintended agricultural experiment are in. There are limits to economies of scale in farming. Moderately sized, family-owned farms tend to be more productive and profitable than large, impersonal factory farms. In other words, there are limits to the synergies that technological innovations can provide, especially when they do violence to the "soft," core factors in the Synergy Model. These factors apply to agriculture as elsewhere in our economy.


ARCHITECTURE

To be an architect is to be a synergist, a builder of "wholes" that serve an almost infinite variety of human purposes and tastes. Partly an artist, partly an engineer, partly a provider of services to clients with varying wants, the architect must strive to blend aesthetics with such practical concerns as where to locate the men's room.

To be sure, the function of a building normally drives such subsidiary matters as siting, the organization and use of space, lighting, selection of materials, and so forth. As the old architectural cliché has it, "form follows function," whether it be a cathedral or a shopping center.

An example, indeed a monument, to what can happen when a construction project is cut loose from any rational, functional constraints is the house built in San Jose, California, by Sarah Winchester, heiress to the vast Winchester Rifle fortune. For 38 years, until her death in 1922, this eccentric, spirit-driven widow devoted herself to the construction of a mansion on her 160-

acre estate. It was a project that continued 24 hours a day, 365 days a year.

The purpose of this round-the-clock construction work was simply to keep building—nothing more. Having been told by a medium that the spirits of those killed by Winchester rifles would take their revenge if ever she stopped the construction of her home, Sarah took the medium's message to heart.

Unfortunately, she had no architect. In fact, she had no plan at all. Rooms were added to the house on impulse, having been sketched on a napkin at the breakfast table, or perhaps suggested by one of the carpenters. The result is a mind-warping maze of rooms without reason. There are stairs that lead nowhere, closets and windows that open to face brick walls, cabinets in odd corners that turn out to be the only means of access to the adjoining rooms.

When the work finally did cease, on the night Sarah Winchester died, this massive, shapeless mansion had 160 rooms with 1,000 windows, 47 fireplaces, and over a mile of meandering corridors. All of these many parts were put together in such an extraordinary jumble that there could be no other practicable long-term use for the house than to serve as museum for future generations of bemused tourists, which is in fact what it is today.


## FRANK LLOYD WRIGHT

At the opposite extreme from this sad relic of our pioneer days is the enduring work of Frank Lloyd Wright, one of America's greatest architects. Like the Winchester mansion, several of Wright's creations also serve as museums today. Some were intended as such, like the stunning Guggenheim in New York City. Others have become museums because of their distinction, and because of the wishes of their owners. In either case, Wright's structures pay homage not to man's potential for irrationality but to a soaring imagination that was able to combine form and function in ways that are at once practical and aesthetically dazzling.

Wright was the complete architect. Though he may have given his imagination a bit too much scope on occasion and made some mistakes, like everyone else, he never made compromises with aesthetic considerations, and he was often brilliantly innovative in combining form and function.

Using a metaphor drawn from the natural world, Wright called his approach "organic architecture." The term referred to Wright's ideal of an architecture in which form, function, and the environment where the building is situated, not to mention its interior decor and its furnishings, are fully integrated and harmonized. A building should blend with its surroundings, just as its interior and exterior should blend with one another.

"Organic architecture is a natural architecture—the architecture of nature, for nature," Wright explained in one of several published expressions of his philosophy. "[It] proceeds from the ground that somehow the terrain, the native industrial conditions, the nature of the materials and the purpose of the building must inevitably determine the form and character of any good building." To Wright, any compromise of this architectural ideal was tantamount to committing a sin, and by his standards many members of his fraternity were deep sinners (which did not endear him to his brethren).


POSITIVE SYNERGY

A striking example of Wright's work is Hollyhock House. Built into a hillside overlooking Los Angeles, the house was designed in the 1920s for a wealthy matron who wanted to be able to display her art collection and hold large musicales and theatricals.

Wright responded to the challenge by designing a structure that has a large interior courtyard containing a semicircular pool that serves to frame the area intended for use as a stage. To take advantage of the terrain, Wright made interesting use of multiple levels, so that the house seems to merge with its surroundings. Indeed, part of the roof can be used like a balcony. In an effort to keep the house close to nature, Wright also brought flowing water into the house itself, where he used it to form a moat around the living room fireplace.

The climate of southern California presented another challenge, and, anticipating some of the energy conservation measures that are more widely employed today, Wright strove to

THE SYNERGISTIC SOCIETY / 223

incorporate climate-control features into the design. To shelter the house from the summer sun, Wright gave the roof a low overhang. The prevailing western winds inspired Wright to design garden walls that would allow the breezes through while still providing needed privacy. The house is also built on a concrete slab that serves to moderate temperature changes during the day-night cycle. Though Wright felt a heating system was unnecessary in southern California, for the occasional chilly day he provided an abundance of fireplaces, some of which are unobtrusively blended into the surroundings while others form focal points, depending on the purpose of the room.

In fact, every detail inside the house is designed to enhance both the utility and the overall effect of the whole. Textured concrete and wood, decorated throughout with a hollyhock motif, form rooms of varying sizes and shapes, each of which was carefully furnished by Wright himself, down to such details as leaded glass windows, hardware, cabinetry, rugs, and furniture items.

Wright also had a strong concern for utility and allowed no space to go to waste. In the "music room," for instance, cabinets especially designed for storing instruments and music have been set into the walls. Even the built-in seats provide extra storage.

Ceiling heights are also varied to suit the purpose of the room: low in family rooms to provide an intimate feeling; vaulted with clerestories and lots of outside light for rooms that are designed for more public purposes, or to display the art collection.

Walking through the house, one gets an extraordinary sense of both variety and unity; the various parts fit together and work together. If innovation was one of Wright's hallmarks, so was synergy.


NEGATIVE SYNERGY

The antitheses of Wright's exalted works are our modern cityscapes, where towering skyscrapers have been crowded together like so many massive slabs to form deeply shaded, glass-walled canyons. One notorious example, a 25-block-square area in midtown Manhattan, provides a classic case of negative synergy; *New*

*York Times* architecture critic Paul Goldberger calls it "an urban horror."

Over the past twenty-five years this small chunk of urban real estate has gained the dubious distinction of having the greatest concentration of high-rise office buildings in the world. Between 1960 and 1983 alone, 172 new structures were added with a total of more than 91 million square feet of floor space, more than the total downtown office space of Houston and Dallas combined. The new buildings are, almost without exception, huge curtain-wall boxes with little or no architectural distinction, while many of the older, more distinguished buildings in the area have been dwarfed and their aesthetics destroyed.

"There is such a thing as being too crowded," writes Goldberger, "and midtown Manhattan has become just that—a place in which enormous buildings block out not just sun and sky, but one another; a place in which traffic moves not just slowly, but almost not at all; a place in which walking is not necessarily more practical than riding, because the sidewalks are as jammed as the streets." At midday in the midtown area, it can take half an hour to go a dozen blocks by taxi. Air quality in the area has also deteriorated markedly, and noise levels greatly exceed federal standards.

A certain level of urban density may well provide positive synergy—an energizing effect—according to recent research and theory in social psychology. Such findings have helped to justify the building boom, though economic factors (or, more precisely, the synergies in skyscraper construction) are the driving force. But, unfortunately, the psychologists have neither data nor theory about overcrowding; they have no idea whether or not there may be a threshold beyond which more crowding is too much. However, if the psychologists were to go ask the people who live and work in the area whether they like their environment and find it exhilarating, we'd be willing to wager on the results.

## THE MILITARY

During the Revolutionary War, the Continental Congress authorized construction of an eighteen-gun frigate for the purpose of harassing British warships. When the USS Ranger was commissioned in the fall of 1777, she weighed a mere 308 tons and carried a complement of 140 men. Nevertheless, under the command of Captain John Paul Jones, the Ranger played an important wartime role, including victorious sea battles against two British frigates.

The modern aircraft carrier Ranger, commissioned in 1958, is the eighth American warship to bear that proud name, and it dwarfs all of its predecessors combined. Some of the statistics are fairly astounding. It displaces 80,000 tons, and it is longer than three football fields laid end to end. On the angled part of its flight deck it is almost a football field wide. If the Ranger were a parking lot, it could park 1,900 cars.

It is also as tall as a ten-story building, from water line to bridge, and there are another 36 feet below the waterline. When it was under construction at Newport News, Virginia, it took several million blueprints and 2 million pounds of welding metal just to put all the pieces together.

Inside the Ranger the statistics are equally impressive. There are 17 decks, in all, that are divided into about 3,000 different compartments. (Many of the crew members never actually get to see all of the ship, and it can take a week for a new man to get "orientated"—to use the navy's idiosyncratic English.)

The Ranger's fuel tanks hold 2 million gallons, its water tanks hold 400,000 gallons (the distillery can produce about 80,000 gallons each day), and the food lockers hold about 3 million pounds. It has two 30-ton anchors with 1,000 feet apiece of anchor chain, each link of which weighs 360 pounds. And there are two five-inch guns just under the flight deck in case of need.

The Ranger is also equipped with four huge airplane elevators that can lift up to 65 tons each, four steam catapults that can fling a 30-ton aircraft into the sky at 150 miles an hour, four hydraulic engines linked to arresting gear cables that can land a jet fighter at 135 miles an hour and bring it to a complete stop in a few hundred feet (navy pilots call a carrier landing a "controlled crash"), plus some 600 miles of electrical cable, a maze of plumbing, sewage and steam pipes, 2,400 dial telephones, a public-address system, and a half dozen other internal communications and signaling systems.

All this incredible bulk can be propelled through the water at speeds in excess of 30 knots, thanks to the Ranger's eight huge steam boilers, which power the ship's four giant turbine engines, which in turn deliver to four 30-foot-wide, 30-ton propellers about 280,000 horsepower.

## A SMALL CITY

It is often said that a modern aircraft carrier is like a small city, and this is no exaggeration. More than 5,000 officers and men are needed to operate the Ranger and its airwing, which must be largely self-sufficient during cruises that may last for several weeks at a time. Accordingly, the Ranger has some fifty sleeping compartments, several mess halls, and a hospital complete with 77 beds, an intensive care unit, a physical therapy unit, an outpatient clinic, a laboratory, a pharmacy, half a dozen dental chairs, and an assortment of battle dressing stations and decontamination stations throughout the ship.

There is also a laundry, a tailor shop, three barbershops, four dry goods stores, a snack bar (or "gedunk shop" in navalese), a post office, a print shop, a library, a chapel, movie projection equipment, and TV and radio stations. To feed a crew of this size, the cooks must prepare each day 1,000 loaves of bread, 10,000 pounds of vegetables, 5,000 pounds of meat, 3,000 pounds of potatoes and serve over 15,000 meals.

And that's not all. To operate the ship and enable it to accomplish its mission, the crew is divided into twelve different departments ranging in size from less than twenty to more than six hundred men.

The deck department does the traditional seaman's work— mooring and anchoring the ship, operating launches, chipping paint, handling transfers at sea from tankers and supply ships, and "calling away" with the traditional boatswain's pipes everything from general quarters to mail call.

The engineering department, with some 650 men, is the shipboard equivalent of a utility company, appliance repair service, and fire department all rolled into one. The ship's power plants, electrical, plumbing, heating, and air-conditioning systems are its responsibility, as well as firefighting and battle-damage control.

The aircraft maintenance department, with over 400 men, operates twenty-seven different work centers where everything from jet engines to radio receivers and radar equipment can be tested and repaired.

The 200 men of the weapons department are responsible for storing, maintaining, testing, and loading the various bombs, missiles, rockets, and conventional ammunition that are used by the ship's aircraft and gun mounts.

The operations department plans and coordinates all flight operations, as well as collecting air intelligence and weather information for the airwing.

The air department handles the launching, landing, and "spotting" on deck of the ship's aircraft, as well as providing local air traffic control whenever planes are airborne.

There is also a navigation department, a medical/dental department, a communications department, a supply department, an administrative department, and a marine detachment under its own commanding officer that is responsible for shipboard security plus various ceremonial functions. All this and more in support of an airwing consisting of half a dozen squadrons and their aircraft, along with the pilots, crewmen, and other squadron personnel.

The payoff is a multi-billion-dollar synergistic effect: the ability to deploy on short notice upwards of one hundred of our best combat aircraft almost anywhere in the world to engage an enemy. We're the only nation on earth that can do that, and we currently have fourteen aircraft carriers and their support ships operating in various parts of the world.

## SYNERGY IN WAR

However, the synergies produced by a single ship, or even an entire task force, pale by comparison with what is required to prosecute even a small war these days. For war is, above all, an enterprise concerned with producing synergies: results that are the combined effect of manpower, technology, organization, training, leadership, strategy and tactics, logistics (the art of moving and supplying an armed force), industrial and agricultural production, and, not least, morale and the will to fight.

If it is not quite true, as General George Patton claimed, that "compared to war all other forms of human endeavor shrink to insignificance," war ranks right up there; the successful prosecution of a war must of necessity be a cooperative effort. Consider the modern classic waged by Great Britain in 1982 against Argentina, a war that was precipitated when Argentine military units seized the Falkland Islands without warning, after 149 years of British occupation.

On paper, the military situation was not promising. With no advance notice, Britain had to assemble a large task force (ultimately numbering more than 100 ships and 27,000 men), complete with fighter aircraft, assault and antisubmarine helicopters, landing craft, assault troops, tanks, troop carriers, artillery, and sufficient supplies and ammunition to last for many weeks. The task force then had to steam 6,000 miles and carry out an amphibious attack against an enemy that was well prepared, well supplied, and had the advantage of being close to its home territory, well within range of its air bases and surface fleet. To top it off, the notoriously harsh South Atlantic winter was setting in, with a likelihood that it would complicate the landings, the logistics, and the movement of troops once ashore.

## A MASTERPIECE OF WARFARE

Nonetheless, the British set out to reconquer the Falklands and within ten weeks scored a brilliant victory, a small masterpiece of modern warfare. There were losses and some heavy fighting, to be sure. The Argentine air force performed surprisingly well and managed to sink several British ships, most notably the frigate HMS Sheffield (which was dispatched with a single Exocet missile). Once ashore, the assault troops encountered stiff resistance at certain points, including some hand-to-hand combat. But British losses were moderate overall, and the tide of battle flowed steadily in their favor. How did they do it?

The battle plan that the British evolved was elegant. First, submarines were used to impose a naval blockade and bottle up the Argentine fleet. When the Argentines tried to test the blockade with the aged cruiser Belgrano, the ship was promptly sunk.

Next, commando units were surreptitiously sent ashore to gather intelligence and identify a location for the landing. This knowledge proved to be vitally important.

Instead of making a frontal attack on the capital city of Stanley, where most of the Argentine troops were located, a decision was made to land on the opposite side of the main island, at San Carlos. The San Carlos site had several advantages. It was sparsely populated and lightly defended; it was in a protected sound, where the assault ships would not be exposed to heavy seas; it had sandy beaches that were ideally suited for small landing craft; it had some hills near the beach that would provide valuable observation posts; best of all, the Argentines were clearly not expecting the invasion to occur at this site and would find it difficult to mount a rapid counterattack from across the boggy terrain, known as "no man's land," that lay between the two sides of the island.

## SURPRISE

To achieve the maximum surprise, the British attack force moved into the sound under cover of darkness, while other British warships and planes engaged in diversionary attacks at Stanley and several other Argentine strongholds. The invasion itself, coming before dawn, was a landing "carried out by stealth rather than force," according to a newsman who was on the scene; the maneuver took four hours. Only light resistance was encountered.

Once ashore, the commandos fanned out to occupy the surrounding hills, while other troops on the beaches set up antiaircraft defenses, laid down landing pads for supply helicopters, unloaded the Scorpion light tanks, Land Rovers, artillery, and supplies (all well suited for the terrain), and did what infantrymen have always done, dug foxholes.

When the Argentines did counterattack, it came from the air. But the British managed to fight off the attackers with a combination of shipboard and shore-based antiaircraft missiles and Harrier "jump-jet" fighters launched from the two British aircraft carriers, which remained at sea and out of range of the Argentine fighters. Later on, some of these versatile, highly maneuverable fighters were moved to shore-based sites, where they could respond to air attacks more quickly.

Once the beachhead was firmly established, the British moved quickly to press the attack. Traveling at night, mostly overland with full packs but also by small outboard motor boats, British parachute troopers were able to capture the twin settlements of Darwin and Goose Green within forty-eight hours, even though they were greatly outnumbered by an Argentine garrison that put up stiff resistance, at least at first. The combination of well-placed artillery, repeated air attacks, and a determined assault by British paratroopers, who fought hand to hand, carried the day and produced 900 prisoners. British casualties were light.

After more slogging overland in driving rain and strong winds, the British were able to seize several strategic peaks around the capital, where they set up artillery, moved in more troops, and began a massive supply operation, partly on foot and partly by helicopter, while Harrier jets and ground-based anti-aircraft missiles kept the Argentine air force at bay.

Next came a softening-up operation using artillery, air attacks, naval bombardment, and air-dropped leaflets urging surrender.

When their troops were ready, the British administered the *coup de grace*: a skillfully executed night attack that caught the enemy by surprise. The Argentine troops woke up to find the enemy in their midst. In some locations there was fierce hand-to-hand fighting, but the resistance soon collapsed. The British, to their surprise, took more than 11,000 prisoners and seized a small mountain of arms and ammunition.

Clearly the British victory was a synergistic effect: the combined result of a brilliant plan, superior intelligence, appropriate (not necessarily better) technology, excellent organization, smoothly coordinated execution by elements drawn from various services, superb training, outstanding leadership, and, not least, high morale, determination, and perseverance. If it was not Britain's finest hour (a term generally reserved for the Battle of Britain against the Nazis in 1940), it was nevertheless one for the history books.

## MILITARY HISTORY

History, which very few of our own military men take the trouble to study deeply today, is replete with examples of defeats in which one or more of the many factors that make for success in war was neglected, or missing. The failure of the Greek city-states to unite against Philip of Macedon doomed them all to conquest and domination. Had the Gallic and British tribes been able to achieve a united front, they might have avoided being incorporated into the Roman Empire. In nineteenth-century Africa, the Nuer tribes, acting in concert, were able to expand at the expense of the disunited Dinka. And the English employed a divide-and-conquer strategy to add the jewel of India to its imperial crown.

Unity is important, of course, but it is not enough. In the 1850s, an outnumbered British force, armed with quick-loading rifles, was able to decimate and finally defeat a splendidly disciplined army of spear-carrying Zulu warriors. In 1940, the Nazi *blitzkrieg* strategy overwhelmed and demoralized a numerically superior French army. And it took more than unity for the Americans to defeat the fanatical, suicidal defenders of the Japanese Empire. The U.S. also had superior numbers, vastly greater resources, better technology, far more production capacity, better intelligence, and, in the end, a lot more ships, planes, tanks, and firepower. Despite a woeful lack of preparedness before Pearl Harbor, in the end we were able to put all the pieces together.

## LOW SYNERGY

These observations may seem to be platitudes, but the fact is that our military leaders (and the politicians who ultimately control the purse strings) seem to be ignoring the lessons that past military history can teach. Instead of having a unified military organization in which all of the pieces fit together and work together toward the common defense, we have been burdened historically with a badly fractionated, bureaucratic system that pits the individual services—army, navy, air force, and marines—against one another; each of the services has prepared to fight its own war, more or less independently of the other services. Indeed, dysergy-producing competition between the services has predominated over synergy-producing cooperation.

Thus the army developed the Apache helicopter for fighting tanks, while the air force developed the A-10 jet for the same role; the army defends against air attacks with the Patriot missile while the air force does the same thing with its fighters. Most absurd of all, each of our four services has the capability for close support of ground troops, an extravagantly wasteful redundancy.

Instead of encouraging a holistic approach in which equal weight is given to all of the factors that make for success in war, with each service playing a complementary role, our system has fostered interservice competition, redundancy, and a preoccupation with the latest piece of military hardware, regardless of the cost or justification for it. And, instead of having well-thought-out, realistic strategies, we have had disjointed planning that, on the one hand, assumes we will do everything but, on the other hand, is cavalier about how to provide the necessary means. Says Senator Sam Nunn, a military affairs specialist: "It has been said that military strategy is the art of looking for danger, finding it everywhere, diagnosing it inaccurately, and prescribing the wrong solution."

The result is dysergy—overlapping roles, duplication of effort, a fascination with high-tech weaponry, and an absorption with winning budget battles and protecting one's own turf, rather than worrying about how to get the job done. Even in World War II, service rivalries cost us dearly. In the Pacific theater, where the army and navy had separate commands, there were some near defeats because of poor battlefield coordination, most notably at the battle of Leyte Gulf. In Vietnam, each of the services fought its own air war, with only a limited effort at cooperation. This didn't improve an already bad situation. And in the (relatively) successful Grenada invasion, lack of coordination between the services prolonged the struggle and made it more costly. (Not even the radios of the participating services were compatible.) In the Falklands war, by contrast, the British operated under a unified command, while the Argentines were hampered by a defense establishment that closely resembled the American model!

## A SYMBOL: THE M-1 TANK

A symbol of much that has been wrong with the American military is the controversial new M-1 tank. The army will ultimately buy over 7,000 of these fifty-five-ton monsters, at a cost of about $20 billion or more (cost overruns have so far put the project about 40 percent over its original budget). Though the M-1s are capable of traveling at high speeds and contain sophisticated electronic fire-control equipment, they have been temperamental and subject to frequent breakdowns. They are so complex that their crews have had difficulty operating them. They require 3.8 gallons of fuel (or more) per mile and have had to stop for repairs approximately every forty-three miles, which offsets their speed and places an additional burden on logistics and repair crews. (The army has estimated that operating and maintenance costs will run 40 percent higher than for the tank it is replacing.) But more important, the new tanks are vulnerable to enemy shells and require the help of a bulldozer whenever they need to dig in.

It is not a tank to inspire confidence. It has not functioned in the field the way it was supposed to on paper; it has some conspicuous weaknesses; it needs a lot of hand-holding; and it is enormously expensive to build and operate. Nevertheless, we are plunging ahead with building more of them. To what end? Only in a major land war in Europe on the scale of World War II would such a large number of heavy tanks make any sense. But does such a war make sense at all in the nuclear age? Even if both sides agreed not to be the first to use nuclear weapons (an agreement likely to be broken by the loser), the sad fact is that the U.S. no longer has many of the other requisites for fighting such a war: the necessary industrial base, the means for deploying a large army across the ocean, and the logistical infrastructure needed to sustain that army for months or even years. There are also deficiencies in organization, training, and, most especially, sound planning.

## A REFORMER

General David C. Jones, retired former chairman of the Joint Chiefs of Staff, has been an outspoken advocate of fundamental reforms in our military establishment. In a professional journal he writes: "We cannot escape the fact that our national security today requires the integration of service efforts more than at any time in our history. . . . We need to spend more time on our war fighting capabilities and less on an intramural scramble for resources." Commenting in the *New York Times Magazine* on our recent military buildup, General Jones warns that: "Fundamental defense deficiencies cannot be solved with dollars alone—no matter how much they are needed. We do not think through our defense problems adequately, and we are getting less capability than we should from our increased defense budget. There is reason to believe that, faced with a contingency requiring a major joint operation, our performance would be below the level we should expect or need."

Senator Barry Goldwater, one of the leaders of a congressional drive to reform the military, is even more blunt. *Time* quoted this prediction: "These problems will cause Americans to die unnecessarily. Even more, they may cause us to lose the fight." (At this writing, a military reform bill was working its way through the Congress. Its effects, if enacted, remain in doubt.)

## GOVERNMENT

If government is often the problem, to use President Reagan's rhetoric, it is equally often the solution. Indeed, government is a prolific producer of both positive and negative synergies, high and low synergies, and competitive and cooperative effects.

On the positive side, NASA, whose past accomplishments most Americans still take pride in despite the recent tragedy, is after all a government agency. And so is Social Security, which has demonstrated time and again that it has broad public support.

Though Americans take less pride in their postal service, consider what it *does* accomplish. In 1900, the total volume of mail was 7.1 billion pieces. In 1980, it was 106 billion pieces, a middle-sized mountain, which 666,800 postal workers in 39,500 postal facilities nationwide were able to deliver safely, if not always on time, to a total of 83.2 million "delivery points." And, despite its image as antiquated and inefficient, the postal service is delivering 40 percent more mail than it did in 1970 with a work force that is 10 percent smaller.

As for the postal service's overall track record, a recent study showed that 95 percent of next-day postal deliveries arrive on time, while 86 percent of the two- to three-day first-class mail reaches its destination as scheduled. And things will get better. By 1989, some 550 automated mail sorting machines will be in place, more than three times the present number. With the new technology, two operators can do a job that currently requires 18 workers using the old method, and they can do it one-third faster to boot. On the other hand, most observers would agree that the postal service still lags in customer service, courtesy, and responsiveness to complaints.

## CONGRESS

Our national legislature, likewise, is a veritable paragon of synergy. Altogether, 435 representatives, 100 senators, and some 20,000 legislative staffers divide up among themselves a vast enterprise: They write, introduce, and process 10,000–12,000 bills each session; they staff 42 specialized committees and 243 subcommittees; they conduct some 7,500 hearings; they write some 850 committee reports; they interact with roughly 15,000 lobbyists; they deal with officials from the White House, 13 giant cabinet-level departments, 80 independent agencies, and over 800 advisory committees and boards regarding literally thousands of government programs; and, of course, they respond to around 1,400 representatives of the news media and several million politically active constituents.

Each year, our Congress collectively produces approximately one million pages of printed matter (sometimes with tens of thousands of copies) in the form mostly of hearings (595,000 pages), bills (96,000), reports (46,000), and the *Congressional Record* (38,000). In addition, the members and their staffs receive some 46,500,000 phone calls (100,000 each) and close to 200 million letters and postcards—about 375,000 each. There are also a total of more than 400 million pieces of franked outgoing mail each year. The annual budget for all this, along with such ancillary support functions as the Library of Congress and the Congressional Budget Office, exceeds $1.6 billion (or about seven dollars per capita).

The ultimate purpose of this monumental effort is the 600 or more laws that are enacted each session. And each floor vote, each head count, is an exercise in producing a combined effect— the aggregation of a sufficient number of individual votes, or blocs of votes, to produce a majority either for or against a given bill. Sometimes the pattern of voting is shaped largely by party ties; sometimes it is shaped by economic interests, or state interests, or regional interests, or constituency pressures, or even patriotism; but many times all of these things and more are blended together to determine the outcome.

In a thoughtful essay called "The Hidden Hand," I. E. E. Thomas stresses the power that one person, or one vote, can have on the course of history. He cites the following examples, among others:

- Oliver Cromwell gained control of England in 1657 by one vote;
- It was one vote that gave America the English language, rather than German, in 1776;
- France made the transition from monarchy to republic in 1875 by one vote;
- Rutherford B. Hayes won the presidency of the U.S. in 1876 by one electoral vote;
- And it was one vote that gave Adolf Hitler the leadership of the Nazi party in Germany in 1923.

Such narrowly decisive votes—for or against—happen occasionally in our Congress too. But, of course, such cliff-hangers are not really the result of one vote. From a synergy perspective, they are merely threshold effects like those we have observed elsewhere. A tie-breaking vote merely tips the result across the threshold from negative to positive synergy (or vice versa, depending on your point of view). A synergistic thinker always keeps in mind the combination of factors that produce such overall results.

## DYSERGY AND LOW SYNERGY

If our governmental machinery is held in low esteem these days, the reasons are not hard to find. Consider just a few examples among the countless cases of dysergy and low synergy in the public sector:

- In a survey, reported in the *San Francisco Chronicle*, almost half the federal government workers queried said they had personally observed examples (mostly unreported) of waste, mismanagement, and outright fraud—stealing, accepting bribes, buying deficient goods, awarding funds to ineligible recipients, giving unfair advantages, tolerating dangerous situations; the estimated cost was $23 billion a year.
- The Federal Office of Management and Budget estimates that, despite recent efforts at paperwork reduction, the average citizen spends at least ten hours a year reading and filling out government forms; and many of us spend a lot more than that.
- The Grace Commission estimated that mismanagement of personnel policies by the federal government (sick leave, for example) costs the taxpayers some $30 billion a year more than is necessary. And "system failures," such as glitches in the Defense Department's inventory management practices, produce excess costs estimated at an astounding $53 billion.
- About 20 percent of the cost of a new house, according to the chief economist at the National Association of Home Builders goes for satisfying various government regulations.
- If you want to start a new business in, say, West Virginia, you must fill out no less than seventeen different government forms from a dozen different agencies. And failure to complete any one of the forms could lead to stiff penalties.
- By stretching out the decisions and procurement cycles on new weaponry, the Congress has greatly inflated the ultimate costs. In 1955, it took eight years to build a new bomber. Now it takes thirteen years. Likewise, it required five years to build a new fighter plane in 1955 versus eight years today. According to the General Accounting Office, each year's delay adds 25 to 30 percent to the final cost.

- In 1960, the number of lawsuits brought against local governments was 270. In 1980, it was 13,534. The cost to the taxpayers for defense against these suits and the burden it places on the agencies that are the targets, whether the case is merited or not, has gone up accordingly.
- It costs the Veterans Administration $61,500 per bed to build a nursing home, four times what it costs a private sector operator.

Journalist Charles Peters, founder of the *Washington Monthly* and a longtime observer of the nation's capital, thinks the country is ill served by its government. The problems, as he sees them: A cautious, self-protective bureaucracy whose sole purpose is "fund-wheedling" and playing "make-believe government"; a survival network of shared purposes and shared efforts linking various lobbyists and government officials; a foreign service that does little significant work; a military establishment that has deteriorated; a legal system that serves lawyers, not people; regulators who favor the industries they regulate; and a press that relies too much on official handouts and pronouncements. Even if Peters is only half right, it is a sorry state of affairs. But more important, it matters—a lot.

## SYNERGY (DYSERGY) AND SOCIETY

What is true of the many parts applies also to the whole. For we are all embedded in a larger system—a collective survival enterprise in which each of us is affected by the actions, or inactions, of many others. A healthy economy is a rising tide that, as the old saying goes, lifts all boats. An efficient telephone system is a national asset—a time and money saver for all of us. Good roads are a public good that impact on transportation costs for all of us. Every innovation that increases farm productivity means (potentially) lower food costs for consumers. And a competent, honest, efficient government is more likely to ensure that its functions will be properly (and economically) performed for the general welfare.

Conversely, an inefficient, unreliable transit system can have ramifying consequences even for many people who do not use the service directly. A high crime rate affects everyone's insurance rates, and we are all victimized by the accident-prone drunk drivers who push up the cost of police services, auto insurance rates, and health care costs (as well as bearing responsibility for about half of our auto accident fatalities). If defense contractors produce "smart" bombs with defective computers, fighter planes with cracked tailfins, or missiles that blow up on their launch pads, such failures put the nation as a whole at risk. Likewise, in the economic sphere, if we allow our educational standards to deteriorate at the very time when changes in the economy demand better educated workers, we run the risk that we will lose out to other nations that are investing more heavily in their "human capital." And if our government is corrupt, obstructionist, or merely ineffectual, we risk losing the race to our foreign competitors in the long term.

## THE JAPANESE MODEL

These days everyone's favorite example of a high-synergy society is Japan, and rightly so. With a population of 115 million people living on a mountainous string of islands with a total land mass roughly equal to the state of Indiana, Japan has few natural endowments. It is required to import one-half of its food calories, 90 percent of its energy, and the vast majority of its raw materials. Moreover, at the end of World War II, its economy was in ruins and its cities were devastated by Allied bombing.

Yet thirty-five years later Japan had risen from the rubble to become the West's second industrial power, after the United States (and some think they've pulled ahead). Japan has seized the leadership of one industry after another: steelmaking, shipbuilding, cameras, watches, motorcycles, consumer electronics, robotics, typewriters, and automobiles, among others. And it has set its sights on doing the same in such industries as machine tools, aircraft manufacturing, microelectronics, communications, biotechnology, and some areas of space technology. One indicator of the Japanese threat is the fact that, with half the U.S. population, Japan now graduates as many engineers as we do. Another indicator is that Japan has surpassed the U.S. in the number of patents granted each year. Robert C. Christopher, a former journalist and longtime student of Japan, declares flatly that it is "the most purposeful and productive society of any great industrial nation in the world." The result, says the noted journalist and Asian scholar Theodore H. White, in an article in the *New York Times Magazine*, is "one of history's most brilliant commercial offensives. . . . Only in another ten years will we know who finally won World War II."

Though there are some features about Japanese society that an American may find unattractive, nonetheless Japan can be credited with some of the most favorable quality-of-life indicators of any nation (based on 1980 data): high life expectancy (seventy-four for males, seventy-nine for females), high literacy (99 percent), very low unemployment (1.2 percent), low crime rates (1.9 robberies per 100,000 people), and a strongly positive outlook among its citizens, as measured by public opinion surveys.

Many analyses have been done recently of Japan's stunning success, and there are an abundance of theories to account for it. The list includes: An ancient and homogeneous culture, a feudal tradition (which stresses authority, reciprocal loyalty, and deference), an ethic of self-discipline and hard work, strong families, a willingness to sacrifice for the common good induced by Japan's crushing defeat in World War II and its inherent economic vulnerability, low labor costs, low defense and social welfare costs (Japan has a relatively young population), a cooperative relationship between government and industry (symbolized by the government's powerful trading authority, MITI), subsidies and protectionist measures by the government to aid the private sector, aggressive innovation, rapid automation, a management style that emphasizes the "soft," core factors (symbolized by the so-called quality circles), the productivity of the individual worker, lifetime employment, a rigorous educational system, and more.

The correct answer, of course, is all of the above. The Japanese juggernaut involves a remarkable blend of feudalism, socialism, and capitalism embedded in a uniquely favorable cultural environment and energized by a strong sense of a collective purpose. Take away any one of the major contributing factors and the outcome would not have been the same.

## THE U.S. MODEL

Japan is not the only model of a high-synergy society, of course. A model closer to home is the U.S. during World War II, a time of extraordinary dedication and national purpose. As historian Gerald D. Nash put it in his *Great Depression and World War II*: "Rarely had the American people shown such self-discipline and unity as they did during World War II. They entrusted the direction of most wartime activities to a vastly expanded federal bureaucracy; they gave wholehearted support to a high degree of centralization in the American economy to achieve maximum production; they relaxed prejudices against minority groups for the sake of wartime unity; and they even organized their cultural activities to boost their morale. More than in any previous conflict, World War II prompted an unprecedented national effort to mobilize materials and human resources for the common effort."

The challenge was immense. Even before the attack on Pearl Harbor the number of military personnel began to increase, due in large part to the first peacetime draft in our history. After Pearl Harbor there was a great flood of volunteers and a procession of draft calls, which ultimately swelled the armed forces to more than 12 million men and women. This huge citizen army had to be housed, clothed, fed, trained, armed, and then transported to every corner of the globe to fight simultaneously against three different enemies.

In addition, America had to serve as the combined arsenal and larder for all of its major allies. It had to ship thousands of tanks, airplanes, and trucks to Russia, supply great quantities of material to the British, equip the army of Nationalist China and the forces of the Free French, build harbors in the Persian Gulf, set up aluminum factories in Canada, and construct airfields all over the world.

Within months, a new War Production Board had commandeered entire industries for the purpose of building tanks, aircraft, jeeps, trucks, landing craft, machine guns, artillery, ammunition, and many other items. Production of automobiles, radios, refrigerators, and a host of other consumer goods was halted completely. Decrees were issued that required manufacturers to save on the use of scarce raw materials ranging from textiles (cuffs were eliminated from mens' trousers and limits were set even on womens' skirt lengths) to copper ("Lucky Strike Green Has Gone to War," read the ads for a new cigarette package with an unfamiliar red dot).

The prodigies of wartime production are legendary, and justly so. In five years, the GNP nearly doubled. Our capital assets, accumulated over many decades, increased by almost 50 percent. Farm production, despite a 17-percent decline in farm workers, increased by one-third. The nation's factories poured forth a cornucopia of arms and munitions: 300,000 airplanes, 86,000 tanks, 71,000 naval vessels (ranging from aircraft carriers to landing craft), and 3,000 merchant vessels.

One of the most remarkable success stories involved the Kaiser shipyards. It took about 300 days in 1940 to build a merchant ship using conventional methods. So Henry Kaiser introduced prefabrication and mass production methods. By 1942, his shipyards were able to cut the time to 80 days. But that was only the beginning. In 1944, Kaiser was launching 10,000-ton Liberty Ships in just 17 days. (Fittingly, Henry was dubbed "Sir Launchalot.")

## GOVERNMENT AND INDUSTRY

Cooperation between government and industry played a vital role in the wartime production effort. Many new factories were built by the government itself (which were later sold off at bargain prices). When supplies of natural rubber from the East Indies were cut off by Japan, the government launched a crash program to develop a synthetic rubber industry, and by war's end we were producing 800,000 tons a year, more than enough to meet our needs. The government also played a key role in doubling our steel output and increasing aluminum production sixfold.

Meanwhile, in response to a flood of government contracts, thousands of small manufacturers shifted over to war production. A canning company, for example, began fabricating parts for merchant vessels; a maker of mechanical pencils started making bomb parts; a bedding manufacturer turned to making mosquito netting; and a soft drink bottler converted its machinery to load explosives into artillery shells.

Rationing of gasoline, tires, shoes, meat, sugar, butter, and other items was imposed by the new Office of Price Administration, and soon everyone had to line up at local rationing boards to get their ration coupons. Many other items, from soap to cigarettes, became hard to get. To prevent inflation, the OPA also imposed price controls on many consumer goods, while the Office of Economic Stablization put a lid on farm prices and wages. Organized labor also cooperated by obtaining a voluntary no-strike pledge from major unions. And, despite some unrest (especially in the coal mines and railroads), work time lost to strikes dropped to less than 1 percent during the war years—less than in besieged Great Britain.

By today's standards, taxes during the war years were astronomical. In October 1942, President Roosevelt, by executive order, set a ceiling on after-tax salaries of $25,000. By the end of the war, the effective tax rate for the top income brackets reached a confiscatory 94 percent. Yet people paid without complaint.

The government also imposed tight censorship over letters and other correspondence, while the Office of War Information, under newsman Elmer Davis, edited "war news" and cranked out favorable propaganda.

The scientific establishment was also enlisted for the war effort, through the Office of Scientific Research and Development, with impressive results. Among the many innovations that contributed to victory were improvements in sonar and radar detection systems, battlefield rockets such as the "bazooka," incendiary bombs, proximity fuses, insecticides such as DDT, drugs such as penicillin, blood plasma (which was responsible for saving the lives of many wounded soldiers), and, of course, the atomic bomb.

To manage the myriad aspects of the total war effort, with all its immense complexity, the size of the federal government increased during the war years from just under one million in 1940 to 3.5 million in 1945. Inevitably there was confusion, waste, du-

plication, and overlapping of responsibilities. Rivalries and conflicts among the various agencies prompted one journalist to describe the situation as "The Battle of Washington."

Nevertheless, the job got done. "What the war experience
revealed to the American people," observes historian Nash,
"was that the federal government, if necessary, could effectively
manage the economy. It could stimulate production, facilitate
full employment, create a higher standard of living, and still
keep the nation solvent." (Not to mention successfully prosecut-
ing the war!) The leadership of President Roosevelt was the glue
that held it all together.

## PERSONAL SACRIFICES

None of this would have been possible, though, without the
wholehearted cooperation and readiness to sacrifice of the
American people—a cliché that is nevertheless profoundly important. Millions of Americans willingly joined the armed forces
and went off to face death in battle. Many millions more had
their lives uprooted as the men went off to war and the women
took jobs in defense plants around the country. In all, some 15
million civilians moved to some other locality to work during the
war years. Housing became tight, especially where new factories
were being rushed into production. Tent cities, trailer camps,
and families doubled up in one house or apartment were a common sight. Public transportation systems became overcrowded.
Long lines became the rule everywhere. There were enormous
strains placed on our shorthanded hospitals, schools, churches,
and local governments.

Everyone had to make do with the old car, the old clothes,
and "Spud" cigarettes (a dreadful wartime substitute). And when
the washing machine broke down, people had no choice but to
do without, or perhaps to borrow the neighbor's machine.

Yet morale was high. Whenever anyone complained, the standard put-down was: "Don't you know there's a war on, buddy?"
Thousands of industry executives dubbed "dollar-a-year men"
volunteered to go to Washington without pay to aid the war effort. Old folks came out of retirement to serve as air-raid war-

dens or take jobs as Western Union delivery "boys." Hundreds
of thousands of volunteers served on draft boards and rationing
boards, recycled tin cans and newspapers, planted "victory gardens," and donated some 12 million pints of blood.

Even Hollywood did its part. In addition to a flood of patriotic
songs and war movies (*Wake Island, Bataan, They Were Expendable,
Wing and a Prayer, Thirty Seconds Over Tokyo, This is the Army*),
Hollywood cranked out hundreds of training films for the military. (Ronald Reagan did a few, and one classic, *Land and Live
in the Jungle,* starring Van Heflin, was still being used with student
aviators fifteen years later.) A number of Hollywood stars volunteered for the armed services, while others spearheaded war-
bond drives (all of which were oversubscribed) or entertained
the troops at the Hollywood Canteen.

The quintessence of that great national effort was captured by
journalist Robert Sherrod in *Tarawa: The Story of a Battle,* an eye-
witness account of the assault against Tarawa Island, one of the
bloodiest battles of the Pacific war:

> To look at row upon row of these pillboxes facing the sea, it seems
> impossible that the Marines ever got ashore D Day. But, in one of them,
> somewhat larger than most along here, I think I find the answer. Inside
> the pillbox there are four dead Japs and two dead Marines. Enough of
> these men in the first wave got ashore, jumped in with the Japs and
> killed them. Thus they knocked out enough machine guns so that others
> in later waves might live and win. Looking down on these two Marines,
> I can say: "These men gave their lives for me. I can understand it
> because this machine gun covered the part of the water I had to wade
> through. They also gave their lives for one hundred and thirty million
> other Americans who realize it, I fear, only dimly." My feeling is one
> of deep humility and respect for such brave men—God rest their souls.
> How much every man in battle owes to every other man! How easy it
> is to see on the battlefield that we are all in this thing together.

Despite Sherrod's disparaging remark about the American
people, our military success in World War II was the result of a
total national effort. Our victory was an example of synergy on
the grandest scale—a common purpose pursued with great
resolve, great resources, great intelligence, and great unity of

effort. Not only was America's performance in that terrible struggle a historical benchmark but, more important, it is a model for how we can, and must, deal with challenges we now face as a nation.

# 12. *E Pluribus Unum*

"From many, one." This, we tend to forget, is our national motto. From many small pieces of stained glass, an awe-inspiring cathedral window. From 1,000 tiny brush strokes, a pointillist painting. From 100,000 blades of close-cropped Bent grass, a putting green. And from the diverse resources, skills, and efforts of the American people, such collective achievements as a telephone system, a military establishment, or an air transportation system.

On the other hand, when any of the parts begins to decline, the whole may suffer. We are all diminished if telephone service declines even as rates and operating costs are increasing. We are all at risk if our military forces cannot perform as they should. We are all affected in one way or another if airline service deteriorates—the negative synergy ripples through the economy. And we are all penalized if jobs and profits flow out of the country, shrinking the tax base, increasing the burden of unemployment and welfare, and reducing the pool of capital needed both for replacing worn-out equipment and for further economic growth.

## APPEARANCES

We have been lulled by our recent economic recovery into a belief, or at least a fervent hope, that as a nation we are now on the right track. We would like to believe that the economic, social, and political troubles of the 1960s, and especially the 1970s ("that slum of a decade," as one writer termed it), are now behind us. Look at the revival of American patriotism. Look in particular at the 1984 Olympics, where our victorious young athletes and an impressively efficient Olympics organizing committee seemed to symbolize a national renewal. "The system is working," the *Wall Street Journal* editorialized at the beginning of 1985, "and success feeds on itself."

The pessimists and doomsayers seem to have been silenced. Silver hoarding has gone out of style, and we hear little these days about "survivalists" who are living in the wild with a year's supply of food and a shotgun at the ready. Indeed, optimism has been institutionalized in the person of President Reagan, while the stock market—that most sensitive of all economic indicators—has been breaking records. We have been assured by many of our economists of continued prosperity, and, as Adlai Stevenson once said: "The contest between agreeable fancy and disagreeable fact is unequal. . . . Americans are suckers for good news."

## THE REALITY

The fact is, however, that the American economy is in a precarious state, and the long-term trend is ominous. Our mounting trade deficits are alarming—an economic hermorrhage that, it has been estimated, has wiped out at least 5 million American jobs to date and devastated entire industries. Some economists predict that a declining dollar will turn the situation around, but in actuality many of our problems are structural and will elude quick fixes.

Worse yet, we owe our recent economic recovery to some dubious causes: the massive, unsustainable deficit spending by the federal government, a huge influx of capital from foreign countries (much of it short-term, liquid assets that were attracted by our high interest rates), excessive levels of corporate and personal indebtedness (at the highest levels in our history), and a grossly overvalued dollar.

The outspoken governor of Colorado, Richard Lamm (dubbed "Governor Gloom" by his critics), describes this country as sitting atop a "souffle economy"—an economy that is in danger of collapsing. Lamm warned in a *Wall Street Journal* interview: "We are violating all the rules of history . . . all the rules of economics."

This nation is in serious trouble, and there are signs of long-term decline. It will take more than a budget cut, economic deregulation, a devaluation of the dollar, or a decrease in military spending to turn around this classic case of low synergy. We cannot survive as a nation that, as Lee Iacocca puts it, sells hamburgers to one another and computer chips to the rest of the world. Indeed, the Japanese are challenging our dominance even in computer chips—and winning.

Nor can we survive with a disorganized, self-destructive family life, with fractionated and dangerous communities, with second-rate schools, unreliable public transit, poor work skills, slovenly (and drug-affected) work habits, short-sighted and greedy management, and, most important, spreading poverty and despair.

As for the grand self-delusion (promoted by some futurists) that we can trade information or management know-how (or even corn and soybeans) overseas in sufficient quantities to pay for millions of automobiles, TVs, cameras, shoes, apparel, and all the rest of our material needs, that's economically naive. Automaking and steelmaking are not "sunset industries" that we can simply write off. If we don't produce cars for the American people, somebody else will, and they will also get the jobs and the profits and, in the long run, our wherewithal for purchasing cars.

It is a dangerous illusion to argue, as some futurists do, that we are simply in the throes of a painful transition from an industrial to a "postindustrial" society. Like all half-truths, it ignores the other half. The reality is that we are also being challenged economically from every quarter (except, ironically, the anemic Russian economy), and in every sector, from avocados to solar cells. Our military rivalry with the Soviets should not be minimized, but the fact is that we are engaged in a two-front war, and the economic war has not been going very well.

## NEGATIVE SYNERGY

To understand what has been happening to this country, and what can be done about it, we must dig deeper. We must consider the "whole" and its many parts. In other words, we must look for negative synergies. It would require a Ph.D. thesis to detail all the interrelated causes of our troubles, but a few of the more significant factors can be identified:

- The lulling effect of our uniquely favored historical experience, especially our European heritage, our vast natural

resources, our geopolitical isolation, and our frontier environment;
- Overconfidence induced by our overwhelming military success in World War II and our economic preeminence in the postwar era;
- A smug complacency arising from our unprecedented material affluence in the postwar era;
- The proliferation in recent decades of adversary relationships between government, business, labor, and consumers, with many negative consequences;
- A political system that only in crises seems capable of asserting an overarching public interest (political scientist James MacGregor Burns calls it "the deadlock of democracy").
- Government regulation run amok, or else subverted to protect (and favor) some dubious vested interests;
- The ascendancy in our economy of a new class of narrow, technocratic, profit-driven business managers;
- The dissolution of our civic culture, most especially the values and ethical norms (and educational standards) that are vital prerequisites for an efficient, productive society;
- A series of wrenching national traumas, including the civil rights revolution, the environmental and energy crises, the assassinations of political leaders, the Vietnam War, and Watergate, all of which corroded our national self-esteem and sense of purpose.

There are many more factors, of course. But perhaps the single most important cause has been our *weltanschauung*—the linear view that it was our "manifest destiny" to have an ever-ascending trajectory of economic growth, material progress, and technological leadership. There was an unspoken national conviction that our well-being could be taken for granted, as if it were our birthright. In the words of Juvenal, the first-century poet: "Luxury is more ruthless than war."

WHO'S TO BLAME?

So who is responsible for our sagging performance as a nation? The answer is our business managers, labor leaders, government officials, politicians, bureaucrats, bankers, educators, social philosophers, psychologists, lawyers, doctors, engineers, workers, parents, and, indeed, all the people who, generation after generation, have earned their livings, raised families, voted (or not voted), and participated (or not participated) in our society. In other words, we all bear part of the blame.

In the introduction to a special issue of *Time* in 1981 concerned with an "American Renewal," Editor-in-Chief Henry Grunwald made this observation: "America's ills are attributed to changes abroad and variously to lack of will, failure of nerve, moral decay, selfishness and sloth, the shattering of community feeling. One can find signs of all these, but the key may be something else: the fact that Americans want just about everything without considering or fully understanding the cost. . . . To use an ungainly but accurate word, we have forgotten the tradeoffs."

We want freedom, but we don't want crime in the streets. We want education, but we don't want to work too hard, or pay very much for it. We want increased incomes, but also increased leisure. We want efficiency, but also more coffee breaks. We want to be competitive, but we don't want some robot taking over our jobs. We want Medicare, Social Security, farm subsidies, aid to education, and all the rest, but we resent high taxes. There is something to be said for Grunwald's point, but our problem is more complicated, and so is the solution.

## VISIONS OF THE FUTURE

"I saw the future," says a character in one of the Calman cartoons, "and it was being repaired."

There is more than one way to interpret that wry bit of crystal-gazing. If you are a utopian—or merely one of the optimists who contributed to a golden anniversary issue of the *U.S. News and World Report* in 1983 entitled "What the Next Fifty Years Will Bring"—the cartoon strikes an unsettling note.

Utopians have a way of leaving out of their schemes the imperfections of the real world. In the futuristic fantasies of the 1939 World's Fair, or of Disney World, it is assumed that the future will be perfectly ordered, perfectly managed, perfectly efficient. Technology will provide for our needs and wants automatically, effortlessly, and we will all flow smoothly through life like water in a quiet-running stream. Somehow, utopia will be free of entropy—of human errors, human strife, human suffering, human vices, or even simple malfunctions.

"An economic boom will give tomorrow's citizens the highest standard of living ever known," claim the editors of *U.S. News* in their anniversary issue. "Floating cities will house thousands of people. Levitating trains will travel at 250 miles an hour. With exotic new energy sources, the U.S. will no longer depend on foreign regions for oil. . . . Freed by technology from much of life's drudgery, people will at last have the time to allow their creativity to flower." (Even Plato, our first great utopian thinker, was realistic enough to know that the key to a harmonious society was not to be found in technology alone; in *The Republic*, Plato focused on making changes in people, society, and the political order.)

Meanwhile, the population explosion continues; the worldwide plague of poverty remains intractable; deadly famines stalk various regions; environmental pollution, it is believed, has already caused measurable climate changes; the arms race continues unabated; and America's future remains clouded with uncertainty as we continue to be outperformed by other nations. If the "prophets of boom" are to be believed, the future will need some major repairs.


PROPHETS OF DOOM

A second way of interpreting Calman's cartoon is as a jibe at the prophets of doom. In the Club of Rome's famous report entitled *The Limits to Growth*, published in 1972, an ambitious computer model was used to project into the future various contemporary trends in population growth, resource consumption, pollution, and so forth. The alarming conclusion was that economic growth had to be stopped in its tracks. If we didn't immediately undertake a transition to a no-growth society, there would be a catastrophic collapse within a century.

Needless to say, such an authoritative-sounding report—

clothed as it was in the trappings of "science"—sparked a heated controversy. The consensus among the critics was that the Club of Rome's computer model (developed by a team at M.I.T.) was too simplistic. Among other things, it did not allow sufficiently for human adaptability. Nevertheless, many experts remain convinced that our future is deeply threatened. A subsequent U.S. government report called "Global 2000," even though it was politically massaged before publication in 1980, still contained some disturbing news: If existing trends continue, 40 percent of the world's remaining forests will be destroyed within twenty years. By the year 2000, 20 percent of the world's remaining animal species will be extinct. And each year an area of cropland the size of Maine is becoming a desert.

The experts' gloom was on parade in 1981 in a public television special called "The Doomsayers." Just listen to some of them:

*Edward Cornish* (World Future Society): "I think the possibility of a very serious economic depression is very real."

*Admiral Gene Larocque, retired* (Center for Defense Information): "I think that we're just simply going to blow ourselves up as a result of our arrogance in a nuclear war with the Soviet Union."

*Anne Ehrlich* (Stanford University): "Starvation is a very real possibility."

*David Brower* (Friends of the Earth): "When you attack, at an exponentially increasing rate, resources that are not renewable, you're headed for trouble."

*Fritjof Capra* (University of California, Berkeley): "The way I see our current situation is a way which has been described by cultural historians many times. Toynbee and many others noted that civilizations or cultures have the tendency to rise, culminate, and then decline and disintegrate."

*Willis Harman* (Stanford Research Institute): "There's a lot of fear, there's a lot of despair. There's a certain basis for both. There's a basis for feeling that our present approaches to the problems of the nation, the problems of the world, are not going to solve those problems."

*Malcolm Muggeridge* (journalist/social critic): "What it amounts to is—human beings imagining that they are in complete control of their own destiny. That men are sufficient. That men can invent this marvelous technology; they can use this technology; they can establish a way of life which will make everyone happy and prosperous and peaceful. And, all of this is untrue."

If subsequent events have not exactly contradicted the doomsayers, the clouds may have lifted a little. Population growth has moderated somewhat; some of the emerging technologies in food production (such as drip irrigation, no-till planting, salt-tolerant crops, and higher-yielding plants) hold the promise of being able to defer the predicted disaster in food production; progress in solar technology points the way to an ultimate transition from highly polluting fossil fuels to an abundant, non-polluting energy source. Finally, our economic recovery, as much as anything else, has made it unfashionable to be a doomsday prophet. Whether or not the doomsayers happen to be right is immaterial; they have lost their audience. In other words, our *imagined* future is being repaired.

## A MIDDLE WAY

A third interpretation of Calman's cartoon is the one we prefer. It is possible Calman meant to suggest (prophetically) that the future can be repaired—that the negative trends that are now so evident in our society and the world as a whole can be reversed. Perhaps he was anticipating that we will face up to our problems and come to grips with them in an effective way.

The implication is that the future certainly can be salvaged, but it will not take care of itself; we must do the repairs ourselves. The invisible hand may be a good carpenter, but it is an indifferent architect. Indeed, when the invisible hand is unrestrained, the results can sometimes be as disorganized as the Winchester mansion. (That is why we have zoning laws, for instance.) It would be a risky gamble simply to turn the carpenter loose and hope that everything will work out alright. That was not how we built this nation. That was not how we fought and won World War II. That was not how we got to the moon—and back. And that is not how our major competitors have been able to challenge our one-time dominance.

But are we facing up to our problems? Have we really mobilized our energies and called in the repair team—the architects, electricians, plumbers, roofers, painters, and so forth? Or is our future still in serious disrepair?

We happen to believe that our efforts to date have been piecemeal and inadequate to the task at hand, and we do not feel comfortable with the upbeat predictions of our pop-prophets— who are prone to criticize others for extrapolating from existing trends and then proceed to do exactly the same thing.

## MEGA-PROPHECIES

Witness mega-prophet John Naisbitt, who assures us that we will win the race with Japan because we are better in "thought ware." A clever turn of phrase, but the data aren't very supportive. The Japanese score a full eleven points higher than we do, on the average, on standardized I.Q. tests. These tests are, to be sure, an ambiguous measure of intelligence, but such a difference in test scores is not trivial either. Japan, as we have noted earlier, educates its citizenry far better than we do, on the whole. It has a much higher literacy rate. It graduates as many engineers as we do (and they are better trained to boot), and it has pulled ahead of us in the patent race. The proof of the pudding, moreover, is Japan's emerging technological leadership; in one field after another, we find ourselves scrambling to catch up—or else already hopelessly outdistanced.

Or consider this prophecy: "It is too late to recapture our industrial supremacy because we are no longer an industrial economy." This is like saying that because only 2.5 percent of our population are farmers we are no longer an agricultural economy. We are fortunate to have such efficient farmers, but the number of farm workers is not a true measure of farming's vital economic importance.

Likewise, we still need steel, automobiles, refrigerators, and almost everything else that our factories were producing in 1950, though maybe not in baby-boom quantities. There is nothing postindustrial about the manufacture of computers. There is nothing postindustrial about the auto plants that were recently built in this country by Honda and Nissan. The joint venture between Toyota and GM is not postindustrial. Even if Ford and GM try to reduce labor costs by having their cars assembled in South Korea, Mexico, or Spain, they are no less industrial as a result.

Or take the claim that "we will have full employment and labor shortages for the rest of the century." To the many millions of unemployed blue-collar workers, destitute farmers, demoralized welfare mothers, and never (gainfully) employed post-teenagers, such prophecies seem totally disconnected from economic reality. Without a reversal of our debilitating trade deficit, and a revival of our industrial and farm sectors, to name two, full employment in the foreseeable future will only be achieved by a statistical sleight of hand.

We happen to think that such imaginative leaps and self-deluding prophecies are not on the whole very helpful. H. L. Mencken observed that "the prophesying business is like writing fugues; it is fatal to everyone save the man of absolute genius." It is certainly useful to look ahead, to consider the implications of existing trends. But it is not helpful to conjure hyperbolic "Third Waves," "Megatrends," and the like, with the clear implication that our society is being swept along by inexorable forces to which all of us must fatalistically adapt. That, unfortunately, is what such portentous, deterministic predictions imply.

## UP FOR GRABS

We, on the other hand, think the future is still very much up for grabs. The goals we set, the decisions and the efforts we make, individually and collectively, may help to make such predictions come true, or perhaps falsify them. That is why prediction is such a risky business, and why so few prognosticators ever show us their batting averages.

We are neither optimists nor pessimists. In our strategic planning work, we are accustomed to looking for strengths and weaknesses, opportunities and threats. That is what we see for our country as well. But we have learned the hard way to avoid making firm predictions in favor of "most-likely" scenarios selected from a range of alternatives in which one or more of the underlying assumptions could very likely change. We always state our projections in if-then terms, to remind ourselves and our clients that the future is contingent.

We also do for our clients what are called "baseline projections"—projections of what will happen if present trends continue and if no action is taken to change course. And it is those baseline projections that frankly worry us about the future of our society and our economy, regardless of the short-term economic picture.

The Joint Economic Committee of the U.S. Congress concurs. In its 1986 report, Chairman David R. Obey wrote: "We must face the fact that, since the mid-1970s, our economic performance has continued to be very disappointing, and *neither political party* has developed economic policies that produce sustained levels of strong economic growth without inflation. . . . The picture that emerges is of an American economy falling far short of its potential. The cost of that failure is a lower standard of living for the American people and weakened American leadership of the free world."

Some experts think the problem is far more serious, and urgent. In its special report earlier this year on "The Hollow Corporation," *Business Week* warned that the U.S. is already well along in the process of abandoning its status as an industrial power, and the decline of our manufacturing sector cannot be offset with more fast-food restaurants. The hollowing of American industry, says *Business Week*, "threatens the entire economy."

## THE EQUIVALENT OF PEARL HARBOR

We see the need for major changes in our existing strategies. We see the need to set clearly defined national goals. We see the need for an all-out mobilization of our talents, and skills, and energies, and resources. *Time*'s Grunwald put it very well: "An American renewal is entirely possible. But it is not inevitable. It will not be accomplished by rhetoric, chest-thumping, self-hypnosis. It will take great and disciplined effort and exact a considerable price." In short, what is needed, we think, is the psychological equivalent of Pearl Harbor.

Just as this nation did in World War II, and as the Japanese have been doing in a less dramatic way ever since, we must focus the energies of the nation as a whole on a clearly defined collective goal: in this case, the goal of restoring our competitiveness and our economic (and cultural) preeminence. Not only is it a worthy goal but it is an attainable goal.

This does not mean we should try to resurrect the past, obviously. Each period in history involves a unique configuration of forces. It would be a mistake to cling to outmoded strategies, or technologies, or weapons systems, or even cultural values for that matter. We must adapt to the changes that have been occurring everywhere in the world, and the root of the problem is that we have been slow in doing so—or have been making short-sighted, expedient responses. In too many ways, our society (and especially its leadership) is still wedded to an out-of-date vision of ourselves and our role in the world. Or to outdated ways of doing business and dealing with the competition from overseas.

## THE SOLUTION

H. L. Mencken used to say that "for every human problem, there is a solution that is simple, neat, and wrong." We tend to be skeptical of solutions that are simple and neat; they are the very antithesis of what the synergy principle teaches.

The way to begin coping with the national dilemma, in our view, is to stop looking for the key. There is no key. Instead we must attend to all of the many parts that affect the performance of the whole. It is not enough to restore our military strength if it is done at the expense of education, and health care, and farmers. It is not enough to make reforms in the values and the modus operandi of our business leaders without also reforming a burdensome and sometimes obstructionist government. And we are whistling in the dark if we think that changes in our national value system will occur without commensurate reforms in our national incentive system—and in a business environment that tolerates cynicism, corner-cutting, and outright cheating. As economist Kenneth Boulding has observed, a society that rewards liars and penalizes honesty will soon be populated with liars.

## A NEW "SOCIAL CONTRACT"

What we need, above all, is a new "social contract"—a new spirit of cooperation and a new sense of national purpose that draws its inspiration from the synergy world view, and from a keen awareness of what is at stake. We need a compact among all of us, in every sector, to work together to minimize (or conciliate) conflict, avoid obstructionism, increase productivity and efficiency—and win the economic war.

This new social contract must in turn be based on the "fair-shares ethic": Everyone must contribute a fair share; the sacrifices must be equitably shared; and everyone must receive a fair share of the rewards. In the end, there is no other way to achieve the kind of unity and cooperation that such a national effort requires. A "fair share" means putting an end to such things as:

- Corporations that pay no income taxes and yet do not invest their windfall tax savings back in the business;
- The "work rules" that unions have negotiated over the years as a thinly disguised means for creating more jobs at the expense of efficiency and productivity;
- Tax cheating (the estimate for California alone is about $2 billion a year), and the abusive tax shelters that enable some people to pay far less than their fair share in taxes;
- Hostile corporate takeovers that line the pockets of a few economic predators (and maybe give shareholders a bonus), while undermining the long-term vitality and competitiveness of the company—in reality a form of economic treason;
- Welfare cheating—a kind of economic parasitism that has long been a way of life in some quarters;
- "Golden parachutes" (excessive severance pay contracts) for high-level corporate executives who don't, in fact, have very far to fall;
- Sloppy work: wallpaper hangers who can't hang wallpaper straight, or painters who can't do a wall without paint spills and "holidays" (the cost is appalling);

- A military pension system which retires our professional soldiers just when they reach the peak of their experience, and value, and allows them to start another career at government expense;
- Bitter labor-management confrontations in which the company seeks to extract unilateral concessions, while the workers resist needed changes to the point of damaging the company's future;
- Cutting corners: Doing the minimum and trying to get away with it—an injustice to those who do an honest job;
- Excessive corporate salary packages; (*Forbes* reported that the CEO's of 258 top U.S. companies last year earned an average of $1.2 million, a 9 percent gain, while Japanese firms were trimming executive pay to cope with the rising yen);
- "Honest graft"—the compaign contributions that poison our political system and, ultimately, undermine the capacity of our government to serve the public interest.

A good place to start a national revitalization—indeed, a fitting symbol (and test) of our resolve—might be a national "give back." What if we all gave back to the economy some of the leisure time we now frequently waste?

For instance, holidays. Newspaper columnist Stephen Chapman recently suggested, less than half in jest, that we ought to stop observing meaningless national holidays that few of us really honor. The federal government, and a lot of businesses, now observe ten holidays a year—almost 4 percent of the total work year. If you add to that the traditional two-week vacation, labor productivity in much of the economy is reduced by nearly 8 percent each year.

Then there's the forty-hour work week. It used to be the case in this country that almost everyone worked at least a half day on Saturdays. In fact, the Japanese, among others, still do. (The average Japanese employee now works 44.8 hours per week while the Koreans average 54.4 hours!) In some parts of this country, moreover, the lunch hour is counted as part of the work day; the effective work day is only seven hours. Indeed, our average work week is only 35.3 hours, 21 percent less than Japan's and 35 percent less than Korea's.

What if we were to start by giving back to the economy—and to our competitive posture as a nation—five of our ten holidays: say, Presidents' Day (what better way to honor our forefathers), Memorial Day (likewise our war dead), Labor Day (an ideal way to help our workers), Columbus Day (no big deal), and Veterans' Day (the jobs they save could be their own). At a stroke we could add perhaps 2 percent to the productivity of our labor force, not a trivial improvement, without seriously inconveniencing most of us. As Chapman points out, those who might nevertheless wish to honor our presidents, our war dead, our workers, Christopher Columbus, or our veterans could still do so around the normal work day, just as many of us now observe St. Patrick's Day and Halloween.

Likewise, a 45-hour work week (or an average of five more hours per week) in the form either of an extra hour a day or a half day on Saturdays would add another 8 percent to our productivity. (Indeed, many Americans already work more than 40 hours per week; one in eight, according to a Bureau of Labor Statistics survey, works at least 60 hours per week.) Would an overall productivity improvement of 10 percent make a difference? It sure would.

But is any such national give-back likely? Only if all of us come to recognize our national peril for what it truly is. And only if the sacrifices are equitably shared. When a beseiged auto manufacturer extracts give-backs from its employees and then uses the money to fatten executive paychecks, buy other companies, or boost profits, instead of cutting prices on its products to make them more competitive, such a betrayal of the fair shares ethic undercuts the effort to win back employee loyalties and improve productivity.

Realistically, the only way a national give-back has any chance of working is if everyone agrees to shoulder a fair share of the responsibility—if managers also work harder, and with less disparity in pay scales; if owners pass along the savings to consumers and reinvest a larger share of their profits back in the business; if capital shows more patience and less concern for instant returns; and if government can get its house in order and reduce the burden of bureaucracy and taxes.

## A NATIONAL MOBILIZATION

Thus a national give-back can only be one part of an across-the-board mobilization of our national will and energies. Equally important, what is needed is a mobilization plan. We think any such mobilization plan requires a high-level cooperative effort somewhat like the Commission on National Goals that President Eisenhower convened in the 1950s. If a new commission were to be convened, however, it should not be a rehash of that exercise in national self-satisfaction. The need is far more urgent today than was the case back then. But more important, it should involve far broader participation by the various stakeholders and political power centers, not to mention the public at large. We are inspired by the Japanese phrase: "None of us is as smart as all of us." Why not ask the American people themselves to suggest what can be done?

It is possible, though, to identify here some of the general areas that must be included in any such national mobilization. (In some of these areas, the need has already been widely recognized, but whatever steps have been taken to date should be reinforced and accelerated, we think.) Our list includes:

(1) *Public Perceptions*: A process of education and leadership is needed if the American people are to be persuaded that business as usual will no longer do; there needs to be a political consensus for making major changes, and the nearest contemporary equivalent to Pearl Harbor, unfortunately, is our trade deficit. It is encouraging, though, that the polls indicate many Americans are aware of our problems and support appropriate actions.

(2) *The Public Philosophy*: The ideology of capitalism is not a dependable guide for organizing our economic system, as we have seen. If we want a high-synergy economy, we need an ideology that points us in the right direction. We have seen what it takes to achieve long-term superiority in the marketplace: high synergy. It takes capital, sound ideas, entrepreneurship, good

management, attention to details, motivated workers, and much more. We should emulate the approach of Jan Carlzon, who turned around an ailing Scandinavian Air System (SAS): "We don't seek to be a thousand percent better at anything. We seek to be one percent better at a thousand things." This can only be accomplished by cooperation, by a team effort in which everyone contributes, and everyone benefits equitably.

(3) *Our Value System*: Individualism was a cultural value that was well suited to a frontier society. Teamwork among individuals with diverse personalities, resources, and skills is more adapted to our era. Not coincidentally, there has been a trend in that direction of late, though it goes under various names: networking, joint venturing, participatory management, support groups, matrix management, and just plain "teamwork."

As for our personal values, we need to rediscover and place a higher value on such vitally important qualities as self-discipline, rigorous training, and superior skill (at whatever trade). Excellence, and its handmaiden perfectionism, is essential to a high-synergy society; it should become a national passion. Many years ago in a slim volume entitled *Excellence*, John Gardner (former HEW Secretary and Common Cause president) berated us for our superficial values. "The society which scorns excellence in plumbing," he wrote, "because plumbing is a humble activity, and tolerates shoddiness in philosophy, because it is an exalted activity, will have neither good plumbing nor good philosophy. Neither its pipes nor its theories will hold water."

Excellence, even on a personal level, can make a real difference. An experiment run by San Francisco's Yellow Cab Company a while back provides a striking illustration. A dozen of the drivers were asked to dress up for two weeks (knotted ties, dress shirts, dark jackets, slacks, short hair, and a neat, clean appearance). Meanwhile, a dozen others in a "control group" continued to do their jobs looking, as usual, like unmade beds. "I'm surprised at the way it turned out," said company vice-president Nate Dwiri afterward. He shouldn't have been. The average gross earnings for the dressy drivers were $1,360 for the two-week period, compared with $1,080 for the non-dressy drivers (or 21 percent more). We need to replicate such experiments on a national scale.

(4) *Family Life*: We must invest in rebuilding family life in this country, because families are the factories where we must hand-tool the competent, mature, well-educated, and well-motivated citizens that this society needs. A simple change in the tax laws to restore the kind of exemption for dependent children that Americans of the 1930s enjoyed would at a stroke take some of the economic pressure off our hard-pressed families. Family allowances, such as many other countries have adopted, would also help.

But more important is the time, love, care, and discipline that parents are willing (and able) to invest in their children, as well as the examples they set. In the end, each of the products of our family factories (truly a cottage industry) affects the whole. In one way or another we are all the beneficiaries of the contributions made by others. Likewise, we are all ultimately penalized by the battered children, the disturbed latch-key children, the school dropouts, the teenage prostitutes, and other horrors. There is nothing quite so sad as the sight of a parent who is wantonly destroying the potential of his or her own child.

(5) *Communities*: Communities matter, a lot. A strong neighborhood, even in a poor area economically, can provide a framework of mutual aid, of collective efforts, of social learning, and personal satisfactions. Conversely, crime and drugs can destroy a "good" neighborhood. Then there are the myriad of functional communities that provide much of our social experience, outside of our jobs: churches, service organizations, recreational groups, social clubs, and so forth. What happens in our communities has consequences that ultimately affect the performance of the whole. Strengthening community life should be a major national priority.

(6) *Education*: If we want good schoolteachers, we need to train them well and pay them well and hold them in high esteem. And if they perform well they should be encouraged and rewarded for continuing to teach. On the other hand, if a due-process system of performance evaluations determines that they are not serving us well, they should be dismissed. It's that simple. Of course, it's easier to prescribe the right solution than to change a system that, over the past few decades, has done just the op-

posite: trained teachers poorly, paid them poorly, held them in low esteem, smothered them with bureaucracy, and shown indifference in equal measure both to incompetence and to outstanding performances.

The sad state of our teaching profession has been more than matched in the past by the abysmal lack of student motivation, and it is unclear whether or not the message about the challenge we face as a nation has yet filtered through to our teen culture.

But then, the rest of us are not much better. We have a daughter who was a member of the Academic Decathlon team in her high school a few years ago. It was very exciting to see her compete in ten different "events" (from history to science to extemporaneous speeches) against teams from the rest of our county, then the state, then finally representatives from thirty-seven other states and foreign countries. What a sad commentary it is on the values of our society that this rigorous competition got less media attention even locally than the high school football team, despite the fact that the football team lost most of its games while the Academic Decathlon team won the national championship. Indeed, how many people have even heard of the Academic Decathlon?

There is also much that we fail to do, or do wrong when it comes to our curriculum. For instance, it has been established that our language-learning ability actually starts to decline after about age twelve. The lack of foreign language skills is one of the most serious educational deficiencies in our society. It can't help matters that our schools have not, traditionally, introduced foreign language instruction until high school.

In an era of two-career families and short summer vacations, we might also consider shifting to year-round schooling (which some districts are already doing)—not to speed up the educational process but rather to permit more of it, and in more depth. (Again, the Japanese are way ahead of us.)

(7) *Business:* In our experience, American companies still have a long way to go. It is encouraging to see a turnaround like the one at Walt Disney Productions. A dynamic new management team is revitalizing an American institution with plans for improvements in its theme parks, television specials, a host of new

movie productions, some joint venturing with Lucasfilm (*Star Wars*), a major new theme park for Europe, and an aggressive new marketing strategy.

Even more encouraging is what has happened to Chrysler. Written off by many "experts" and ideologically hidebound jeerleaders, the company recovered far more quickly than even the optimists expected. Not only that but Chrysler has been getting the jump on the competition recently (as well as an increase in its market share), most notably with a new mini-van that the public has judged superior to both domestic and foreign alternatives. (This is another example of fruitful government-private sector cooperation, however grudging the aid may have been.)

Despite such success stories, American business as a whole is still in trouble. Behind the mask of a booming stock market, our economy is in turmoil. Consider our auto manufacturers.

When the invasion of Japanese cars began, back in the 1970s, Detroit launched a much-ballyhooed counterattack: management reorganizations, massive investments in new technology, employee give-backs, renewed emphasis on quality, and so on. Most dramatic was the Saturn Project, GM's plan for a brandnew, high-tech production facility that would leapfrog the Japanese advantage.

Well, the results are now coming in. The 1986 member survey in *Consumer Reports* magazine indicates that, ten years later, Detroit's cars remain on the whole higher priced, have a higher number of manufacturing defects, and a higher overall frequency of repairs. Indeed, there is still some evidence of the corner-cutting that contributed to Detroit's troubles in the first place—most notably in the crash resistance of its bumpers.

Even more ominous for the future has been Detroit's inability to narrow the gap in production costs. The outgoing chairman of Ford Motor Company acknowledged recently that the gap is "as great as it's ever been." At GM, costs are so high that the company could not justify launching a new generation of domestic small cars. So it plans to buy them from abroad and resell them here. Indeed, GM's return on sales is the lowest in the industry and its earnings are expected to fall by fifteen percent this year. As for the Saturn Project, still several years from coming on line, GM is reportedly having second thoughts.

Without acknowledging the fact, the American auto manufacturers are in retreat. For the Big Three, plans for the next five years or so involve shutting down perhaps as many as ten more domestic plants and buying more cars (and parts) abroad. *Business Week* predicts that by 1990, the Big Three could be manufacturing two million fewer cars each year, while their overall share of the U.S. car market (to say nothing of the overseas market) could slip to less than two-thirds. At the same time, Japanese companies are planning to build more plants here. The list includes Subaru, Mazda, Nissan, Toyota, Honda, and Mitsubishi.

What still remains of our industrial sector will also soon have to decide whether and how to make a massive shift to robotics and automated factory operations, as this nascent technology reaches the take-off stage and as our major competitors press ahead on this front. At present, neither labor nor management seem prepared to deal effectively with the transition.

What should we do about the industries that are being wiped out by foreign competition, or survive only because of import restrictions? To write them off without a thorough examination of the causes and consequences is something we may later regret. We should not just take our chances, or else blindly follow our ideological proclivities.

(8) *Government*: There has been much talk in recent years of developing a national industrial policy. The idea hasn't been popular with a free-market administration, but such determined inaction by the government shows ignorance of what other governments are doing, not to mention the historic role that the public sector has played in creating, subsidizing and also destroying industries, sometimes intentionally and sometimes not. Equally important, a laissez faire attitude avoids making any systematic assessment of the piecemeal policies which are already in place and which are modified regularly in response to this or that pressure group. By the same token, the successive rounds of budget cutting and tax tinkering by the present administration are, in many particulars, implicit changes in our national industrial policies.

We need to think through more carefully, and in a broader and longer-range perspective, the role of our government in helping our industries to hold their own with foreign competitors whose governments are already deeply involved in playing a supportive role. Indeed, international economic competition has always been entwined with government, ever since the days of the East India Company, and only those who wear ideological blinders think otherwise.

## A NATIONAL REDEVELOPMENT PLAN

Our preference, though, would be for an approach that is broader in scope than what is connoted by the term "industrial." We need to consider every aspect of our relationships with other countries from a long-term perspective. We prefer the term "National Redevelopment Plan."

The overall strategy that we need to develop must be aimed at making us more effective cooperators at home and more aggressive competitors overseas. We need a policy that will help us to take full advantage of the synergy principle—one that will enable the many parts to achieve a high-synergy whole. And that, as we have tried to show throughout this book, is no small task.

## INTERNATIONAL COOPERATION

This is not to say that we should be less cooperative toward other nations. As we stressed earlier, competition and cooperation can go hand in hand. If it is in our interest as a nation to be more effective competitors, it is equally in our interest to cooperate with other nations where there are synergies to be had.

Our vitally important relationship with Japan is perhaps the primary case in point. Just as we must be a stronger competitor, we must at the same time retain and expand the close cooperation that has existed between our two nations ever since World War II.

Japan's diplomatic interests closely parallel ours, and she has been a strong supporter in various international crises of recent years. She shares with us the desire to contain Soviet expansionism and to help advance China's evolution. Her growing foreign aid commitments have been directed increasingly toward countries that we think are strategically important—Pakistan, Turkey,

Egypt, and the nations of Southeast Asia. In fact, Japan is the anchor of American security in the entire western Pacific area.

Japan and the United States also have a strong shared interest in maintaining and improving the international financial structure, and Japan's financial strength can contribute significantly to that end.

If the U.S. presses ahead with the plan for a space mission to Mars, the Japanese will be increasingly in the position to help underwrite and participate in that venture. A Mars mission might even provide a major opportunity for closer cooperation with the Soviet Union, as former NASA administrator James Beggs among others has proposed.

A synergy-oriented approach to foreign policy has been argued persuasively by Secretary of State George Schultz: "We have a kind of competitive ethic in the United States. It starts in football. We're brought up in a culture which is totally different from, say, the Japanese culture. But certainly the skills of cooperation need a lot of nourishment in our attempts to build alliances and maintain them."

## SUPREME DANGER

A clear warning about our long-term peril has been sounded in recent months by one of our most distinguished political commentators, Joseph Kraft. Noting some similarities between America in the 1920s and in the present decade, he concluded: "No one can be clear as to how the current chapter will end. Forecasting another great crash is like predicting a return to flagpole-sitting. But the élan of the present is based on illusion. Confidence cannot change anything, nor can buoyant leadership. Generals matter, but armies make the big difference. So if Americans are lucky, we will rediscover a sense of social purpose before we are again threatened by a supreme danger."

The fact is that we already *are* threatened by a supreme danger. The time to rediscover a social purpose is now. In the words of philosopher John Locke: "Hell is truth seen too late."

Whatever the outcome of any "macro-level" efforts to revitalize America, each one of us can make more effective use of the synergy principle at the "micro-level." And if each of us can achieve a high level of synergy in our personal lives, our families, our communities, and our work, the combined result will surely be a high-synergy whole.

# INDEX

A&P, 182
Additive vs. multiplicative effects, 77–78
Advertising, 169
Agglomeration effects, 147–48
Aggregated demand, 150–51, 173
Agriculture, 43–44, 68, 99–100, 112, 213–20, 238, 254, 258
Airlines, 44, 116–17, 117–18
Alliances, 90
American Conservatory Theater (A.C.T.), 211
Antitrust law, 124, 186
Apple Computers, 104, 184
Architecture, 14–15, 18, 45–46, 220–24, 254–55
AT&T, 103, 183
Atlantic City, New Jersey, 161
Automobile-induced dysergy, 43, 45
Automobile industry, 36–40, 41, 76, 91; Japanese advantage, 197–98, 266–67

Baltimore, Maryland, 153–54, 164–67
Baltimore Orioles, 200–202
Banks, 3, 90–91, 97, 100
Biochemical synergies, 24–25
Biological synergies, 12–13, 15, 24–34, 67–68
Burger King, 119, 120
Bushnell, Nolan, 191–92, 194
Business: diversification, 179–80; dysergy in, 48–49, 94–95, 187–94, 237, 250; fair-shares ethic for, 259–60; family, 67, 76, 137, 143; franchising, 180–92, 194–97; prophecy dangers, 255–56; regional competition for, 151–52; 7-S model for, 124–27; small-business successes, 184–87; success rate, 193; synergy in, 92–93, 104–5, 122–24, 127–33, 168–98; Synergy Model for, 123, 127–29, 194–98; synergy strategy role, 258, 259–62, 261, 265–68. See also Competition; Cooperation; Mergers; specific kinds

Cab drivers, 153, 263
Capitalism, 95–105; synergistic ideology vs., 42, 105–6, 107–10, 262
Caravansary, 185–86
Carpet-cleaning business, 115, 117
Center for Integrated Systems, 16

Century 21, 181
Challenger, 47
Charitable organizations. See Organizations
Chemical synergies, 12, 13, 14, 23–24
Chrysler, 172, 266
Cities as communities, 148–49; dysergy in, 156–64, 223–24; synergy example, 153–54, 164–67
Club Med, 18
Club of Rome, 252–53
Coalitions, 91
Cogeneration systems, 18, 170
Common Market, 90
Communications, 100, 170–71, 238. See also Telephone system
Communities, 146–67; agglomeration effects, 147–48; aggregated demand in, 150–51; as families, 142; formal organizations in, 153–56; informal, 152–53; latent, 156; regional, 151–52; synergy strategy role, 264, 269–70. See also Cities
Compaq, 112, 194
Competition: capitalist manipulation of, 101–2; dysergy from, 93–95; in families, 143–44; interplay with cooperation, 25–26, 33, 85–92, 93–95, 102–6, 198, 206–7, 268–69; synergy as edge in, 17, 33, 62, 173–74; synergy produced by, 92–95
Complementarities, 76–77, 119, 120, 169–70, 172
Computers, 41, 43, 71, 76, 80–81, 100
Condominiums, 205–6
Congress, as synergy example, 235–36
Cooperation, 28–29, 85, 123–24, 259, 263; antitrust laws vs., 124, 186; cost and use sharing, 69–71; negative forms of, 94–95. See also Competition
Cooperatives, 155, 170, 172–73
Copy Mat stores, 174
Corporations: in agriculture, 215–16, 219–20; conglomerates, 182–84, 186–89; joint ventures, 172, 263. See also Business; specific corporations
Cost and use sharing, 69–71
Crime, 4–5, 240; community and, 50, 152–53, 157; family dysergy and, 142–43

Darwinism, 28, 41, 198
Defense Department. *See* Military
Depression, 52–55, 100
Deregulation, 116–17, 117–18
Detroit, Michigan, 162–64
Disney Productions, 265–66
Diversification, 179–80
Divestitures, 186, 188, 189
Division of labor, 64–67; agglomeration
    effects and, 147–48; in early
    communities, 146, 147; in families, 135–
    36, 138–39; symbiosis, 67–68
Divorce, 5, 140–41
Doomsayers, 252–54
Dysergy, 43–55; additive vs. multiplicative
    effects, 77–78; causes of, 249–51; from
    competition, 93–95; diseconomies of
    scale, 159–60; examples, 43–46, 47–55,
    115–18, 187–94; 248–50; future visions
    of, 252–54; impact of, 238–39, 247;
    social, 46, 150–51, 248–50; social/
    psychological, 79–80; synergy vs., 55–
    57; threshold effects, 78–79; ubiquity
    of, 56–57, 84

Economic Darwinism, 198
Economics: appearances vs. reality, 247–
    49, 256; baseline projections, 257;
    dysergy in, 52–55, 248–50, 257; Great
    Depression, 52–55; public vs. private
    sector, 98–101; strategic
    recommendations, 257–62, 265–69;
    symbiosis in communities, 148, synergy
    in, 42, 238. *See also* Capitalism; Socialism
Economies of scale, 70–71, 149, 204;
    negative aspects, 147, 159–60, 219–20
Education, 5–6, 239, 258, 264–65
Electricity, synergy principle in, 24. *See also*
    Energy
Electronics industry, 4, 6, 24
Emotional synergy, 137–38
Energy: dysergy examples, 45, 46, 250;
    promising technologies, 18, 170, 254
Engineers, 5, 6, 239, 255
Environmental crisis, as dysergy cause, 250
Equity, as value, 85. *See also* Fair-shares
    ethic
Ergonomics, 67, 74
Evolution, synergy principle in, 23–34
Excellence, 61–62, 84, 263
EXXON, 182, 183

Fair-shares ethic, 108–10, 144–45, 259–60
Falkland Islands war, 228–30, 232
Families, 135–45; in business, 67, 76, 137,
    143; dysergy in, 5, 139–41, 142–43,
    144; synergy in, 67, 135–39, 141–42,
    144–45; synergy strategy role, 264, 269–
    70

Fast-food businesses, 119, 120, 194–97
Financial supermarkets, 172
Ford, 37, 38, 256
Foreign policy, 268–69
Fortuitous combinations, 69
Fort Wayne, Indiana, flood response, 156
Franchising, 180–82, 194–97
Fujitsu Fanuc, 68, 172
Fuller, Buckminster, 10, 18
Future, visions of, 251–57

Games, 73–74
Gardening, 212–15
General Electric, 183
General Motors, 103, 183; dysergy
    examples, 109, 127, 266; foreign
    assembly plants, 256; Fujitsu Fanuc and,
    172; Toyota and, 76, 90, 256
Gestalt approach, 80, 113–14
"Give-backs", 109, 260–62
Gold Rush, 35–36
Government: agriculture role, 217–18,
    219; airline deregulation problems, 117–
    18; cooperation with private sector, 98–
    101, 166, 242–44, 266, 267–68; dysergy
    in, 234, 237–38, 239, 250; services
    provided by, 99–101, 149–50; synergy
    in, 234–36, 238; synergy strategy role,
    258, 262, 267–68; World War II synergy
    role, 241–44
Great Britain, military synergy by, 228–30,
    231, 232
"Greatness," 61–62
Grenada invasion, 232
Group rates, 173
Groups. *See* Organizations

Harborplace, 154, 165–66
Hardware synergies, 175–76
Health: community size and, 157–58;
    dysergy examples, 47–48; infant
    mortality, 4, 157
Health care, 43, 115, 117, 119–20, 121;
    cooperatives, 155; synergy strategy role,
    258. *See also* Hospitals; Physicians
Hewlett-Packard, 105
History, synergy and dysergy in, 34–41,
    52–55
Honda, 256, 267
Hospitals: cooperation vs. competition
    among, 87; high vs. low synergy
    examples, 59–61, 131, 133; multi-
    hospital systems, 183; outpatient centers
    vs., 115, 117
Hostile takeovers, 188, 259
Human body, synergy principle in, 12–13,
    26–28
Human evolution, synergy principle in,
    31–34

IBM, 103, 104, 112, 183, 184
Ideology, 83–110; fair-shares ethic, 108–10, 259–60; outmoded, 106; synergy strategy role, 262–63
Individualism, 84, 263
Industry: national industrial policy recommendation, 267–68; productivity, 2, 4, 240, 260–62. *See also* Manufacturing; *specific kinds*
Insurance, as synergy example, 70
Intended vs. unintended synergy, 73–74
International cooperation, need for, 268–69
Iranian hostage rescue, Entebbe vs., 46
ITT, 183, 187, 189

Japan, 10, 239–40; auto manufacturing advantage, 197–98; business philosophy, 105, 125, 193, 240; need for cooperation with, 268–69; technological leadership in, 6, 239–40, 255; U.S. auto plants, 256, 267; work week in, 260
Joint ventures, 172, 263

Labor relations. *See* Personnel
Language, synergy in, 15
Lease-a-staff, 175
*Limits to Growth* (Club of Rome), 252–53
Linear vs. synergistic thinking, 111–14
Lionel Corporation, 48–49
"Live Aid", 18
Lucasfilms, 184, 266

McDonald's, 119, 120, 194–97, 198
McKinsey & Co., 124–27, 187
Mafia, 142, 144
Management: dysergy in, 50–51, 190–94; high- vs. low-synergy, 59–61; Japanese-style, 105, 125, 240; models, 123, 124–32; professional, 174–75; synergy strategies, 263
Manufacturing: dysergy example, 190–91; factory closures, 2; synergy examples, 173, 177–79, 184, 185; synergy strategies for, 266–67; World War II synergy, 241–44. *See also* Industry; *specific kinds*
Medicine. *See* Health care; Hospitals; Physicians
Merchant associations, 173
Mergers, 91, 186–87, 189; dysergy produced by, 43, 48, 187–89; hostile takeovers, 188, 259; synergistic, 169–70
Mesta Machine Company failure, 190–91
Miami, Florida, crime problems, 161–62
Military: aircraft carrier synergy, 225–27; combined marketing to, 186; dysergy in, 231–34, 232, 237, 239; scandals, 3, 6, 115, 117; synergy in, 224–31; synergy strategy role, 258, 260

Mitsubishi, 172, 267
Models, management consulting, 123, 124–32
Mom-and-pop businesses, 67, 76, 137
Motivation, 104, 125
Movies, 168–69, 245
"Mr. Build," 181–82
Multilevel synergy, 26
Multiple synergies, 72–73
Multiplier effects, 77–78
Mutual funds, 70

Nabisco, merger with Standard Brands, 169–70
Nader, Ralph, 156
NASA, 47, 104, 234
National Redevelopment Plan, 268
Natural selection, 28–29
Natural vs. man-made synergy, 74–75
Negative synergy. *See* Dysergy
Neighborhoods, 152–53, 264
Networking, 171, 263
New York City, 49–52, 149, 150, 152, 160, 161, 202, 223–24; Broadway theater, 208–10
Nissan, 256, 267
Nuclear power, 6, 47

Office sharing, 170
OPEC, 56
Organizations, 16, 91–92, 152–56, 173

"Pacifier Leash," 175–76
Patents, to other countries, 4, 239
Pearl Harbor, response to, 241–46; contemporary equivalent, 257–58, 262
Perfectionism, 84, 263
Personal life: dysergy in, 47–48; synergy in, 71–72, 121–22, 244–45; synergy strategy role, 263, 269–70
Personnel: dysergy examples, 4, 51–52, 237, 260; synergy examples, 174–75, 194–96; synergy strategies, 259, 260
Photography, one-hour photo services, 186
Physical universe, synergy principle in, 23–24
Physicians, synergy used by, 17, 119–20, 121, 173, 175. *See also* Health care; Hospitals
Pin factory, 65–66, 70–71
Pizza Time Theatre, 191–92, 194
Politics, dysergy causes in, 92, 250, 260
Pollution, 43, 45, 160
Population growth, 43, 44, 77, 78, 254
Postal service, 234–35
Postindustrial society, as myth, 249, 255–56
Printers, 174, 189–90
Proctor & Gamble, 109–10, 187, 198
Productivity. *See* Worker productivity

Professional managers, 174–75
Professionals, solo successes, 185
Psychological synergy, 79–81, 79–82, 137–38
Public services, 149–50, 158

Real estate, synergy in, 202–7
Regulatory agencies, 100–1
Religion, cooperation vs. competition in, 86
Rental services, 172
Restaurants, 58–59, 72–73, 91, 120, 121
Retailing, 118, 120, 153, 168, 171–72, 173, 176–77, 185
Roads, 4, 37, 39, 45
Robots, 68, 172
Rockford Headed Products, 177–79, 184

Safeway, 118, 120
7-Eleven stores, cab drivers and, 153
7-S model, 124–27
"Shopsteading," 166–67
Small businesses, synergy examples, 184–87
Smith, Adam, 64–66, 71, 75–76, 97, 102, 147
Smith, Bucklin & Associates, 174–75
Social action organizations, 155–56
Social contract, in synergy strategy, 259–62
Social dysergy, 46, 150–51, 248–50
Socialism, 42, 106, 107–10
Social/psychological synergy, 79–82
Social Security, as synergy example, 234
Social synergy, 15–16, 81–82; dysergy vs., 46, 150–51, 248–50; future visions of, 251–57; strategies for achieving, 257–69
SONY, 105
Soviet Union. See USSR
Space exploration, 269
Sports, 86, 92, 94; Academic Decathlon vs., 265; dysergy example, 47; synergy examples, 15–16, 199–202
"Stakeholders" ideology, 107
Standard Brands, merger with Nabisco, 169–70
Standard Oil of New Jersey, 182
Statistics, unfavorable comparisons, 3–5
Sunflower oil innovations, 218–19
Supermarkets, financial, 172
Superstores, 171–72
Symbiosis, 29–30, 67–68
Synergy, defined, 12
Synergy Model, 123, 124, 127–29; applied to McDonald's, 194–97; Factor Analyzer,

Synergy Model (continued)
131, 132; Japanese management style and, 240; Systematizer, 129–30

Tandem Computers, 14
Tax system, 115, 117, 259, 264
Teaching profession. See Education
Teamwork, 85, 104, 105, 263; in families, 140; in sports. See Sports
Technology: in agriculture, 216–17, 220; combined marketing in, 186; hardware synergies, 175–76; Japanese leadership, 6, 239–40, 255
Telephone system, 7, 66–67, 170–71, 238
Theater, 207–12
Threshold effect, 78–79, 219–20, 224, 236
Timesharing, 173, 205–6
Tools, 67, 68, 75–76. See also Models
Toyota, 76, 90, 256, 267
Trade associations, 16
Trade deficits, 1, 112, 248, 256, 262
Transportation: dysergy in, 6, 44, 45, 46, 47, 49–52, 238–39; synergy in, 75, 238. See also Automobiles; Roads

Unemployment, 2, 240, 256
Unions, 259, 260
United Way, 92
Urban renewal, 164–67
USSR, competition vs. cooperation with, 85, 87–88, 91, 269

Vacations, 18, 43, 205–6
Values, 84–85, 250; synergy strategy role, 258, 259–60, 262–63
Vaughn, Johnny, 185
Venture capitalism, 102
Victor Technologies, 111–12
Vietnam War, 232, 250

Walt Disney Productions, 265–66
War, synergy and, 100, 227–31, 232
Watergate, 92, 250
Welfare cheating, 259
Welfare state, 97–98, 107, 108
Weltanschauung. See World view
Winchester mansion, 220–21, 254
"Wino Park," 160
Worker productivity, 4, 240, 260–62
Work ethic, 84, 259, 260–62, 263
Work week, 260–61
World view (Weltanschauung), 8, 9, 10, 41–42, 83, 250
World War II, 232, 241–46; synergy strategy from, 257–58
Wright, Frank Lloyd, 221–23